CAREER READING SKILLS

CAREER READING SKILLS

Judith Mallegol Cardanha
Educational Consultant

Homewood, IL 60430
Boston, MA 02116

Executive editor: Carol A. Long
Senior developmental editor: Jean Roberts
Developmental editor: Anna Drake
Project editor: Rebecca Dodson
Production manager: Mary Jo Parke
Designer: Annette Spadoni
Compositor: The Clarinda Company
Typeface: 11/13 Times Roman
Printer: Webcrafters, Inc.

ISBN   0-256-13836-2

Printed in the United States of America
1 2 3 4 5 6 7 8 9 0 WC 0 9 8 7 6 5 4 3

Preface

Career Reading Skills has been developed to be part of a reading improvement program for students in career schools. After being exposed to specific reading improvement methods in Part 1, the student will be able to read, with improved comprehension, the high-interest career selections in Part 2. These newly acquired reading skills will motivate them to practice on these selections. With an awareness of word meanings and of the structure of paragraphs, students will better comprehend what they are reading.

Part 1, "How to Improve Your Reading," teaches the student specific methods for improving reading ability and comprehension. Part 2, "Practicing for Reading Improvement," is the vehicle for students to practice the skills they learned in Part 1. Part 1 is where the learning is done. Part 2 is for practicing what was learned. With the full use of *both parts* of *Career Reading Skills,* students can expect to become better readers.

Each selection begins with a list of vocabulary words and definitions. The lengths of the lists vary because some of the selections deal with careers that involve more difficult or technical language than others. Some lists might contain 5 or 6 words, while others might contain 10 or 11 words. The length depends on the nature of the selection. Each reading selection is followed by five comprehension questions and by a vocabulary test that check understanding of main ideas and of facts and details. The student can check all the answers to the exercises, comprehension questions, and vocabulary tests in the Answer Key at the end of the book. Checking the answers gives the student immediate feedback, and, if checking the answers shows that the student has not yet mastered the skill, he or she can review that skill right away and try another selection.

No matter what the age or career goal of a student, learning and practicing the skills taught in this book will make reading easier and more enjoyable. When students want to read and are skillful readers, they will be able to absorb what is being read and be better able to learn.

◆ Benefits from Using This Book

By using *Career Reading Skills,* students will be introduced to all the reading skills they will need to be effective readers and, thus, effective learners. Some careers might require reading material that is technical and more difficult than usual; but if a student has built a solid foundation of vocabulary and reading skills, he or she will be able to use those skills to attack any level of reading.

Students will gain an *appreciation of vocabulary* and an understanding of the ways to figure out the meaning of an unfamiliar word.

Students will understand the *structure of a paragraph* and will be better able to grasp the main idea of a paragraph.

Students will be shown that there are different *speeds of reading* and will be helped to see when each reading technique is most appropriate.

Students will be given a *study system*, the PR4 System, to use while studying with their new reading skills.

Students will read *high-interest selections* that have been chosen to appeal to students in all career fields. Even if the selection is about being an auto mechanic and the student is preparing to be a computer programmer, he or she will enjoy reading and learning about what someone else does.

Students will *increase their vocabulary* by using the vocabulary lists at the beginning of each reading selection. They will take a vocabulary test at the end of the selection and can receive immediate feedback by checking their answers with the Answer Key at the back of the book.

Students will *check their understanding of facts and details* in each reading selection by answering five comprehension questions at the end of each reading selection. They will check their answers in the Answer Key and will be able to watch their progress by recording their scores on the Progress Chart at the back of the book.

Students will have *more confidence* in their reading ability, having been given definite reading skills, and will approach all reading with a more positive attitude.

◆ Skills to Be Learned

Working through Part 1 of *Career Reading Skills*, students will learn various skills needed to be effective readers:

Word skills: Students will learn to figure out the meaning of an unfamiliar word from analyzing the word and its various components and from context clues. Using a dictionary to find a particular meaning of a word is presented.

Paragraph skills: Students will learn to identify the topic and the main idea of a paragraph. They will learn to pick out a sentence that summarizes a paragraph, and they will learn to appreciate the logical order of sentences in a paragraph.

Reading skills: Students will learn to use the reading techniques called *skimming* and *scanning* and the purpose of each.

Study skills: Students will learn to use the steps of the *PR4 Study System:* preview, relate, read, review, and recall.

Comprehension skills: Students will use their new reading skills for reading comprehension and will answer comprehension questions that appear with each reading selection.

◆ Users of *Career Reading Skills*

Career Reading Skills can be used by any student who wants to improve reading and studying skills. The book is not just an anthology of reading practice selections. Practice does improve reading skills somewhat. But practicing reading with improved reading and studying skills will give students a new appreciation of what they are reading and a new confidence in their ability to read and comprehend the material in their course texts.

This book can be used by students in *any* career program. The examples in Part 1 and the selections in Part 2 of the book cover many areas of career study in which the students might be involved. The book can also be used by students of any post-high school age. The content of the examples and selections will appeal to men and women in all career fields and at any point in their career training.

◆ Learning Features

Part 1—How to Improve Your Reading

Lesson titles are straightforward indications of what is presented in the lesson.

Objectives for each lesson appear right after the title to focus both the instructor and the student on the goal(s) of the lesson.

Key terms appear in bold type in the text and in bold in displayed definitions.

Examples are given in the lesson to illustrate the concepts being taught and to prepare the student to do the practice exercises.

Practice exercises, with one or more answers already given, allow students to try out the skills that have just been learned.

Tables of prefixes and suffixes and of words with those prefixes and suffixes are provided for the student as a learning tool and as a handy reference guide.

Answer Key to all the exercises in Part 1 appears at the end of the book so the students can check their progress and so that the book can be used in a self-teaching manner. The pages are perforated so that the instructor can remove them if students are not to have them.

Part 2—Practicing for Reading Improvement

"How to Use Part 2" appears right before the reading selections so students know exactly how to use the features of the reading selec-

tions. They are told how to score the Comprehension Questions and the Vocabulary Tests.

Vocabulary Previews appear before each reading selection. The lists vary in length depending on the difficulty of the words and the way in which they are used. Difficult words tend to be used in the more technical selections and need to be defined. Words that have many possible meanings are defined so that the student is clear on the meaning for that particular selection.

Vocabulary words appear in boldface type in the selection so that the student recognizes the word in its context.

Comprehension Questions follow each reading selection to check the student's knowledge of the facts and details of the selection.

Vocabulary Test is the last item in each reading selection and tests the student's learning of the words in the Vocabulary Preview.

Answer Keys appear at the end of the book for the Comprehension Questions and for the Vocabulary Tests. The students can score themselves according to the instructions given in "How to Use Part 2." Immediate feedback is a useful learning tool for many students, but the pages are perforated in case the instructor wishes to remove the Answer Keys.

Progress Chart for the Comprehension Questions appears at the end of the book so that the students have a record of their performance and are able to see what progress they are making.

The *Instructor's Manual* contains detailed plans for each lesson and flowcharts illustrating how the program can be implemented in a 36-hour or 24-hour course. Supplementary Activities and Chapter Quizzes are provided. All Answer Keys are included.

Acknowledgments

The comments, observations, and suggestions of the following reviewers were a great help in preparing the manuscript:

Mary C. M. Anderson	DeVry Institute
Jane Ann O. Benson	Southern Ohio College
Kirk W. Bromley	P.S.I. Institute
Kathy Grimes	Trend College
Beth A. Tarquino	Bryant & Stratton
Linda C. Werner	Trend College

I am very grateful to Carol Long, who shared her many insights with me and who believed in me and in this book, and to Anna Drake, my developmental editor, for all her motivational and organizational help. My thanks to the editors and designers who put the final product together. To my research assistant, Peter Dujardin; my typists, Madeline Brewster, Diane Drake, and Evan Cardanha; and my computer consultant, Brian Cardanha, a special thanks for helping me get all the pieces of the manuscript ready on time.

Judith Mallegol Cardanha

To the Student

Reading is something you do all day, every day—from course lists to street signs, from package labels and prices to newspaper stories and want ads, from greeting cards and invitations to tax forms and textbooks. The whole purpose of reading is to get information and to make that information your own. The purpose of *Career Reading Skills* is to make it easier for you to get and own the information contained in what you read. This book will help you learn skills needed not only to read efficiently and to get the most from your reading, but specifically to help you in your career.

Whatever you read has been written by someone who wanted to tell you something, to communicate. What you read is written language. *Written* language demands more of both the writer and the reader than does *spoken* language. The writer tries to express ideas as clearly as possible. You, the reader, cannot ask questions of the writer, as in a conversation, nor can you see facial expressions or hear tone of voice. You must depend on your own ability to read well and on the writer's ability to write well. You have no control over the ability of the writer, but you can control your reading ability. You can learn all the skills presented in the first part of this book and then practice them while reading the selections in the second part.

Part 1 of *Career Reading Skills* is called, "How to Improve Your Reading." The purpose of Part 1 is to help you learn skills that will improve the way you read and your reading comprehension. Part 2, "Practicing for Reading Improvement," helps you practice those skills that you learned in Part 1. The skills must be learned in Part 1 before you can practice them in Part 2. And you practice the skills in Part 2 so that your comprehension of the reading you do in all your course texts will improve.

Each chapter in "How to Improve Your Reading" deals with a different aspect of reading, and each lesson in the chapter treats one reading skill, beginning with a stated objective to guide and focus your learning. The skill is then explained and examples are given. You then have the opportunity to practice and reinforce the skill and to become confident in using it. The examples and exercises relate to the various careers for which you might be preparing.

The selections in "Practicing for Reading Improvement" have been chosen for their relevance to the experiences of career students like yourself. Each one relates to the program in which you might be involved or a program with which you might be familiar (e.g., secretarial, travel, medical assistant) or to the program of someone you know (e.g., auto-body repair, computer technician, travel agent). Thus, the selections are ones you will want to read as you practice your newly learned reading skills.

It is important that you work in the best environment for you. Maybe you work best at a desk or table, while others like to lean on cushions piled on a bed or on the floor. Some people need absolute silence. Others like music playing softly to blur out distractions. Still others work best with their favorite rock music filling the room. Maybe you do your best studying with a friend or two, while other students need to work alone. Some people can get a job done early in the morning, but maybe you feel most alert at night. Identify your best working conditions and make sure you use them.

Remember that when you read better, you learn better—and you are learning so you can begin a rewarding career. You need to work at improving your reading skills, but remember that work has its rewards and lifelong satisfactions.

Contents

How to Improve
Your Reading

1

Vocabulary

Reading is a form of communicating, as are listening, speaking, and writing. All these forms of communicating need words. For the message to be understood, the words must be understood—their meaning must be known.

The entire group of words known to you is your *vocabulary*. The group of words that you can use correctly in speaking is your "speaking vocabulary." You also have a reading vocabulary (usually the largest for an adult), a listening vocabulary, and a writing vocabulary.

As a very young child, when you first began to speak, you learned one word at a time: *no, cat, ...* You did not know what the word looked like, nor did you look in a dictionary to find its meaning. Someone probably pointed to a cat, said "cat" to you, you repeated "cat," and you then had "cat" in your vocabulary. You probably had a few hundred words in your speaking and listening vocabularies before you could read or write.

As you got older, you began your reading and writing vocabularies, and that might have been before you went to school. You probably recognized your name on greeting cards and recognized names on food packages. Then you began the job of learning to write—that difficult job of forming letters and combining the letters into words and sentences and paragraphs. You learned also to read those words and sentences and paragraphs.

Now you pick up many different types of reading matter, and, even though you can read them, you probably come to unfamiliar words now and then. You could carry a dictionary around so you could look up the meaning of the words, but that is not really practical. This book will help you to discover the meaning of unfamiliar words using two common methods. The first reveals clues to the meanings of a word by looking at the structure of the word (the parts that make up the word). The second reveals clues by looking at the context in which the word appears (the words and sentences around the unfamiliar word). The clues revealed by either method or both will help you uncover the meaning of an unfamiliar word without the use of a dictionary.

LESSON 1.1

Base Words

Objectives   To recognize prefixes and suffixes.
To recognize and identify base words.

The **base** is the foundation on which something else is built or attached. A **base word** is the beginning or center of a longer word.

A base word is often contained, or hidden, in a longer word. Look at the word *multifunctional.* It can be separated into three parts:

multi   function   al

The base word is *function; multi-* is attached to the front of *function,* and *-al* is attached to the end.

A group of letters that is added to the front of a word is called a **prefix:** *multi-* is the prefix in *multifunctional.*

A group of letters that is attached to the end of a word is called a **suffix:** *-al* is the suffix in *multifunctional.*

The following are lists of common prefixes and suffixes. You will learn their meanings in the next lesson.

Prefixes			
a-	ab-	ante-	anti-
bi-	circum-	co-	com-
contra-	dis-	ex-	extra-
il-	im-	in-	inter-
intra-	macro-	mal-	maxi-
micro-	mini-	mis-	mon-
mono-	multi-	non-	post-
pre-	pro-	re-	semi-
sub-	super-	trans-	tri-
un-	uni-	ultra-	

Suffixes

-able	-al	-ance	-ant
-ary	-ate	-ation	-ee
-en	-ence	-ent	-er
-ery	-ese	-ess	-est
-ful	-ian	-ible	-ic
-ical	-ing	-ion	-ism
-ist	-ity	-ive	-ize
-less	-like	-ly	-ment
-ness	-ology	-or	-ous
-ry	-ship	-y	

EXAMPLE

Identify the base word in *unfavorable.*

   un- is a prefix, and *-able* is a suffix.

   Remove *un-* and *-able* from *unfavorable,* and *favor* is left.

   favor is the base word.

EXAMPLE

Identify the base word in *configuration.*

   con- is a prefix, and *-ation* is a suffix.

   Is *figur* the base word? No, the letter "e" was dropped from the real base word *figure* when the suffix was added.

EXAMPLE

Identify the base word in *dragging.*

   -ing is a suffix.

   Is *dragg* the root word? No, the letter "g" was doubled when the suffix was added to the real base word *drag.*

   When identifying a base word, you may have to add an "e" to or remove a double letter from the end of the word to find the base.

PRACTICE

Identify the base word and write it on the line. The first one is done for you.

1. minicomputer   <u>computer (mini- is the prefix)</u>
2. discoloration   _____
3. biweekly   _____
4. dictation   _____
5. substandard   _____
6. microchip   _____
7. prearrangement _____
8. trifold   _____
9. prolabor   _____
10. assistant   _____
11. invalidate   _____
12. replace   _____
13. unacceptable   _____
14. indicator   _____
15. deletion   _____
16. horizontally   _____
17. subscript   _____
18. superimpose   _____
19. misinform   _____
20. originate   _____

LESSON 1.2

Using Prefixes—Prefix List

Objective   To use a prefix to learn the meaning of a word.

When a **prefix** is added to the front of a base word, the meaning of the prefix is added to the meaning of the base word.

The meanings of many common prefixes are given on pages 7–8. Look at each prefix, its meaning, and the example(s) given. The prefix will change or modify the meaning of the base word in some way.

EXAMPLE

Many people **misspell** *occurrence.*

What is the meaning of *misspell* in that sentence?

mis- means "wrong," so *misspell* means "spell wrong."

spell means "to name, in order, the letters that make up a word," so *misspell* means "to name the wrong letters that make up a word or to name in the wrong order the letters that make up a word."

EXAMPLE

If you enroll in the program early enough, you can **preselect** your classes before you start the term.

What is the meaning of *preselect* in that sentence?

pre- means "before," so *preselect* means "select before."

select means "choose," so *preselect* means "choose before."

PRACTICE

Use the prefix to explain the meaning of each word. The chart of the prefixes and their meanings will help you. The first one is done for you.

1. malfunction   mal- means "bad, badly," so malfunction means "function or perform badly."

2. untitled   _____

   _____

3. depart   _____

   _____

4. reformat   _____

   _____

5. preset   _____

   _____

6. bimonthly   _____

   _____

7. transatlantic   _____

   _____

8. immovable _____

_____

9. extralegal _____

_____

10. co-worker _____

_____

11. disassociate _____

_____

12. subtitle _____

_____

13. multistage _____

_____

14. mismanage _____

_____

15. monosyllable _____

_____

16. antifraud _____

_____

17. minivan _____

_____

18. interbranch _____

_____

19. ultramodern _____

_____

20. semiannual _____

_____

Prefixes

Prefix	Meaning	Examples
a-	not	asymmetric
ab-	from, away from	abnormal
ante-	before, in front of	anteroom
anti-	against, opposite	antilabor

Prefixes

Prefix	Meaning	Examples
bi-	two	biannual
circum-	around, on all sides	circumvent
co-, com-, con-	together, with	cooperate, commission, contact
de-	from, away, opposite	debug
dis-	separation, reversal	disassemble
ex-	out of	export
extra-	outside of, beyond	extraordinary
il-, im-, in-	not	illegal, impossible, invalid
inter-, intra-	among, between	interoffice, intrastate
macro-	large, long	macroeconomics
mal-	bad, badly	malpractice
maxi-	very large	maxiskirt
micro-	small	microchip
mini-	very small	minicomputer
mis-	badly, wrong, lack of	misinterpret, mistrust
mon-, mono-	single, one	monoxide, monocolor
multi-	many	multifunction
non-	not	nonindustrial
post-	later, behind, after	postdate
pre-	before	prearrangement
pro-	favoring, supporting	promanagement
re-	again	recalculate
semi-	half	semimonthly
sub-	under	subprogram
super-	above, over	superstructure
trans-	across, beyond	transcontinental
tri-	three	triplicate
ultra-	beyond, extremely	ultracompact
un-	not	unauthorized
uni-	one, single	unicellular

LESSON 1.3

Using Suffixes—Suffix List

Objective   To use a suffix to learn the meaning of a word.

When a **suffix** is added to the end of a base word, the meaning of the suffix is added to the meaning of the base word.

The meaning of many common suffixes are given on pages 10–12. Look at each suffix, its meaning, and the example(s) given. The suffix will change or modify the meaning of the base word in some way.

EXAMPLE

His **leadership** qualities will make him go far.

What is the meaning of *leadership?*

-*ship* means "having the quality of," so *leadership* means "having the quality of a leader."

EXAMPLE

The new **typist** started work today.

Give the meaning of *typist.*

-*ist* means "one who," so *typist* means "one who types."
(Note that the "e" on *type* was dropped when the suffix was added.)

PRACTICE

Use the suffix to explain the meaning of the word. The chart of the suffixes and their meanings will help you. The first one is done for you.

1. activate   -ate means "to cause to become," so activate means "to cause to become active."

2. instruction   _____

3. replacement   _____

4. sterilize   _____

5. computerese   _____

6. bindery   _____

                  _____

7. assistance   _____

                  _____

8. employee   _____

                  _____

9. auditor   _____

                  _____

10. seasonal   _____

                  _____

11. translatable _____

                  _____

12. printer   _____

                  _____

13. usefulness   _____

                  _____

14. accountant   _____

                  _____

15. successful   _____

                  _____

16. poisonous   _____

                  _____

17. judgeship   _____

                  _____

18. energetic   _____

                  _____

19. professionally _____

                  _____

20. viruslike   _____

                  _____

Suffixes

Suffix	Meaning	Examples
-able	capable of, tending to	perishable
-al	of, action of	directional
-an	of, belonging to	American
-ance, -ancy	action of, quality of	performance
-ant	one who	claimant
-ary	of, belonging to, relating to	budgetary
-ate	cause to become, function of	administrate
-ation	action or process of	accommodation
-ee	receiver of (an action), performer of (an action)	appointee
-en	of or belonging to, cause to have	golden lengthen
-ence, -ency	state of being, condition of	dependency
-ent	one who	correspondent
-er	one who	buyer
-ery	place of (doing), character of being	refinery bravery
-ese	pertaining to (a place or thing)	legalese
-ess	female	heiress
-est	superlative	quickest
-ful	full of, having the quality of	powerful masterful
-ian	skilled in	mathematician
-ible	capable of, tending to	credible
-ic	having the nature of	electronic
-ical	having the property of	symmetrical
-ion	act or process, result of	regulation
-ious	full of, having the quality of	ambitious
-ism	practice of, state of	professionalism
-ist	one who, one who specializes in	artist
-ity	quality of, degree of	legality
-ive	performs or tends	indicative
-ization	action, process, or result of	industrialization
-ize	cause to be or conform to	unionize
-less	not having	faultless
-like	resembling, having the quality of	machinelike
-ly	in the manner of, recurring regularly	fatherly weekly

Suffixes

Suffix	Meaning	Examples
-ment	result of, place of	development
-ness	state of (being)	business
-ology	study of	criminology
-or	one who	auditor
-ous	full of, having	industrious
-ry	place of doing, character of being	dentistry
-ship	having the quality of, position of (being a)	leadership
-y	characterized by, instance of	inky inquiry

LESSON 1.4

Context Clues

Objective   To use context clues to figure out the meaning of a word.

> **Context** is the words and sentences surrounding an unknown word that may reveal clues to the meaning of the unknown word. The clues from those surrounding words and sentences serve as hints to the meaning of the unknown word and are called **context clues.**

EXAMPLE

> Employees of nursing homes often work with *invalids* who need special care. Nurses, nurses' aides, and other attendants need to keep up with the new skills and technology available for caring for people who have difficulty moving and doing things for themselves.

What does the word *invalids* in the first sentence mean? Look at the context of the paragraph to find clues to the meaning of *invalid*.

Clue 1: "invalids who need special care"—invalids are people with special needs.

Clue 2: "Employees of nursing homes often work with invalids"—invalids are in nursing homes; people in nursing homes are usually sick.

Clue 3: "caring for people who have difficulty moving and doing things for themselves"—invalids cannot move easily or take care of themselves.

Putting all those clues together, you could define an *invalid* as "a sick person who needs special care because they cannot move easily or take care of themselves."

EXAMPLE

The technician told Mr. Flynn not to eat or drink anything but water for 14 hours before the blood tests so that the test results would be accurate. During the night, he forgot and drank a glass of milk. So the results of the tests were *invalid*.

What is the meaning of *invalid* in the last sentence? In this context, does it seem that *invalid* means a sick person who cannot move around? No. Look at the context of the paragraph to find clues to the meaning of *invalid*.

Clue 1: "results of the tests were invalid"—*invalid* is describing *test results*.

Clue 2: "not to eat or drink anything . . . so that the test results would be accurate"—the test results depend on not eating or drinking.

Clue 3: "he forgot and drank a glass of milk"—the directions for the test were not followed; if you do not follow directions, things usually do not come out right.

Putting all those clues together, you could decide that *invalid* in this paragraph means "not correct."

PRACTICE

Use context clues to find the meaning of the boldfaced word. Locate and underline the clues. Circle the letter of the definition that seems the best. The first one is done for you.

1. After a few puffs (on a cigarette), the level of nicotine in the blood **skyrockets.** The <u>heart beats faster</u> and <u>blood pressure increases.</u>
   a. goes down   b. crashes
   c. stays the same   d. quickly goes way up

2. The computer screen remained blank. Ms. Aveci **peered** under the desk to see if the computer was still plugged in.

   a. peeked   b. looked closely
   c. felt around   d. crawled

3. Mary listened to the traffic report before she left work for the day. She heard that an overturned truck had blocked all the **outbound** lanes on the highway she usually used to drive out of the city. Mary would be late getting home.

   a. tied up   b. high-speed
   c. directed to go away from a center   d. coming in

4. **Produce** is the first department at one of the store's two entrances. Customers buying fruits and vegetables can choose from common salad items and local favorites, such as five kinds of chili peppers.

   a. made things   b. fruits and vegetables
   c. bread and cake   d. canned goods

5. In the 1930s, the **forerunners** of the first computers were being developed in university research centers. In 1951, the first computer was used to process the U.S. census. In 1954, the first computer was used in private business. Since then, public and private industries, universities, and other research centers have been developing many different kinds of computers.

   a. fast machines   b. old computers
   c. samples that showed what was to come d. failures

LESSON 1.5

Using the Dictionary

Objective   To use a dictionary to learn the meaning of a word.

A **dictionary** is a book listing words, usually in alphabetical order, with their meanings, histories, variations, pronunciations, uses, and so on.

In order to look up a word, you must know its correct spelling so you can find it in the alphabetical list. To find the meaning, or definition, of a word, you must know how the word is being used.

EXAMPLE

Define the word *margin,* as in "Set the margin on the typewriter."

1   The spelling is m-a-r-g-i-n.

2   Go to the "M" section of the dictionary.

Find the "m-a-" listings.

Find the "m-a-r-" listings.

3   Look down the list until you find *margin.*

mare	marge
marengo	margent
margarine	**margin**
margarita	marginal
margay	margrave

4   Read the definitions and decide which is the one that best fits your use of the word.

margin |mar-jen| *n* [L *margo* border] 1: the part of a page outside the main typing   2: the outside limit and the surface joined to it; edge ⟨the margin of the sea⟩   3: a spare amount allowed for emergencies ⟨margin of error⟩   4: a limit past which something is not possible or desirable ⟨margin of good taste⟩   5: the difference between sales and cost of merchandise ⟨profit margin⟩

Definitions 1, 2, and 4 all give an idea of what a margin in typing is. You know your use of margin has nothing to do with emergencies or profits. It is the limit of a page, the edge of the typing, the limit past which you do not want to see any symbols typed.

PRACTICE

Use a dictionary to define the underlined word as used in the sentence. The first one is done for you.

1. <u>cursor,</u> as in "The cursor on my computer screen is an arrow." _____
   <u>A figure on a computer screen that indicates where data is to be entered;</u>
   <u>it is usually controlled by hand.</u>

2. <u>brief,</u> as in "Mr. Corley's legal assistant prepared the brief for him." ____

3. <u>pipe</u>, as in "You should replace that lead pipe with a copper one." _____

_____

_____

4. <u>pen</u>, as in "He likes to use a fine-tipped pen for all his letters." _____

_____

_____

5. <u>crown</u>, as in "During the soccer game, Alice's tooth was broken, and the dentist replaced it with a crown." _____

_____

_____

6. <u>reservation</u>, as in "You should make your plane reservation several weeks in advance to get the lowest fares." _____

_____

_____

7. <u>program</u>, as in "What is your favorite word processing program?"

_____

_____

8. <u>patient</u>, as in "That hospital has beds for 134 patients." _____

_____

_____

9. <u>outlet</u>, as in "The only thing you should put in an electrical outlet is a plug." _____

_____

_____

10. <u>counter</u>, as in "The salesman put three calculators out on the counter so I could decide which one to buy." _____

_____

_____

11. <u>order</u>, as in "If you place your order before 10 A.M., it will be delivered the following day." _____

_____

_____

12. <u>pressure</u>, as in "A reading of 120/80 means that your blood pressure is fine." _____

_____

13. <u>run</u>, as in "If you wash your new uniform in cold water, the colors will not run." _____

_____

_____

14. <u>diet</u>, as in "A healthful diet is low in fat and high in complex carbohydrates." _____

_____

_____

15. <u>hardware</u>, as in "Computer hardware is very different from what it was 20 years ago." _____

_____

_____

16. <u>breaker</u>, as in "My boss installed a separate circuit breaker for each computer when he remodeled the office." _____

_____

_____

17. <u>frame</u>, as in "I am going to frame my diploma." _____

_____

_____

18. <u>officer</u>, as in "I had to see one of the bank's officers in order to make such a large withdrawal." _____

_____

_____

19. <u>manual</u>, as in "Manual typewriters are not seen very often since electronic ones became so inexpensive." _____

_____

_____

20. <u>tissue</u>, as in "They removed some tissue from her leg for the biopsy." __

_____

_____

2

Paragraphs

In the first chapter, you studied words. Words can be joined together to form a sentence. Sentences can be joined together to form a paragraph. Paragraphs can stand alone or can be joined together to form anything from a short passage or article to the longest textbook.

A **sentence** is a word or group of words that expresses a complete thought.

A **paragraph** is a group of sentences that deal with one point or idea. It is usually part of a longer composition, but it is complete in itself.

Paragraphs are written for various purposes:

- To develop an idea.
- To describe an object.
- To present the ordered steps in a sequence of events or a set of directions.
- To compare or contrast ideas, things, or events.
- To show the relationship between a cause and an effect.

The following paragraph is from an article on building an office in your own home. As you can see, *sentences* make up the *paragraph*.

sentence   *I could work down in the unfinished basement.* The basement does   main idea

sentence   offer plenty of space and easy access to electrical and telephone
lines. But callers would have to enter through a door in the

sentence   kitchen—better than walking by the bedrooms but still not quite   supporting sentences
what I wanted. Also, the space was not clean, the ceiling was

sentence   about a foot lower than upstairs, and a water meter and a bunch of   supporting
sentence   columns and beams were visible. When I thought it through,   sentences

sentence   though, the basement was irresistible. I could "commute" from my   summary
sentence   bedroom to the office in my home *and* be isolated from the   sentence
family.

Usually, one sentence of a paragraph states what the whole paragraph is about. This sentence is called the *main idea,* or topic sentence. Other sentences explain the main idea and supply facts and details about the main idea. These sentences are the *supporting sentences,* or information sentences. Often, there may be a sentence at or near the end of a paragraph that pulls together all the details of the paragraph. It prepares the reader to move on to the next paragraph and to find out more information. This sentence can be called a *summary sentence* or a transition sentence.

In some paragraphs, the main idea is not stated directly. You must identify the main idea of the paragraph in your own words. Being able to identify the main idea, either in a sentence from the paragraph or in your own words, is a good skill to learn. It helps you to remember what you read.

LESSON 2.1

Topics

Objective   To identify the topic word in a list.

The sentences in a paragraph are all about one **topic,** or main idea.

Another word for *topic* is *category.* The topic or category of a paragraph will point to the main idea and will help you to find and identify the main idea.

EXAMPLE

The words in the following list all have something in common. They belong in the same category—they relate to the same topic. One word or term in the list names that topic or category. A topic word is a title word for all the other words. Can you identify the topic word?

keyboard   disk drive
computer parts   cable
monitor

Look at each word. Is that word a title for all the other words?

keyboard—No, all the other words are not keyboards.

computer parts—Yes, all the other words are computer parts.

monitor—No, all the other words are not monitors.

disk drive—No, all the other words are not disk drives.

cable—No, all the other words are not cables.

The topic word is *computer parts*.

PRACTICE

Identify the topic word. Circle it. The first one is done for you.

1. hammer
   (tool)
   screwdriver
   pliers
   wrench

2. secretary
   chef
   dental assistant
   welder
   career

3. dictionary
   computer manual
   diary
   catalog
   book

4. motel
   hotel
   bed and breakfast
   lodging places
   inn

5. hiking
   sailing
   touring
   vacation
   fishing

6. memo
   letter
   report
   requisition
   typed things

7. transmission
   brakes
   muffler
   auto parts
   battery

8. computer command
   delete
   return
   save
   escape

9. blood pressure
   temperature
   respiration
   reflexes
   vital signs

10. department
    stores
    hardware
    stationery
    grocery

LESSON 2.2

Main Idea

Objective   To identify the main idea in a paragraph.

The **main idea** of a paragraph can be stated in any sentence in a paragraph.

The main idea is often the first sentence. If it is the first sentence in the paragraph, then the other sentences in the paragraph explain and add to the first sentence. Sometimes the main idea is not found in the first sentence but in another sentence in the paragraph. Wherever it appears in the paragraph, it always explains the overall point of the other sentences.

EXAMPLE

Identify the main idea in the following paragraph.

1   Read the paragraph.

2   Think about how you would name the paragraph if you had to give it a title.

3   Look at each sentence in the paragraph and decide which one is most like your title—expresses the topic of the rest of the paragraph.

Microwave-oven use shows no signs of slowing down. Across the United States, more homes have microwave ovens than VCRs, toasters, or dishwashers. Microwaves are expected to be in 80 percent of homes by the year 2000. The owners of restaurants also have good reason to take another look at how they can use a microwave to its full potential.

The main idea is expressed in the *first sentence:* "Microwave-oven use shows no signs of slowing down." All the other sentences explain and give examples of how the use is not slowing down. Go back to the paragraph and underline or highlight this sentence.

EXAMPLE

Identify the main idea in this paragraph.

Look under the hood. Do you see frayed cables, loose clamps, or corrosion? Are fan belts loose, cracked, or worn smooth? Do hoses feel soft or look discolored? Are the oil and antifreeze dirty or below prescribed levels? All are signs of a poorly maintained vehicle loaded with potential engine and starting problems.

Which sentence is a title for all the other sentences? In this paragraph, the main idea is in the *last sentence*. It is the topic sentence—it tells what all the other sentences are about.

PRACTICE

In each paragraph, two sentences are underlined. One of them is the main idea. The other is not. Identify the main idea, and copy that sentence onto the blank lines. The first one is done for you.

1. At Peoples Bank, Bridgeport, Connecticut, employees watch a video of an angry customer talking to a teller. <u>Then the employees discuss what might have happened to the customer before coming to the bank.</u> "You can't control events in your customer's day," says the director of personnel development. <u>Employees must learn self-management techniques.</u> "Instead of blaming themselves when faced with an angry customer, employees must learn to remain calm and to ask themselves 'What can I do to improve the situation?'" Callahan says.

    <u>Employees must learn self-management techniques.</u>

    _____

2. Anyone who has ever tried to give up smoking cigarettes knows the meaning of being hooked. <u>Of those who succeed in quitting for the first time, 75 percent go back to smoking.</u> Recently, the U.S. Surgeon General made official what everyone has recognized for a long time. <u>Tobacco, like cocaine or heroin, is addictive.</u>

    _____

    _____

3. <u>There is so much equipment in the avionics field that technicians usually specialize in one area.</u> That area might be radio equipment, radar, computerized guidance, or flight-control systems. <u>New specializations are constantly opening up as new developments occur in avionics.</u> The development of the new specializations requires avionics technicians to keep informed about their special fields. They read technical articles and books and attend seminars, and they take courses in new developments, often sponsored and offered by manufacturers.

    _____

    _____

4. New Orleans is an old city, as American cities go. It was founded in 1718. <u>In the past 25 years, it has changed more than it did in its first 200 years.</u> It has grown so fast that although I have lived here nearly all my life, I'm constantly amazed. Swamps and marshes have been drained and filled. <u>Suburbs stretch up and down the river and into the pines near the shore of Lake Pontchartrain.</u> The woods where I once hunted for Indian relics have become shopping centers and parking lots.

_____

_____

5. <u>You won't get AIDS from clothes or a telephone or a toilet seat.</u> You won't get it by donating blood to a blood center. You won't get it from dishes or glasses, or from using the same desk or word processor, or from sharing an elevator. <u>In other words, you don't have to worry about ordinary living or working with someone who carries HIV.</u>

_____

_____

LESSON 2.3

Stating the Main Idea

Objective   To identify the main idea when it is not directly stated in one sentence.

For some paragraphs, you have to decide on the main idea yourself. You may not find an actual main idea sentence anywhere in the paragraph. It is not stated directly in a sentence in the paragraph. In order to find out what the paragraph is about, you read the paragraph and identify the topic of the paragraph. A good way to identify the topic, or category, of the paragraph is to ask yourself what would be a good title for the paragraph.

EXAMPLE

State the main idea of the paragraph that follows these instructions.

1   Read the paragraph.

2   After you have read the sentences of the paragraph, try to pull them all together to form one simple idea.

3 Use that idea to decide on what would be a good title for the paragraph.

4 State the main idea in a sentence.

> Many claims have been made about the ecological benefits of using soy-based inks. It is true that soybean oil is better for the environment—is more biodegradable—than petroleum oil. However, once made into an ink with colors, waxes, and other additives, a soy-based ink is no easier to dispose of than the usual inks. While not considered toxic to the environment, the colors in an ink still require that it be disposed of in the proper manner, which means transportation to licensed landfills or incinerators.

The paragraph is not about the benefits of soy-based inks, and it is not just about its bad effects. The main idea would be: *While there are benefits to soy-based inks, there are drawbacks, too.*

PRACTICE

Two statements are given for each paragraph. Choose the one that states the main idea, and circle that letter. The first one is done for you.

1. Changing paper not only takes time, but printing one simple memo can interrupt the flow of work. Even worse, printing the memo can shut down the whole system while operators are alerted not to send documents to the printer until the memo is sent and printed. Thus, the electronic typewriter has an advantage that would be a disadvantage in a word processing system. You still insert one page or form, type or print it, and remove it from the printer.
   A. Electronic typewriters are better than computers.
   B. It is no trouble for an electronic typewriter to print one memo at a time.

2. Do you know what ranks as one of the three top industries in over half the states in our nation? If you guessed tourism, you're right. And where do these tourists stay during their travels? Most likely, they occupy one of the 2 million rooms in the 37,500 hotels and motels in operation from coast to coast. Lastly, what do these hotels and motels offer besides rooms for travelers? The answer, of course, is jobs. There are 800,000 Americans working in the hospitality industry, with an additional 35,000 being added each year.
   A. It is good to work in the hospitality industry because there are so many jobs.
   B. Travelers like to stay in hotel and motel rooms.

3. Keeping cool may be the last thing on your mind during the winter months. But when it comes to your car's automatic transmission, excess

heat is as likely on a snowy winter day as it is during a long summer-vacation drive. That is why winter and summer are the busiest times of the year for transmission-repair shops.

A. Automatic transmissions need to be kept cool.

B. Automatic transmissions can overheat in winter or summer and need to be repaired.

4. Senior citizens don't have to run marathons to reap the benefits of physical fitness. Brisk walking, swimming, and simple weight-lifting benefit people at any age. Recent studies show that even leisure activities—gardening and bowling, for instance—burn off calories and help maintain overall fitness. What's most important, say experts, is to find an enjoyable activity, exercise on a regular basis, and consult with a physician before leaping into a program.

A. Senior citizens can benefit from simple leisure exercise on a regular basis.

B. Senior citizens should exercise if they like it and see a doctor first.

LESSON 2.4

Summarizing

Objective   To identify a summary sentence in a paragraph.

Some paragraphs end with a sentence that summarizes the paragraph—restates the main points that have been discussed. It is called a **summary sentence.**

The summary sentence pulls together all the sentences of a paragraph one last time to reinforce the main idea for the reader and to prepare the reader to move on to the next paragraph. If a paragraph has a summary sentence, it helps you to remember what you read in the paragraph.

EXAMPLE

Read the following paragraph. The last sentence is underlined. Is it a summary sentence?

1   Read the paragraph.

2   Decide if the last sentence restates the ideas of the paragraph.

The use of temporary employees is of great value to management in controlling costs. For example, all businesses are subject to seasonal demands of one kind or another: inventories, fiscal closing, tax season, and budget preparation. <u>For all of these tasks, and many others, temporary employees may be the answer.</u>

The last sentence states: "For all of these tasks, and many others, temporary employees may be the answer." This sentence pulls together all the individual pieces of the paragraph. It is a summary sentence—it draws the whole paragraph together.

PRACTICE

Read each paragraph. Write yes or no on the line to tell whether the last sentence of the paragraph is a summary sentence. The first one is done for you.

1. Catholic churches, built in the shape of a cross, are true architectural treats. Many of the worshippers coming from Sunday morning Mass have enjoyed a Saturday night dance to fiddle and accordion music. Cajun folk music has fans all over the country. But no preachers are needed here to bring out believers at countless places every weekend. Ask around and you'll find them, too. _____No_____

2. Doctors had determined the health benefits of having a pet. Now psychiatrists and psychologists began to identify the reasons why. Having a pet helps to relieve stress. It can also prevent cases of extreme depression in which people feel that their lives cannot be improved and are not worth living. In short, pets give people a reason to live. _____

3. The really maddening thing about computers is that they do exactly what you tell them to do. The stupidest typing error you make when entering the program will come back to haunt you because the computer is too dumb to correct it. This explains why some of the programs we buy for our personal computers produce "computer errors" that seem really ridiculous._____

4. I could work down in the unfinished basement. The basement does offer plenty of space and easy access to electrical and telephone lines. But callers would have to enter through a door in the kitchen—better than through a bedroom but still not as professional as I wanted. Also, the space was not clean; the ceiling was about a foot lower than upstairs (and it was covered with pipes); and there was a water meter on the wall and a bunch of columns and beams holding up the house. _____

Sequencing

Objective   To be able to arrange a group of sentences in logical order.

The sentences in a paragraph are written in a certain order. One sentence leads to another in a logical order that expresses a clear idea. The sentences that are written in logical order are called a **sequence.**

Some sequences that might be familiar to you would be

- The instructions for filling out your tax forms.
- The directions for changing a tire.
- The steps in applying for a loan.

The following is a list of steps for mailing a letter after the boss has handed it to you.

1. Fold the letter.
2. Put the letter in the envelope.
3. Address the envelope.
4. Put postage stamps on the envelope.
5. Seal the envelope.
6. Mail the letter.

Think about the order in this list. Could any of the events be done in a different order?

- Step 1 must be done before Step 2.
- Steps 1 and 2 must be done before Step 5.
- Steps 1, 2, 3, 4, and 5 must be done before Step 6.

These are the "musts" of the sequence. For the other steps, some variety in the order is possible.

- The envelope can be addressed and stamped after it is sealed.
- The letter can be put into the envelope after it is addressed and stamped.

Using the numbers 1 through 6, write a sequence for the steps of mailing the letter that is different from the one given. _____

So, there is an order to a sequence of events, but within the sequence, sometimes some of the events may happen at different times. You must think about each step and decide if it could come before or after another step.

Read the following paragraph. Follow the writer's thought from one sentence to the next. Decide if the order of the sentences could be changed.

Food production starts at the ingredient issue-and-assembly area. All ingredients are weighed, measured, and stored before being sent to the cook-and-chill area. All ingredients then move to the various production areas. Hot food is cooked in steam-jacketed kettles. When the cooking is completed, the product is pumped into plastic casings of various sizes, sealed with stainless steel clips, and labeled. The food is quickly chilled and held in refrigerated storage. The shipping dock is the final point along the product flow line. Then the food is trucked to the various schools.

The steps in this food-preparation sequence cannot be changed without changing the taste of the food or making it unsafe to eat by giving bacteria a chance to grow.

Put these events in order. Write the proper number on each line. Number 1 and number 10 are marked for you.

Pumping Gas

_____ Squeeze handle to deliver gas.

_____ Insert nozzle into car's tank opening.

_____ Lift hose nozzle from holder on pump.

_____ Remove nozzle from tank opening.

___1___ Remove gas cap from car's tank.

_____ Turn on gas pump by moving lever.

_____ Replace gas cap on car's tank.

_____ Turn gas pump off.

___10___ Replace nozzle on holder.

_____ Release pump handle when desired amount of gas has been delivered.

The following sentences are from an article on how a video-game designer might invent a game. They are not in order. Read all the sentences. Decide which one is first and copy it onto the first blank line below. Then decide which sentence is second and copy it. Continue until you have completed the paragraph. One sentence is done for you.

a. Others believe it's the best type of work imaginable.

b. Behind all computer games is a designer who performs a series of steps that are both technical and tedious.

c. At big companies, designers use state-of-the-art equipment.

d. Using whatever equipment they can afford, they try to invent games that will catch the fancy of game companies.

e. For some, it's a lonely, frustrating job.

f. Freelance designers work for themselves.

g. At small companies, they may work with little more than home computers.

h. How the work is done depends in part on which company the designer works for.

1. _____
   _____

2. _____
   _____

3. a. Others believe it's the best type of work imaginable. _____

4. _____
   _____

5. _____
   _____

6. _____
   _____

7. _____
   _____

8. _____
   _____

3

Different Kinds of Reading

You read for different reasons. You read the manual that comes with a new word processing program so you will know how to use it. That would be careful reading. You do not want to miss anything.

You might read a magazine on the bus. That would be relaxed reading. You just sit back and enjoy the articles.

You read a birthday card or a letter from a friend for the feelings or news that it contains. You might even read it a second time.

You read the Yellow Pages of a phone directory to find a dentist's office. You read the white pages of a phone directory to find the phone number of a printer that has been recommended to you. Both of these tasks would mean glancing down a list, looking for a particular word, until you find the information that you want.

You might read a job search book as carefully as you would the word processing manual, but for a different reason. You are reading for facts and general ideas, not for directions.

You might read for directions, for fun, for inspiration, for news, for information, or for facts and ideas. You might read because you want to or because you have to. Different techniques can help you get the most out of your reading, whatever the reason. Different purposes of reading mean reading at different speeds.

◆ Different Speeds of Reading

Without realizing it, you probably read at different speeds depending on what is being read and why you are reading. If you like the verse on a greeting card, you may read it slowly once or even twice. If you are trying to understand the instructions for filling out income tax forms, you probably read them slowly so you will understand them completely. You might read a car owner's manual quickly to get to the root of a problem.

You probably use different reading methods. If you were reading an article in the newspaper just to see if there were something in it that interested you, you could *skim* it; that is, you would read the main title, the first paragraph, the section titles, any boldface or italic terms, and the last paragraph. You would get the main idea and a few facts.

You could read a magazine article at an average rate of speed. If you went back over it to show someone a part you liked, you would probably *scan* it; that is, you would glance down each column until you found the part in which you were interested.

There are many ways to read and different speeds of reading. Each has its purpose. Knowing when and how to vary your reading speed will make you a better, more efficient reader.

◆ Skimming

Skimming is covering a lot of reading material at a faster-than-usual speed.

You might skim just because you are in a hurry. You might skim because you are familiar with what you are reading. You might skim because what you are reading is not that important to you—you are looking over the description of a resort to see if it might interest you. Some people might think that skimming is a kind of speed reading. It is not—it is a method of reading. To skim, you read particular parts of the material you want to cover. This will be explained in the following lesson.

Skimming is a valuable skill because it allows you to cover a lot of material in a short time. Remember, though, that fast reading means low comprehension. In skimming, you get the main idea of the material and a few facts. You would not skim the manual to a new word processing program the first time you read it. You might skim if you were going over a manual for a program that is very much like one you already use.

◆ Scanning

Scanning is actually a locating technique used when you are looking for a specific piece of information, usually in some sort of list.

The list you are scanning might be the alphabetical listing in the telephone book. It could be TV listings, which are arranged according to time of day. The list might be a table of contents, which is arranged according to page number. To scan, you need to know what you are looking for and the type of list you are reviewing.

LESSON 3.1

Skimming

Objective   To learn and use the skimming method of reading.

If you are reading an article just to get the main idea and a few facts, then use the *skimming method.* The following list shows you the steps to follow in skimming.

Skimming is not a substitute for reading. A student should not skim a textbook on the first reading. You can skim when it is all right to absorb only about half of what you read. This might be when you are "reading" the sports page to check up on your favorite teams or when you are looking over a magazine article to see if you really want to read it.

◆ How to Skim

1   Read the first paragraph. This is the introduction.

2   Read the last paragraph. This is the summary.

3   Read all subheadings.

4   Read the first and last sentence of each paragraph that you have not already read. They are often the main idea and summary sentences.

5   Read all italicized or boldface words or sentences.

EXAMPLE

Skim the following paragraph. Use the last two steps from the above list, since this is only one paragraph. Look for the main idea.

> Shorter hospital stays are the rule for nearly every type of admission these days. The federal government recently added 100 procedures to its list of **approved outpatient surgeries.** And Blue Cross/Blue Shield, the Chicago-based insurance giant, now lists 400 procedures that should be carried out on a one-day basis, including **hernia operations, some plastic surgery, breast biopsies, and the removal of tonsils.** Some areas of medicine have been completely changed: cataract surgery is now a 95 percent outpatient procedure.

Now decide which of the following is the main idea:

1.   Shorter hospital stays are the rule for nearly every type of admission these days.

2. The federal government recently added 100 procedures to its list of approved outpatient surgeries.

The federal government's list is not the main point of the paragraph. The widespread use of short hospital stays is. So sentence 1 is the main idea.

PRACTICE

Skim each paragraph. Then circle A or B to identify the main idea. The first one is done for you.

1. Every business needs an organization chart. The family business is no exception. To design one for your company, first determine what jobs exist within the business. Then develop clear descriptions for these jobs, listing the responsibilities. Put this information on a chart so that everyone in your company understands how the business is organized and how it works.
    A. A family business needs an organization chart.
    B. An organization chart shows each job and its responsibilities so everyone knows how the business works.

2. If you're in the market for new office equipment or an upgrade but can't figure out what to buy, try calling a users' group. Industry experts regard users' groups as one of the best sources of useful and reliable information. You don't have to be a member to call and ask a question or two before buying equipment. These clubs are particularly helpful because members are constantly discussing the equipment they own and how they've solved technical problems. "Users' groups are great educators," says an editor of a computer magazine. "They work because no one's trying to sell you anything."
    A. Computer users' groups are a good source of information on computer equipment.
    B. There is a users' group for every computer owner.

3. How can hotels clean up their act and not lose inquiry calls? First, do not let inexperienced people answer incoming calls. Before an employee takes on that job, he or she should know about the hotel, know who works in which department, understand the workings between departments, and have a cheerful voice that can be understood.
    A. Only experienced employees who know the workings of a hotel should answer incoming calls.
    B. Anyone answering a phone should have a cheerful voice.

4. The history of medical-laboratory technology shares many of its important historical milestones with the history of medicine itself. Both medicine in general and medical-laboratory technology go back to the time of the Greeks. Some of the main achievements

shared by both medicine and medical-lab technology include Jan Swammerdam's discovery of red blood corpuscles in 1658, Leeuwenhoek's use of a microscope to observe microorganisms in the second half of the 1600s, and the discoveries of Koch and Pasteur in bacteriology in the 1870s. Through these efforts and others like them, medical professionals became aware by the end of the 1800s of the valuable information and possible cures that were available from bacteriology (the study of microorganisms in the human body), cytology (the study of human cells), histology (the study of human tissue), and hematology (the study of human blood). The growth of these medical specialties created a steadily increasing need for laboratory personnel.

A. Medical-lab technicians help make medical history.

B. The growth of medical-lab technology follows the growth of medical advances.

LESSON 3.2

Scanning

Objective   To learn and use the scanning method.

If you are reading a list to find one particular item—one name, one word, one course listing—then use the *scanning technique.* You do not read each item in the list. Your eye moves rapidly down the list until you find the scan clue. The *scan clue* is the item for which you are looking.

Usually the material being scanned is in a particular order. The phone book is in alphabetical order. If you are scanning a table of contents, the items are in numerical order.

So, to scan, you must know

1. How the information is organized.

2. What you are looking for.

Then you must scan carefully. Accuracy is very important in scanning. It does no good to scan a list and come up with the wrong phone number or page number.

EXAMPLE

Look at the following section of a catalog index. You want to know if you can find *paper clips* in this catalog.

1 Note that the index is arranged in alphabetical order.

2 Decide where you are going to start looking—in the Ps because *paper* begins with "p."

3 Move your eye, with or without the aid of your finger, down the P list until you find words that start with "pa."

4 Continue looking until you come to *paper.* The first entry is simply *paper.* The next entry is *paper clip dispenser.* You look farther, and the next entry is *paper clips.*

5 You *can* find paper clips in this catalog on page 29.

You might also use scanning in reading an article in a magazine or a newspaper or an encyclopedia. You do not read every word in the paragraph. You look for a scan clue—the word or phrase that alerts you to the information that you want.

EXAMPLE

The following paragraph discusses finding tire damage. You are looking for information on how to know if there is enough tread on your tires. You do not *read* the *entire* paragraph, you just scan it, line by line, and look for the word *tread* to see if the paragraph would have any information for you.

Spotting Damaged Tires

- After striking anything unusual in the roadway, have the tires checked.

- Inspect your tires for cuts, cracks, splits, or bruises in the *tread* and ←tread sidewall areas. Bumps or bulges may indicate a separation within the tire body.

- Inspect your tires for uneven wear. Wear on one side of the *tread* or ←tread flat spots in the *tread* may indicate a problem with the tire or vehicle. ←tread

- Inspect your tire for adequate *tread* depth. When the tire is worn to ←tread 1/16 or less *tread*-groove depth or the tire cord or fabric is exposed, ←tread the tire is dangerously worn and must be replaced immediately.

- Inspect your tire rims also. If you have a bent or cracked rim, it must be replaced.

As you scan the paragraph, you see the word *tread* five times. This looks like a good paragraph to read for information.

PRACTICE

This list is part of a table of contents. The titles are in the order in which they appear in the book, listed by page number. Read the questions below. Then scan the table to find the answers.

Table of Contents

1. On what page would you find the topic "Grooming and Dress"?

2. Is "Letter Writing" covered in this section?

3. What will you find on page 12?

The following is a listing of the last, or most recent, price of some stocks, along with the price change, up (+), down (−), or no change (...), for one particular day. Most of the stock listings are abbreviations.

The first stock name under "J" is "Jaclyn." Its last price was $8 ⅝. It went down $1/4, or $0.25.

Read questions 4–6 on page 39. Then scan the table to find the answers.

	Last		Net chg		Last		Net chg
Insteel	$9^5/_8$	+	$^1/_4$				
Instron	$10^1/_4$	−	$^1/_4$	———— L ————			
InsSy pf	6	−	$^1/_4$	LSB Ind	$4^5/_8$	+	$^1/_2$
InstSy	$6^1/_8$	−	$^1/_8$	LSB pf	$34^1/_4$	+	$4^1/_8$
IntigS n	$1^1/_2$		...	LaBarg	$2^1/_8$	−	$^1/_8$
InCtPd	8		...	Lancer	6	−	$^1/_8$
InFinSv	14	−	$^1/_8$	Landur	$15^3/_8$	+	$^1/_4$
Intrmk	$^1/_4$	+	$^1/_{16}$	LdmkS	$11^1/_2$		...
IntCoin g	$7^1/_8$	+	...	LndsPc	$4^5/_8$	+	$^1/_8$
IntlCor n	$4^1/_2$	+	$^1/_8$	Larizz	$2^1/_8$		...
IntMobil	$6^1/_8$	−	$^1/_2$	Laser	$3^3/_8$		...
IntMovie	$1^1/_8$		...	Lawson	8	+	$^3/_8$
IntMur	$14^7/_8$	−	$^1/_8$	LazKap	$5^7/_8$	−	$^1/_4$
IntMur wt	$6^1/_8$	−	$^3/_8$	LeePhr	$1^1/_2$		...
IntPwr	$2^3/_8$	−	$^1/_8$	Lfetme	$1^1/_2$		...
IntTich	$^3/_8$		...	LilVern	$13^3/_4$	−	$^1/_8$
IntTest	$7^1/_4$	−	$^1/_8$	Lilly un	$^1/_4$		...
IntThr	3	+	$^1/_8$	LinPro	$^3/_4$		...
InThr pf	$4^1/_2$		...	LincNC	$4^3/_4$		...
IGC	3	−	$^1/_8$	viLionel	$^5/_{16}$	−	$^1/_{16}$
IntPly n	$9^3/_8$	−	$^1/_4$	Litfld	$9^5/_8$	+	$^1/_8$
IvaxCp s	$24^1/_4$	−	$1^1/_4$	Lumex	$12^5/_8$	−	$^1/_2$
				Luria	$7^3/_8$	−	$^1/_4$
———— J ————				LynchC	$18^3/_4$	−	$^1/_4$
Jaclyn	$8^5/_8$	−	$^1/_4$				
JanBell	$16^1/_8$	−	$^1/_2$	———— M ————			
Jetron	$^1/_2$		...	MC Shp	$5^1/_8$		...
JhnPd	$15^1/_4$	−	$^1/_2$	McRae A	$5^1/_8$	−	$^1/_8$
JoneInt	$11^1/_8$	+	$^1/_8$	Medch S	$11^3/_4$	−	$^1/_8$
				MedcR	$17^3/_4$	+	$^1/_4$
———— K ————				Medeva	$17^5/_8$	−	$^1/_4$
vi KLH	$^1/_4$		...	Media	$18^3/_8$	−	$^1/_2$
KV B s	$13^7/_8$	−	$^3/_8$	MedPro	$^{11}/_{16}$	−	$^1/_{16}$
KV A n	$13^7/_8$	−	$^1/_4$	Mdcore	1		...
Keane	$17^1/_2$	−	$^1/_4$	Mediq	$4^1/_2$		...
Keithly	$12^5/_8$	−	$^1/_4$	Mediq pf	$4^1/_2$	−	$^1/_8$
KelyOG	$14^3/_8$	−	$^1/_8$	MercAir	$1^3/_4$	−	$^1/_4$
Kerkhff	3		...	MercA pf	$7^5/_8$	−	$^3/_8$
Ketema	$11^1/_4$		...	MerPt6	$1^7/_8$	+	$^1/_8$
Kinark	$5^3/_4$	+	$^1/_8$	MerP6 pf	$2^1/_4$	+	$^1/_4$
Kirby	$13^1/_2$	−	$^1/_8$	MerPt7	$3^1/_4$	+	$^1/_8$
Kit Mfg	$6^5/_8$	−	$^1/_2$	MLDM	$^1/_4$	−	$^1/_8$
KierVu	$7^3/_4$	−	$^1/_8$	MetPro	$13^1/_8$	+	$^1/_4$

	Last		Net chg		Last		Net chg
Metrbk	$11\frac{3}{8}$	+	$\frac{1}{8}$	NY Tim	$30\frac{1}{2}$	−	$\frac{7}{8}$
MichAnt	$3\frac{3}{8}$	+	$\frac{1}{8}$	NichisA	$8\frac{3}{4}$	+	$\frac{1}{8}$
MidABc	16	+	$\frac{1}{8}$	NichisC	$8\frac{1}{2}$		...
MMaine	$3\frac{3}{4}$	...	...	Norex	$5\frac{1}{4}$	+	$\frac{1}{8}$
Midlby	$3\frac{1}{4}$	+	$\frac{3}{8}$	NARec n	4		...
MinP pf	$92\frac{1}{4}$	+	$1\frac{1}{4}$	NA Vac s	$10\frac{7}{8}$	−	$\frac{1}{2}$
Minven			...	NCdO g	$12\frac{1}{8}$	+	$\frac{1}{4}$
MoneyS n	$14\frac{5}{8}$		...	Nthby s	$18\frac{3}{8}$	−	$\frac{1}{4}$
MoogA	$5\frac{3}{4}$		...	NIPS pf	$50\frac{1}{2}$	−	$1\frac{1}{8}$
MMed	$6\frac{5}{8}$		...	NuHrz	3	−	$\frac{1}{8}$
MorgnF	$1\frac{3}{8}$		...	Numac	$4\frac{1}{4}$	+	$\frac{1}{8}$
Munvst	$10\frac{3}{4}$	−	$\frac{1}{4}$	NNYM n	$12\frac{1}{4}$	−	$\frac{1}{8}$
Myerln	$23\frac{1}{4}$		...				
— N —				**— O —**			
NFC	$24\frac{3}{8}$		...	OOkiep	$9\frac{3}{8}$	+	$\frac{1}{8}$
viNVR	$\frac{3}{4}$	−	$\frac{1}{16}$	OBrien	$4\frac{3}{8}$		...
Nabors	$7\frac{1}{8}$	−	$\frac{3}{8}$	OSullvn	$8\frac{1}{4}$	+	$\frac{1}{8}$
Nabr wt	$2\frac{1}{8}$	−	$\frac{3}{8}$	OdetB	7		...
Nantck	$6\frac{5}{8}$	−	$\frac{1}{8}$	OdetA	$6\frac{1}{4}$	−	$\frac{1}{8}$
NapaVl	$11\frac{1}{8}$	−	$\frac{1}{4}$	Olsten	$30\frac{1}{4}$	−	$\frac{1}{4}$
NatEnv	$\frac{1}{16}$	+	$\frac{1}{32}$	OneLb	$15\frac{7}{8}$	+	$\frac{1}{8}$
NHltC	$12\frac{1}{4}$	+	$\frac{1}{8}$	Oneita	$15\frac{1}{2}$	+	$\frac{3}{8}$
NtPatnt	$4\frac{1}{8}$		...	Orgngn	$12\frac{7}{8}$	−	$\frac{5}{8}$
NtlRlty	$21\frac{1}{8}$	+	$\frac{1}{8}$	OriolH B	$9\frac{5}{8}$	−	$\frac{1}{4}$
NewLine	$12\frac{1}{2}$	−	$\frac{1}{16}$	OxfEgy	$\frac{1}{2}$	−	$\frac{1}{16}$
NMxAr	$7\frac{3}{8}$	−	$\frac{1}{8}$				
NYTEl	$10\frac{5}{8}$	+	$\frac{1}{8}$	**— P —**			
				PEC s	$13\frac{3}{8}$		...

4. Find the stock named *MercAir.* What was its last price?

5. Find the listing *Lfetme.* How did its price change on that day?

6. Is there a listing for *NewLeaf?*

Scan each paragraph to answer the question. The scan clue is underlined.

7. Are any <u>free</u> tours mentioned in this article?

The National Trust for Historic Preservation trains volunteers that offer free tours of the renovated station. The Union Station tour program is a first for the National Trust, which never before offered its architecture and history-oriented tours to public buildings. It does, though, give such tours of some historic houses owned by the National Trust itself.

8.   Is <u>mechanical</u> drawing mentioned in this article?

Because a drawing is a set of instructions that a worker must follow, it must be clear, correct, accurate, and complete. The ability to draw does not in itself make a person a draftsman. A draftsman must have creative ability, a wide range of technical knowledge, and specialized knowledge in his or her own field. The various specialized fields are as different as the branches of industry. Some of the main areas of drafting are mechanical, architectural, structural, and electrical drafting. Technical drawing is the term applied to any drawings used to express technical ideas. When drawings are made with the use of instruments, they are referred to as instrumental drawings. If instruments are not used, drawings are referred to as sketches. The ability to sketch ideas and designs and to make accurate instrumental drawings is a fundamental part of this graphic language.

PR4 Study System

While you are in school, much of your learning is done with the aid of textbooks. Later, when you are finished with school, on the job, and in all areas of life, you will still be learning from books and other written materials. That is why reading skills are so important.

Learning is more than just reading. Learning involves not only retaining and being able to recall facts and ideas, but also being able to relate what you learn to your experiences and to the experiences of others. Studying is the work you do to learn. The PR4 Study System gives you a way to read efficiently so that you learn as much as possible for your efforts.

PR4 stands for five steps in a system that will help you learn to read to the best of your ability:

P— Preview

R1—Relate

R2—Read

R3—Review

R4—Recall

When you are reading your textbooks or doing other reading assignments, you should perform each of the five steps in order. (If you are preparing for a quiz or exam, you will have to use only the Review and Recall steps.) Maybe you think this looks like too much work. Just plain reading is good enough, you might say. Why is PR4 so important?

PR4 is important because it directs your mental activities while you are reading. It helps to eliminate distractions. It gives you a program for consistency in your reading. It ensures that you will give the same attention to your work every time you sit down to read. It encourages you to think along the same lines as the author. PR4 helps you *learn while you read.*

The next five lessons will help you practice the Study System. The reading selection "Highway Robbery: The Scandal of Auto Repair in America" has been reprinted here so you can tear it out of the book and use it for the practice lessons. It does not matter if you are a salesperson who travels a lot, an auto mechanic, or a person who drives to school or work every day. You will be concerned about auto repairs at some time, and this is a very interesting article for anyone to read.

When you have finished the five practice lessons, you will be ready to approach any reading and to organize your study time using this system. It may take a while to get used to the PR4 System, but you could not do less and do a good job. As you practice the system, you will be able to do all the steps in a shorter time, and you will find that you remember more than you ever did before. When it comes time to study for a test, all you have to do is go over your outlines, and you will be thoroughly prepared. You will not have to spend hours cramming material that you cannot remember.

When you have mastered the PR4 Study System, it will actually save you time. Learning in organized stages takes less time and effort and is more effective than reading without any plan. Make this study system a habit, and you will find that your reading is much more rewarding than it was before.

Trade and Technical

Highway Robbery: The Scandal of Auto Repair in America

By Robert Sikorsky

◆ Introduction

Are Americans getting a square deal for the $65 billion they spend each year to maintain their cars? To find out, Reader's Digest *bought a used car—a 1984 Oldsmobile Cutlass Ciera sedan with 20,000 miles on the odometer.*

The car was made "like new": engine tuned, transmission serviced, new spark plugs, brakes, shock absorbers, struts, fan belts, and hoses. Every vital part was checked and, if there was any doubt, replaced. Then we put our Olds on the road. Behind the wheel was automotive columnist Robert (Bob) Sikorsky, author of "Drive It Forever" and veteran of hundreds of road tests. His assignment was to travel the country, pick repair garages at random, and see how they treat a customer in need. (The survey hoped to show what an average motorist in need of car repair might encounter.) Bob pulled the same single spark-plug wire loose from the V-6 engine just before each stop, thus making the motor run roughly. Reattaching it to the plug was all that was necessary to put our car in perfect running condition. But many mechanics either didn't spot the problem or dishonestly "corrected" it by selling or recommending a wide array of parts, oils, and solvents.

What Bob Sikorsky discovered after stops at 225 garages should be a warning to every car owner.

My experiences with garages strongly suggest you have a less than 50-50 chance of getting a good, fair repair on your first try. It is important to take some simple precautions.

The "Prevent" Defense

Know your car. Read the **owner's manual.** Understand the basics. Does your car have a carburetor or fuel injection? Four cylinders or six? Have a mechanic point out the basics under the hood so you can check your oil and coolant levels, spot a loose wire or hose. Follow a **regular maintenance plan**—oil changes and such—to prevent trouble. Most on-the-road breakdowns could be avoided by a **"check before you drive"** inspection.

A Regular Customer

*When you find a good, honest garage, use it **regularly.*** The few dollars you may think you're saving with a bargain oil-change here, a cut-rate tuneup there, cannot compare with work done at a garage that knows your car and wants to keep you as a customer.

Symptoms

*Be **specific** in describing your car's symptoms.* Try to speak directly to the mechanic. If possible, go with him on a **test drive.** If major work is recommended, insist on getting a **second opinion.** At the second garage, describe the trouble without giving the first shop's opinion. If the opinions match, chances are the recommendation is correct.

Written Estimate

*Insist on a detailed **written estimate.*** Make sure that no extra work will be done without your permission. This is required by law in some states. Moreover, be wary of **scare tactics** ("Lady, I wouldn't drive this car another mile"). Also be wary of someone who tries to rush you into a major repair, insisting he can do it "right away."

Useful Complaining

*When precautions fail, **complain.*** This is the most important rule. Do not accept even small rip-offs. Often you will find that what seems to have been fraud was a mistake or misunderstanding that can be straightened out agreeably. But when bad work or dishonesty is obvious, complain effectively. **Complain in writing** to the consumer-fraud unit of the local or state government, to the Better Business Bureau, and to any national organization connected with the shop, such as the American Automobile Association.

Preview (P)

Objective   To become familiar with the steps to use in previewing reading material.

Too many readers jump right into a start-to-finish reading of assignments. This puts them at a disadvantage. When you read without a *Preview,* you are not aware of the author's purpose and style of writing. Your mind has to deal with unexpected ideas as they occur. The *Preview* helps you anticipate the author's ideas and ways of presenting them so that you understand the writing more quickly and completely. Here are the steps you should follow to perform an efficient Preview:

1 Read the title of the article or chapter.

2 Read any section headings or titles.

3 Read any **boldface,** *italicized,* or <u>underlined</u> words or phrases.

4 Examine briefly any pictures, diagrams, maps, or tables.

5 Read the entire first paragraph.

6 Read the entire last paragraph.

7 Glance through the entire selection.

The reading selection that is printed on pages 43–44 also appears on page 61. It has been printed here with some special changes so you can use it to practice some of the steps of the PR4 Study System.

Examine each of these steps:

1 Reading the title usually tells you the subject of the material to be read. The title might be a catchy line designed to attract your attention and make you want to explore further. It might express an opinion and give you a clue to the author's stand on the subject. In looking at a title, then, you can expect to learn the subject and/or the author's opinion on the subject.

Copy the title onto the following line: _____

_____

What are you going to be reading about? _____

_____

What does the word *scandal* tell you about the author's feelings toward auto repair in America?_____

_____

2 Reading any *section headings* or *titles* (sometimes called *subheads*) in the selection tells you more than the main title did of what you will read in the chapter and something of the author's plan of organization.

This selection is unusual because it starts with a three-paragraph introduction. It makes the article that follows more interesting because you have been told how it all started—you feel like an insider. For this activity, copy onto the lines all the subheads.

_____

_____

_____

_____

_____

_____

Circle the best answer to each question.

To whom is the author speaking?   repairpeople   car owners

Does the author seem to believe you can get a good repair job done if you are careful?   yes   no

3 Reading any **boldface,** *italicized,* or <u>underlined</u> words or phrases gives you a more detailed look at what you will be reading and tells you items that the author thought were important. It gives you an idea of the material on which you should concentrate as you read.

Write on the following lines any boldface, italicized, or underlined words that appear in the main article. _____

_____

_____

4 Looking at any *illustrations and/or tables* in the selection can tell you about the who, where, and when of what you are reading. They can make it easier to remember facts from your reading and can point out some of the important information.

This article does not have any pictures or tables, but there is a symbol near the title that gives you an idea of the career area to which it belongs.

What is it? _____

5 The *first paragraph* usually gives you (1) the purpose of the selection, (2) background needed to understand the selection, or (3) a look at what is to come in the reading. Occasionally, an author will begin a section with a story to get the reader started or to encourage the reader to continue.

The first paragraph (other than the introduction) is not very long, but it does tell you the main idea of the article. Complete this sentence: To have a better chance of getting a good, fair auto repair on your first try, _____

_____

_____

6 The *last paragraph* usually summarizes the important facts of the selection as a brief review. It may draw a conclusion based on the facts that have been presented.

The last paragraph of this selection tells you what to do if you did *not* get a fair repair. Write the idea here: _____

_____

_____

7 *Looking over the entire reading selection* helps you see the author's overall plan, noticing again the important terms and main points.

The author made five important points, one from each paragraph, in his article. Write the main points on the following lines. The first one is done for you.

a. Get to know and understand your car, and do basic maintenance

   regularly.

b. _____

   _____

c. _____

   _____

d. _____

   _____

e. _____

   _____

LESSON 4.2

Relate (R1)

Objective   To learn how to Relate reading material to previous knowledge and experiences.

To *relate* means to make *connections*. Being related to a person means you have family connections with that person. Relating what you read means you make connections between what you are reading and what you already know. You will be more interested in reading material if you can relate to it, and it is easier to learn something if you are interested in it. You will be using what you already know to help you learn more.

The Relate step in the PR4 Study System requires you to make connections in your reading. If you were reading Chapter 3 of a book, you could relate it to what you read in Chapters 1 and 2. If you were reading just a section, you could relate it to the previous section. If you were just beginning a book, you could relate it to what you read last year or in some other course.

You can also relate your reading to experiences from your own life or from the lives of family members or friends. If you were reading about caring for the elderly, you might relate it to the care that you saw being given to a grandparent. If you were reading about how to write a good résumé, you could relate it to any job-hunting experiences you have had.

In addition to relating your reading to past experiences, try also to connect it to things to come. Mentally question the author on what you can expect to read in the future, that is, later on in the article or chapter or book. If you are reading about the experiences of a legal secretary, you might ask: "Can I expect to learn what a lawyer does? Will trials be described? Will I ever have to be in a courtroom?" You will get the most out of what you read if you develop at least a temporary interest in the subject.

When answering the following questions, use complete sentences.

1. Look at "Highway Robbery: The Scandal of Auto Repair in America." The introduction describes how the Reader's Digest Association made the 1984 Cutlass like new. Can you relate to that?

    On the lines that follow, describe how you fixed something up, or tried to make it like new.

    _____

    _____

    _____

2. How would you relate to the idea of knowing about your own car? You could describe what jobs you can do or have done to your own car or that you have seen someone else do. You could describe other do-it-yourself jobs that you do.

    _____

    _____

    _____

    _____

3. Is there some business or store that you deal with regularly? Relate that experience to dealing with one reputable garage.

_____

_____

_____

_____

4. Have you ever had to describe a symptom of a car problem to a mechanic? Maybe you had to tell a repairperson what was wrong with a computer or a copy machine. Relate those experiences to that of dealing with a garage.

_____

_____

_____

_____

5. Has anyone ever tried to rush you into a deal? Have you ever gotten a bad deal because you did not have a written estimate or a guarantee? Relate your experience to the article.

_____

_____

_____

_____

6. Relate the consumer advice in the last paragraph to some complaint you made. What were the results of your complaint?

_____

_____

_____

LESSON 4.3

Read (R2)

Objective   To learn to Read actively.

Suppose you have to read a chapter on "Uses of Computers in Business." In the PR4 Study System, you would already have *previewed* the chapter. (Look back at Lesson 4.1 for the steps in a Preview.) Then you would have *related* what you learned in the Preview to what you already know about uses for computers and anticipated what you might learn in the future.

Now you are ready to Read intelligently. Whatever your assignment is, it will be much more than just a number of pages to be covered. You can control your reading speed, reading slowly any ideas that are new or unfamiliar and reading quickly ideas covered during Preview or Relate. This is active reading, the kind that gives you the best results.

Underline or highlight any material that seems important to you. Take notes in the margins as you go along so you will not need to give this material a complete reading again.

Refer to the selection "Highway Robbery: The Scandal of Auto Repair in America." Before you start to read, go over the definitions in the Vocabulary Preview on page 61. The definitions are given to fit the context in which they appear in this selection. Look at the word *square,* for instance, in the first sentence. Does it mean "a deal with four equal sides"? No, it means "an honest and fair deal." Reading the definitions in the Vocabulary Preview puts you into the style or flavor of the selection. You start reading in the correct frame of mind.

Now read the introduction to the selection (in italic type), something that is different in this selection. It was written by the Reader's Digest Association so you, the reader, would understand the condition of the car before Robert Sikorsky went out testing garages across the United States and the experiences Sikorsky had in the garages. This is a very interesting selection, almost like a story, and you might find yourself reading it rather quickly. You might read slowly other selections that are more technical or less familiar to you. Sometimes your rate of reading will be governed by the reading material and other times by you.

After the introduction, the selection begins with the word *My.* That word lets you know that now you are reading the author's advice to car drivers—the advice he feels is necessary after his experiences with the Oldsmobile Cutlass.

Each paragraph is a different piece of advice. Be sure you get the main idea in each paragraph.

Remember to take notes in the margin or to underline or highlight statements that you think are important. Perhaps you would underline "Have a mechanic point out the basics under the hood" in the paragraph titled "The 'Prevent' Defense." Maybe in the last paragraph, you would underline "Better Business Bureau." In the margin, you could write the address and/or phone number of your local Better Business Bureau, which you will find in the phone book.

The last paragraph tells you how to register an official complaint against a repair shop that has not satisfactorily dealt with your complaint to them. Such a procedure not only protects your interests, but also makes sure that other car drivers who ask about that shop will know that it does not satisfy complaints. Some government agencies might take action against a

garage to put them out of business or to fine them for improper repair practices. If you have not been treated fairly by any kind of business, you do not
just have to put up with it. You can take action, and after reading this article, you will have some idea of what to do.

As you read, do not *regress* in your reading; that is, do not let your eyes
wander back up the page to reread lines you have already read. That slows
you down and breaks up the flow of the reading. It could also confuse you if
you forget what you had been reading or how far you had gotten. There is a
place for going back over what you have read, but that is in the next lesson, "Review."

LESSON 4.4

Review (R3)

Objective   To learn to Review material that has just been read.

After you have finished doing any reading, you should do the review immediately while it is still fresh in your mind. But suppose you have just read a
chapter on auto transmissions, and you are tired. You do not feel like continuing to work, going over the same material right away. All right, then;
take a short break. Have a snack or call a friend; but set a time limit—no
more than 10 minutes. Then go back to your book and do the following:

1 Preview again, and Relate.

2 List important points to remember. Use your margin notes to help
you.

3 Read over the points you listed.

4 Close the book.

Look again at "Highway Robbery: The Scandal of Auto Repair in
America."

1 Redo the Preview, and as you Preview, recall any relationships you
made with the information as you first did the Relate step.

Read the main title and any subheads, from "Introduction" to
"Useful Complaining."

Read any boldface, italicized, or underlined words, such as **check
before you drive** and **second opinion.**

Look at any tables, illustrations, or graphic symbols.

Read the first paragraph, glance over the next several paragraphs,
and read the last paragraph.

2 Make a list on paper of the phrases or sentences that you underlined or highlighted. Also write down your margin notes.

3 Read over the list you just made.

4 Close the book. You have finished your Review.

In addition to the Review after every reading session, you should also have a Review session at the end of every week. Then when it is quiz or exam time, you will be prepared because you have constantly kept the material fresh in your mind.

Recall (R4)

Objective   To learn how to perform the Recall step.

This step is performed after you have finished a complete chapter or other major section of reading, right after you have finished the Review (R3). The object of the Recall is to see how much of the material you remember without rereading the text. It is especially useful right before an examination.

1 Prepare by writing on a sheet of paper the title, subtitles, and any important terms from what you have just read. Leave a few lines of space after each item.

2 Then fill in the ideas that belong under each section. One idea will probably trigger another until you have a rather complete outline of what you have read. Refer to your textbook or other reading to check your facts if necessary.

3 Find the review questions or the questions that check understanding that most textbooks include at the end of sections and chapters. Read each question. Try to identify the place in the outline you have created where you could find the answer to the question. Put the number of the question beside that place. Now, with that link, try to answer each question without looking in the book; but check your answers to be sure you are correct and complete.

    Compare your outline with the way the chapter or section is actually organized in the book. If you find anything that you omitted, add it to your outline.

4 If you have a tape recorder, you might want to record everything you can recall about your reading at this point. Talk about the chapter as if you were telling someone else about it. When you have recalled all you can about the chapter, replay the tape as you go through the material in the book. If you find anything that you omitted, add it to your written outline.

This process will ensure that you know the material as completely as possible. You can walk in to any exam and feel confident that you will do well. You have gotten as much as possible from your reading, and that is the purpose of reading.

The following is what your Recall of "Highway Robbery: The Scandal of Auto Repair in America" might look like.

1. Compare the selection with the following outline, and then fill in the details you remember reading.
    Highway Robbery: The Scandal of Auto Repair in America _____

    _____

    _____

    Introduction _____

    _____

    The Prevent Defense _____

    _____

    owner's manual _____

    _____

    regular maintenance plan _____

    _____

    check before you drive _____

    _____

    Regular Customer _____

    _____

    regularly _____

    _____

    Symptoms _____

    _____

    specific _____

    _____

    test drive _____

    _____

second opinion _____

_____

Written Estimate _____

_____

scare tactics _____

_____

Useful Complaining _____

_____

complain _____

_____

complain in writing _____

_____

2. Go to the Comprehension Questions at the end of the selection (page 63). Read each question and place its number in the outline where you think the answer is. For instance, the answer to question 1 is in the Introduction. Write #1 under "Introduction."

3. If you have a tape recorder or can borrow one, try telling the story of "Highway Robbery" in your own words and recording it. Then play it back for yourself and compare it with your outline. Add to the outline any details that you forgot to write down but remembered when you recorded and remind yourself of any details that you had written in the outline but forgot when you recorded.

Practicing for Reading Improvement

How to Use Part 2

As the title of this part points out, you are now going to practice for reading improvement. You are going to practice the skills to which you were introduced in Part 1. Those skills—identifying main ideas, finding the meaning of words, scanning, and so on—will improve as you practice them while reading the selections to come, and your reading comprehension will improve as you read using those skills.

1 Read the title of the selection and note the career field symbol. Is the topic new to you or familiar? Is this your career field or that of someone you know?

2 Look at the words in the *Vocabulary Preview.* These are words that either are difficult to understand or have more than one meaning. The definitions are given in the Preview so you will correctly understand the word when you read it in the selection. (The words will be in boldface type in the selection.) Also, you can increase your vocabulary by learning these words.

3 You may want to read the *Comprehension Questions* that appear after the reading selection first. They check your understanding of the *main idea* of the selection and your grasp of various *facts and details* in the selection. Looking over the Comprehension Questions before you read the selection helps to focus your reading and should make it easier to answer the questions at the end.

4 Perform each preview step that you learned in the PR4 Study System (skipping step 1, since you already did it). In step 3, you will see the words from the *Vocabulary Preview.* When you get to step 7, *read* the entire *selection.* (Since these are short reading selections—not a whole chapter of a book—the method is a little different.) You have prepared to read the article, and you should be able to understand it easily. Take your time—there is no need for speed. You are reading for comprehension. Enjoy the chance to learn something new.

5 After you finish reading the selection, catch your breath and get ready to answer the *Comprehension Questions*. Two questions will be about the general idea of the selection, and three will be about facts and details that you should be able to recall. Read the question and then read the four answer choices. Even if you think choice **a** would be the best answer, *read all four*. As you read each choice, if you know it cannot possibly be the answer, draw a line through the letter.

Often you can eliminate two choices immediately and then decide between the remaining two choices. Read them carefully, and choose the one that you think is the best answer. Try to answer the questions without rereading the selection, but if you are unsure of an answer, then go back over what you read.

When you have answered all the questions, check your answers with the *Answer Key* on page 281. (Looking at the answers before you make your choices is just cheating yourself of an opportunity to improve your reading comprehension.) Give yourself 20 points for each correct answer, and use a dot to record your score in the correct place on the Progress Chart on page 296.

1 correct—20 points

2 correct—40 points

3 correct—60 points

4 correct—80 points

5 correct—100 points

6 Having read the Vocabulary Preview and then the selection, you should be ready to take the *Vocabulary Test*. Some are matching columns, and some require filling in the blanks with the correct word.

As you decide on a match or fill in a blank, put a small mark next to the word or definition so that it is eliminated from the possible choices. Continue making eliminations one by one until you have finished the test. Then check your answers with the Answer Key on page 281. Figure your score in the following table. (For example, if there were 9 answers in the test and you had 7 correct, your score would be 78.)

7 When you are finished with the test, take a moment to think over all you have learned from the reading selection. Take time to enjoy your progress and newfound knowledge.

Number Correct

Number of Answers in Test	1	2	3	4	5	6	7	8	9	10
5	20	40	60	80	100					
6	17	33	50	67	83	100				
7	14	28	43	57	71	86	100			
8	13	25	38	50	63	75	88	100		
9	11	22	33	44	56	67	78	89	100	
10	10	20	30	40	50	60	70	80	90	100

Score

Career Selections

Highway Robbery: The Scandal of Auto Repair in America

By Robert Sikorsky

Vocabulary Preview

consumer: someone who buys and uses goods and services

fraud: a dishonest act in which someone is cheated

odometer: an instrument for measuring and recording the distance traveled by a vehicle

opinion: a judgment based on special knowledge

precautions: actions taken to prevent error

random: without pattern; by chance

solvents: something that can dissolve other substances

square: honest

struts: structural pieces designed to resist pressure or shock

tactics: acts designed to accomplish some purpose

veteran: a person who has had much experience in an activity

vital: very important and necessary

wary: on guard; suspicious of

---

*Are Americans getting a **square** deal for the $65 billion they spend each year to maintain their cars? To find out,* Reader's Digest *bought a used car—a 1984 Oldsmobile Cutlass Ciera sedan with 20,000 miles on the* **odometer.**

*The car was made "like new": engine tuned, transmission serviced, new spark plugs, brakes, shock absorbers, **struts,** fan belts, and hoses. Every **vital** part was checked and, if there was any doubt, replaced. Then we put our Olds on the road. Behind the wheel was automotive columnist Robert (Bob) Sikorsky, author of "Drive It Forever" and **veteran** of hundreds of roads tests. His assignment was to travel the country, pick repair garages at **random,** and see how they treat a customer in need. (The survey hoped to show what an average motorist in need of car repair might encounter.) Bob pulled the same single spark-plug wire loose from the V-6 engine just before each stop, thus making the motor run roughly. Reattaching it to the plug was all that was necessary to put our car in perfect running condition. But many mechanics either didn't spot the problem or dishonestly* *"corrected" it by selling or recommending a wide array of parts, oils, and* **solvents.**

What Bob Sikorsky discovered after stops at 225 garages should be a warning to every car owner.

My experiences with garages strongly suggest you have a less than 50-50 chance of getting a good, fair repair on your first try. It is important to take some simple **precautions.**

The "prevent" defense. Know your car. Read the owner's manual. Understand the basics. Does your car have a carburetor or fuel injection? Four cylinders or six? Have a mechanic point out the basics under the hood so you can check your oil and coolant levels, spot a loose wire or hose. Follow a regular maintenance plan—oil changes and such—to prevent trouble. Most on-the-road breakdowns could be avoided by a "check before you drive" inspection.

When you find a good, honest garage, use it regularly. The few dollars you may think you're saving with a bargain oil-change here, a cut-rate tune-up there, cannot compare with work done at a garage that knows your car and wants to keep you as a customer.

Be specific in describing your car's symptoms. Try to speak directly to the mechanic. If possible, go with him on a test drive. If major work is recommended, insist on getting a second **opinion.** At the second garage, describe the trouble without giving the first shop's opinion. If the opinions match, chances are the recommendation is correct.

Insist on a detailed written estimate. Make sure that no extra work will be done without your permission. This is required by law in some states. Moreover, be **wary** of scare **tactics** ("Lady, I wouldn't drive this car another mile"). Also be wary of someone who tries to rush you into a major repair, insisting he can do it "right away."

When precautions fail: complain. This is the most important rule. Do not accept even small rip-offs. Often you will find that what seems to have been fraud was a mistake or misunderstanding that can be straightened out agreeably. But when bad work or dishonesty is obvious, complain effectively. Complain in writing to the **consumer-fraud** unit of the local or state government, to the Better Business Bureau, and to any national organization connected with the shop, such as the American Automobile Association.

Comprehension Questions

1. **The author went from garage to garage to_____ .**
   a. get the best price
   b. find the best mechanic
   c. check the skill and honesty of some mechanics around the United States
   d. see how different mechanics do the same job

2. **Mr. Sikorsky believes that most on-the-road breakdowns could be avoided by _____.**
   a. making sure your spare tire has air
   b. dealing with one garage
   c. keeping your owner's manual in the glove compartment
   d. knowing your car and checking it out before you drive

3. **The author advises sticking with a good, honest garage when you find one because   .**
   a. the garage will know your car and want you to stay its customer
   b. the mechanic will become your friend
   c. you may get a discount
   d. you will know who made any mistakes

4. **If you have some bad work done on your car, the article states you should _____.**
   a. complain in writing
   b. try somewhere else
   c. ask for your money back
   d. tell all your friends

5. **This article might also be titled _____.**
   a. Fixing a 1984 Oldsmobile
   b. Avoiding Auto-Repair Rip-Offs
   c. Garages around the U.S.A.
   d. How to Get a Good Tune-Up

Vocabulary Test

On each line, write the word that completes the sentence.

consumer	opinion	solvents	tactics
fraud	precautions	square	veteran
odometer	random	struts	vital
			wary

There are many government agencies to protect a _____ against _____. One trick that dishonest car salespersons use is changing the number on a car's _____. If you are looking for a used car, get the _____ of a reliable mechanic on the car's condition. It is _____ not to fall for phony sales _____ and to be _____ of any deal that sounds too good to be true. _____ checks of car dealers show that most of them are honest, but it never hurts to take _____ to avoid a bad deal.

Working in the Hospitality Industry

By Arnold R. Deutsch

Vocabulary Preview

accommodations: lodging, food, and services or traveling space and related services

bellhop: a hotel employee who escorts guests to rooms, assists them with luggage, and runs errands

fraught: well supplied or accompanied

maître d': headwaiter

metropolitan: relating to a large, important city

prerequisite: something that is necessary in order to attain or do something else

proliferating: increasing rapidly in number

refurbishment: a brightening or freshening up of something

stamina: staying power; endurance

upkeep: the act of maintaining in good condition

Do you know what ranks as one of the three top industries in over half the states in our nation? If you guessed tourism, you're right. And where do these tourists stay during their travels? Most likely they occupy one of the 2 million rooms in the 37,500 hotels and motels in operation from coast to coast. Lastly, what do these hotels and motels offer besides **accommodations** for the traveler? The answer, of course, is jobs. There are 800,000 Americans working in the hospitality industry, with an additional 35,000 being added each year.

Remember Arthur Hailey's book *Hotel*? It depicted the large **metropolitan** hotel as a city within a city, **fraught** with more high-powered drama than Broadway. In many ways, Hailey was not exaggerating. For those whose pleasure is working with people, hospitality work may prove fascinating—even without the diploma that is the **prerequisite** for so many other jobs today.

Consider for a moment all the tasks that must be performed in the hotel/motel industry: housekeeping, maintenance, and laundry services; millions of meals to be prepared and served; miles of lawns and grounds to be manicured; catering of receptions; meeting and convention planning; and greeting and escorting guests.

And then there's the resort industry. It takes a vast network of employees to create, establish, and service the hotel/motel chains that are **proliferating** on every continent. Jobs are as diverse as those in large industrial corporations and range from clerical jobs to middle-management and top-level executive positions.

Three out of five hotel workers are service employees—elevator operators, parking attendants, doormen, chambermaids, laundry assistants, pool attendants, kitchen help, maintenance workers, **bellhops**, and waiters and waitresses. More than a fourth of all hotel workers are concerned with keeping the premises clean and inviting.

Average gains in the number of employment openings are expected for most of these slots in the near future, with the brightest outlook for waiters and waitresses. Opportunities for advancement in this field, however, are somewhat limited. Consider bellhops, for example. Hotels may employ a dozen people to work in this capacity, but there is only one bell captain. Besides limited advancement, prospective hotel workers should consider another factor: work in many locations is seasonal, necessitating periodic reductions in the work force. On the other hand, because of their seasonal nature, these positions are frequently sought by students.

Opportunities for getting ahead *do* exist. Hotel/motel housekeepers may become executive housekeepers, supervising the work of large staffs, preparing budgets for their departments, purchasing supplies, and pointing out needs for repairs or **refurbishment**. Custodians, too, can begin with general maintenance tasks and rise to supervisory positions that involve overseeing **upkeep** of entire buildings.

What are some of the advantages of employment in the hotel/motel industry? Except for the seasonality aspect at resorts, the work is generally steady. Free meals are often provided, especially to restaurant and food-service personnel. Tips are usually a substantial part of take-home pay. (The Internal Revenue Service [IRS] expects the worker to declare tips as income. For example, the IRS is aware that 25–75% of a bellhop's income comes from tips.) One of the great allures of this field, no doubt, is the array of personalities one meets on a daily basis.

What attributes can help you along the motel/hotel career path? A desire to please and be helpful, an outgoing personality, trustworthiness, and reliability are important strengths when coupled with the **stamina** to work on one's feet much of the day. Furthermore, most service positions are accountable to a higher authority, so that the employee must be willing to answer to one or even several bosses.

If you have some college credits or at least a high school diploma, it can substantially broaden your choice of opportunities. The hospitality industry uses a full complement of front-desk staff, cashiers, banquet managers, convention coordinators, chefs, **maître d's**, and clerical workers to accept reservations, prepare bills, provide information, distribute mail, and collect payments. Behind the scenes there are cashiers, bookkeepers, telephone operators, secretaries, and personnel workers, just as in any big business. An increasingly popular position is the hotel employee who, in the European tradition, is known as the concierge. This person is, in essence, a human data bank of information for guests. He or she can offer advice on almost everything—hiring limousines, entertaining VIPS, activities around town, etc.

More and more managers and others in training for key positions are college educated. In fact, courses leading to degrees in hotel administration are on the rise throughout the country. Course work in these programs covers the gamut from preparing hors d'oeuvres to stocking appropriate wines to maintaining effective public relations to running the financial end of the business. Hotel administration trainees begin with average salaries, but skilled, experienced managers earn salaries and bonuses to match their counterparts in business and industry. There are additional benefits for key staff members, such as free stays at other hotels of the chain and meals in the dining room.

Among the universities now offering degrees in hotel management are New York State's Cornell University (Ithaca, N.Y.), the University of Massachusetts (Amherst campus), Florida International University (Miami, Fla.), the University of Hawaii, and the University of Houston.

Comprehension Questions

1. **The hospitality industry** _____ .

    a. takes only college graduates
    b. employs a great number of people
    c. is good for young people
    d. is shrinking

2. **According to Arthur Hailey's book, a hotel is like** _____ .

    a. a city within a city
    b. a ship
    c. a TV show
    d. any small town

3. **Three out of five hotel workers are** _____ .

    a. cooks
    b. women
    c. men
    d. service employees

4. According to this article, the choice of opportunities in the hospitality industry is much greater if _____ .

    a. you have some experience

    b. you are over 25

    c. you are a woman

    d. you have some college credits or at least a high school diploma

5. One of the most important reasons for considering a job in the hospitality industry is that _____ .

    a. the work varies according to the season

    b. you can get free food and rooms

    c. there is a variety of jobs to cover almost everyone

    d. a lot of people make good tips

Vocabulary Test

On each line, write the word that matches the definition.

accommodations	bellhop	fraught
maître d'	metropolitan	prerequisite
proliferating	refurbishment	stamina
upkeep		

1. _____ something that is necessary in order to attain or do something else

2. _____ well supplied or accompanied

3. _____ the act of maintaining in good condition

4. _____ increasing rapidly in number

5. _____ a hotel employee who escorts guests to rooms, assists them with luggage, and runs errands

6. _____ lodging, food, and services or traveling space and related services

7. _____ relating to a large, important city

8. _____ headwaiter

9. _____ staying power; endurance

10. _____ a brightening or freshening up of something

Cable-Television Technician

Trade and Technical

Vocabulary Preview

acute: sharp; extremely accurate

amplifying: increasing in power

coaxial cable: a conducting line used to transmit telegraph, telephone, and television signals of high frequency

corrosion: wearing away by chemical action

deficiency: a shortage or lack

preventive maintenance: the upkeep of property or equipment in order to prevent major repairs later on

schematic: showing the design or outline of something

splicing: uniting by interweaving the strands

Cable-television technicians work in a variety of settings and perform a wide range of activities. These technicians inspect, maintain, and repair antennas, cables, and **amplifying** equipment used in cable-television transmission systems. Television cables usually follow the routes of telephone cables, running along poles in rural and suburban areas and through tunnels in cities. Working in tunnels and underground cable passageways, technicians inspect cables for evidence of damage and **corrosion.** Using **schematic** diagrams and blueprints, they trace cables to locate sites of signal breakdown. They may also work at pole-mounted amplifiers, where they analyze the strength of incoming television signals, using field strength meters and miniature television receivers to evaluate reception. At customers' terminal boxes, they explain the workings of the cable system, answer customers' questions, and respond to complaints that may indicate cable or equipment problems. When major problems arise, they repair or replace damaged or faulty cable systems.

Cable-television technicians use electrical measuring instruments (voltmeters, ohmmeters, capacity meters) to diagnose causes of transmission problems. They also use electricians' hand tools (screwdrivers, pliers, and so forth) to dismantle, repair, or replace faulty sections of cable or disabled equipment, such as amplifying equipment used to boost the signal at intervals along the cable system.

An important aspect of the work of cable-television technicians involves implementing regular programs of **preventive maintenance** on the cable system. Technicians inspect connections, insulation, and the performance of amplifying equipment, using measuring instruments and viewing the transmitted signals on television monitors.

A large part of the technician's time is spent on ladders or in confined spaces. As with all electrical maintenance work, there is some danger of electrical shock. The **coaxial cables** used to transmit television signals are from two to three inches in diameter. Because of their tough shielding and thick insulation, they are heavy and awkward to handle. When a section of cable is replaced, heavy-duty lifting and pulling equipment is put to use. Cables still have to be manipulated into position for **splicing,** which involves medium to heavy physical work.

Cable-television technicians must be able to deal with people, to analyze clients' descriptions of reception problems, and to explain cable system costs and operations when necessary.

The activities of these technicians require care and precision. The work is moderately heavy, involving occasional lifting of up to 50 pounds. Cable-television technicians work both indoors and outdoors and must be able to climb utility poles and work at heights comfortably. **Acute** vision, with no color-perception **deficiency,** is essential for analyzing cable reception. Technicians must be physically able to bend and stretch and to work in confined spaces easily. They should feel comfortable working with electrical equipment and with electricians' tools.

Comprehension Questions

1. **The main qualifications for a cable-television technician are** _____.

    a. skill with the cable system and ability to deal with customers
    b. no fear of heights and good vision
    c. knowledge of electricity and skill with hand tools
    d. ability to trace cables and to work in tight places

2. **Cable-television technicians must be fairly strong because** _____.

    a. they need to climb utility poles
    b. television sets are heavy
    c. coaxial cables are heavy
    d. they need to be able to handle tools

3. **According to this article, one of the dangers of cable-television work is _____.**

   a. muscle strain   **c.** color blindness
   b. electrical shock   **d.** frostbite

4. **Much of a cable-television technician's time is spent _____.**

   a. dealing with customers   **c.** tracing cable routes
   b. checking TV reception   **d.** on ladders or in confined spaces

5. **A cable-television technician's work would be most like _____.**

   a. a carpenter   **c.** a plumber
   b. an electrician   **d.** a TV repairman

Vocabulary Test

On each line, write the number of the word that matches the definition.

1. **deficiency**

2. **schematic**

3. **acute**

4. **splicing**

5. **coaxial cable**

6. **preventive maintenance**

7. **corrosion**

8. **amplifying**

_____ **a.** wearing away by chemical action

_____ **b.** the upkeep of property or equipment in order to prevent major repairs later on

_____ **c.** a shortage or lack

_____ **d.** showing the design or outline of something

_____ **e.** a conducting line used to transmit telegraph, telephone, and television signals of high frequency

_____ **f.** sharp; extremely accurate

_____ **g.** uniting by interweaving the strands

_____ **h.** increasing in power

Video Game Designers—How Do They Make Their Magic?

By Scott Stuckey

Vocabulary Preview

flawless: without defects or flaws

freelance: independent; working in a profession without commitment to an employer

graphics: visual part of a program; drawings and illustrations

gruesome: awful; causing shock or horror

insignificant: lacking meaning; unimportant

jettison: to drop from an airplane or spacecraft

nautical mile: a unit of distance used for sea and air navigation; 6,076.115 feet

piecemeal: put together bit by bit, not in any order

promoted: to present for buyer acceptance through publicity

routine: ordinary; commonplace

tedious: boring; tiresome

unleash: to let loose; to free

Through the Space Shuttle's windows, you see clouds drifting lazily over the launchpad. Your instrument panel warns that liftoff is only seconds away. Suddenly the main engines ignite. The ship shudders violently, and soon you're blasting through the clouds headed for outer space.

Although only a **routine** shuttle flight, this one takes place right in your living room, made possible by an inexpensive game computer.

It is, of course, just a video game (or "simulation," as its designer prefers to call it). And like most good video games, it is an almost magical combination of color, sound, and action. Once you fall under its spell, you can barely pull yourself away.

Video games *are* fun. And in the years since they first appeared in America, thousands have been made, some good, some bad. The bad ones are quickly abandoned. The good ones devour your hours without your even noticing.

That doesn't happen by accident. Every speck of color, blip of sound, and sequence of movement is programmed into the game by an eager game designer hoping to create a hit. Thousands try their hand at it. How do they do it?

The making of the Space Shuttle simulation described above is a good example. It shows just how much work can go into a game—in this case, two and a half years' worth.

The designer, Steve Kitchen of Woodside, Calif., started it not with an idea, but a goal: "I wanted to get people interested in the space program," he says.

Instead of the usual cosmic shoot-out, however, Kitchen decided to re-create the flight of an actual spacecraft. He vowed to make his shuttle simulation authentic. He would include no laser cannons nor alien warships, but only what happens in a real shuttle mission.

For the next year and a half, with NASA's cooperation, Kitchen did little else but research: He attended shuttle launches and landings. He studied documents and blueprints. He even rode in the shuttle simulator used for flight training.

All the while, he gathered details for his game. The real Space Shuttle, for example, **jettisons** its solid rocket boosters at 26 **nautical miles** and orbits at 210. Kitchen's shuttle would, too. For the next 13 months, he struggled with the computer coding that would make it all happen.

Writing computer code is anything but glamorous. It means sitting for hours at a computer keyboard, typing countless lines of computer-language commands. The designer hopes the commands will work. Often they don't, and the designer has to try again.

Finally, after plenty of 12-hour workdays, Kitchen finished. And in late 1983, Activision launched his "Space Shuttle, A Journey into Space."

Few game designers devote so much time to a single game. But behind all computer games is a series of steps that are both technical and **tedious.** For some, it's a lonely, frustrating job. Others believe it's the best type of work imaginable.

The strategies of game design vary. How it is done depends in part on which company the designer works for. At big companies, designers use state-of-the-art equipment. At small companies, they may work with little more than home computers. **Freelance** designers work for themselves. Using whatever equipment they can afford, they try to invent games that will catch the fancy of game companies.

Designers have no secret formula for clever ideas. They draw them from books, magazines, movies, dreams—from their entire life experience. Don Bluth, creator of the arcade videodisc games *Dragon's Lair* and *Space Ace,* offers this advice: "To design a good game, you have to look very closely at human nature. You need to understand life's struggles."

Bluth, 46, who has a degree in English, says he gained helpful insights for his games and animated movies by reading the life-and-death struggles in classical literature. (He recommends reading such masters as Shake-speare, Melville, and Hawthorne.)

In a fan newsletter, Bluth advises would-be animators to search their past for **gruesome** people, such as mean schoolmates, who might make good animated characters.

If that doesn't work, they should combine ideas from books, movies, and other sources. "You **piecemeal** your way to a design, like Dr. Frankenstein robbing graves to create one body," he says.

Creating game ideas can sometimes bring unexpected rewards. At least that's what happened to Will Harvey, a 17-year-old Eagle Scout (Troop 175, Foster City, Calif.).

A couple years ago, Harvey was designing a video game. He wanted to add music, but he didn't know how to get the notes into the computer. In fact, he didn't even know how to read music.

He decided to write a computer program that would help. What resulted was more exciting than the game itself: his program allowed him to "construct" music right on a TV screen.

Harvey spent the next eight months refining his "music constructor," which eventually comprised about 5,800 lines of code. He had help from an engineer sent by a software company, Electronic Arts. One big challenge was getting three-note chords to come out of computers designed to produce only one tone at a time.

His efforts paid off. In its first four months in the stores, Harvey says, the Electronic Arts *Music Construction Set* sold thousands of copies—at $40 each.

Good ideas can bring success, yet many designers believe ideas are the easiest part of video game design.

"Really, the initial idea is almost **insignificant** to the end result," says Activision senior designer Steve Cartwright. "The game concept might take you only five seconds, but that's just the beginning of the work."

After an idea takes shape, most designers try to get it down on paper. Rough sketches—of spaceships, submarines, monsters, or whatever—might be refined into full-color drawings.

A sequence of sketches or drawings, called *storyboards,* might be presented for group criticism. And *flowcharts,* or *block diagrams,* which depict a game in words and boxes, can help check whether game action seems logical.

Whatever any designer accomplishes must be done through programming, or coding, the biggest part of game design. (In fact, game designers used to be called simply "programmers.") The designer might first program the game's basic display **graphics,** using a loop (a section of code that repeats itself over and over). Next, he might code the main action sequences, building in a degree of randomness so that game action is less predictable. Then he might add obstacles and enemies. Finally, he might put in the "extras," such as a musical jingle.

Each line of code must be **flawless** in syntax (the computer's language rules) and logic, or else the game will malfunction. "Debugging" the program (removing errors) is a tough but important step.

"The computer will alert you to syntax errors," says Mark A. Van Alstine, a designer for Creative Software, a small company in California's Silicon Valley, "but not to errors in logic, which might make a spaceship fly off the screen even though you didn't intend for it to."

"It's a constant rewrite," says Activision's Steve Cartwright. "In the process of designing a game, I might go through 100 different sets of (game) rules before I find what I want."

When a designer thinks his game is ready, he'll **unleash** his fellow designers on it for testing. "Then everybody gets a big kick out of trying to make it crash (stop working)," says Glenn Hicks, another designer at Creative Software. "That's part of the fun of the job."

Cartwright says, "Once I think a game (of mine) is finished, it's really a month or two away from being really finished."

When the game design *is* finished, a company might test it further before mass production begins. Atari, for example, invites local kids to play new games, watching their reactions through a two-way mirror.

If a game passes the tests, next comes mass production. Finally, the game is packaged, distributed, advertised and **promoted**.

Making videodisc games, such as *Dragon's Lair,* involves some different steps. These games are like short movies, except that you get to control the action instead of just watching it. For Don Bluth's animated games, 24 different color drawings are needed for each *second* of game play. Bluth's production team of 165 creates 28 *minutes* of animation per game—at a cost of $100,000 per minute.

What does the future hold for video games and their makers? Most industry observers believe the games will survive for many years to come. And they will get better. As computers become more powerful, video games will become more complicated. Designing them will demand ever more skill.

Comprehension Questions

1. **The author makes it clear that designing a video game is**

   _____.

   a. not too hard   **c.** done quickly
   b. a lot of work   **d.** mostly fun

2. **A sequence of sketches or drawings is called a _____.**

   a. storyboard   **c.** block diagram
   b. flowchart   **d.** program

3. **One of the extras in a video game is _____.**

   a. action   **c.** music
   b. graphics   **d.** rules

4. Steve Kitchen prefers to call his game _____.

   a. a computer program   **c.** animation
   b. a video game   **d.** a simulation

5. The main steps in a game design are _____.

   a. sketching and drawing
   b. an idea, the sketches, and the computer program
   c. drawing and testing
   d. an idea, debugging, and selling

Vocabulary Test

On each line, write the number of the word that matches the definition.

1. **insignificant**   _____   **a.** a unit of distance used for sea and air navigation; 6,076.115 ft

2. **nautical mile**

3. **promoted**   _____   **b.** to drop from an airplane or spacecraft

4. **freelance**   _____   **c.** boring; tiresome

5. **tedious**   _____   **d.** awful; causing shock or horror

6. **routine**   _____   **e.** to present for buyer acceptance through publicity

7. **flawless**

8. **gruesome**   _____   **f.** to let loose; to free

9. **jettison**   _____   **g.** ordinary; commonplace

10. **unleash**   _____   **h.** without defects or flaws

                         _____   **i.** lacking meaning; unimportant

                         _____   **j.** independent; working in a profession without commitment to an employer

Cajun Country

By Bryce Moreland

Hospitality and Tourism

Vocabulary Preview

bayou: a shallow, slow-moving stream that drains a swamp or shallow lake; term used in areas of Louisiana, Texas, and Mississippi through which the Mississippi River drains

Cajun: a native of Louisiana whose family were French-speaking people from Acadia (now Nova Scotia) in Canada

commercialism: preoccupation with profit-making businesses

crawfish (also crayfish): a freshwater lobsterlike being, but much smaller than a lobster

Creole: a descendant of French or Spanish people who settled around the Mississippi delta

ethnic: relating to a large group of people classed according to common racial, national, and cultural origin or background

gumbo: a vegetable soup thickened with okra pods; usually contains meat and/or seafood

mainstream: the current or popular direction of activity

moss-draped: having Spanish moss hanging from it (real moss is made up of tiny green plants growing so close together as to look like a velvet pad; Spanish moss is not real moss but a flowering plant with long, gray stems that look like hair)

okra: a tall plant grown for its long pointed pods that are used alone as a vegetable or in soups and stews for flavor and thickening

quarter horse: a compact, muscular saddle horse known for achieving great speeds for a short distance (about a quarter mile)

savory: very tasty due to seasonings

storefront: the front side of a store at street level and facing the street

St. Martinville, Louisiana, is small-town America but with a big local difference. Its quiet streets, old **storefronts,** and corner coffee shop are a typical American scene. But when you order your coffee, you clearly hear the voice of an almost unchanged region in your waitress's **Cajun** accent.

She speaks Cajun French as well as she speaks English. It is hard to tell—even by her—which is her first language. Local conversations switch from one language to another as easily as her children switch television channels. It's a fact of life in St. Martinville that French is alive and well in many families. But it's also true that television, education, and **commercialism** have washed out some of the local color in communities in Acadiana.

Which brings us to the point: Acadiana—also called Cajun Country—is a travel experience of enjoying people in small towns and out-of-the-way places. Because these people, these Cajuns, are often farmers and fishermen, it's also an experience of the land and sea.

What you do in Cajun Country is dig into a culture. Wonderfully seasoned food. Real folk music. Friendly conversation. Hard-betting **quarter horse** racing. Backroad sights of marshland, winding **bayous,** acres of swampland, and square miles of rice, soybean, and sugar cane fields. Here you'll find your typical Louisiana of **moss-draped** oaks, dark waterways, and spicy food. But if you go about it right, you'll also find a pattern of life that would still comfort the French Canadian farmers exiled here from Nova Scotia—they called it Acadia—in 1755.

Industrial cities of Lake Charles, Morgan City, and Lafayette (Acadiana's unofficial capital) are mostly Cajun-populated cities. However, you get your real feel for **ethnic** Acadiana outside the cities where grass-roots Cajun culture can, for the most part, escape being absorbed into **mainstream** America.

Besides the language, Cajun life is characterized by spicy, **savory** food, close family ties, distinctive folk music, Roman Catholicism, and traditional occupations that harvest from the land and sea.

The finer restaurants in Lafayette have raised Cajun cooking to a level equal to New Orleans' best **Creole** dishes. But food like pork sausage (called boudin), rice and dark gravy, rich chicken and **okra gumbo,** and **crawfish** stew over rice (etouffée) is served up in cafés and authentic Cajun restaurants everywhere.

Your most unforgettable dining experience will no doubt be your first meal of boiled crawfish (crayfish to the rest of the world). This dish is prepared the same as boiled shrimp à la Louisiane . . . with enough cayenne pepper to kill them if the water didn't. These critters are a delicious, unmistakable Cajun gourmet discovery.

Catholic churches, built in the shape of a cross, are true architectural treats. Many of the worshippers coming from Sunday morning mass have enjoyed a Saturday night dance to fiddle and accordion music. Cajun folk music has fans all over the country. But no preachers are needed here to bring out believers at countless places every weekend. Ask around and you'll find them, too.

Along Bayou Teche, the land is planted in sugar cane and the towns are shaded by large oaks. St. Martinville is here; the Atchafalaya Swamp is not far away. Westward is the Vermilion Bayou and Abbeville with its two town squares and, like all the other places, its language, crawfish, Catholic church, and surrounding farmland. Rice and soybeans are the cash crops on the prairie. Southward to the coast, some farmers double as trappers, harvesting furs from the marshes each winter.

Rural and quiet, with a few cities and all the comforts, Acadiana takes you back to life's basics: family, friends, the good earth, and faith. It's for people who like local color—in language, food, music, work, and the land—and want to travel a way different from mainstream America.

Comprehension Questions

1. **The main topic of this reading selection is _____.**

   a. two specific Cajun communities in Louisiana
   b. what to expect from Cajun food and restaurants
   c. the language patterns of Acadiana
   d. an area strong in a particular ethnic way of life

2. **One of the features of the land in Cajun country is _____.**

   a. many different religions
   b. rice fields
   c. Creole cooking
   d. rock music

3. **The Cajun people came originally from _____.**

   a. Acadiana
   b. France
   c. Louisiana
   d. Nova Scotia

4. **The food is described as _____.**

   a. always having fish as an ingredient
   b. rich and spicy
   c. boring
   d. vegetarian

5. **Each of these statements comes from the selection. Which one best gives the main idea?**

   a. What you do in Cajun country is dig into a culture.
   b. You get your real feel for Acadiana outside the cities.
   c. Some farmers double as trappers.
   d. Local conversations switch from one language to another.

Vocabulary Test

On each line, write the number of the word that matches the definition.

1. **commercialism**
2. **mainstream**
3. **crawfish**
4. **bayou**
5. **savory**
6. **gumbo**
7. **Cajun**
8. **ethnic**
9. **quarter horse**
10. **storefront**

_____ **a.** a shallow, slow-moving stream that drains a swamp or shallow lake

_____ **b.** a native of Louisiana descended from the Acadian French

_____ **c.** preoccupation with profit-making businesses

_____ **d.** a small freshwater lobsterlike being

_____ **e.** relating to people classed according to common racial, national, and cultural background

_____ **f.** a vegetable soup thickened with okra pods

_____ **g.** the current or popular direction of activity

_____ **h.** a compact, muscular horse known for racing short distances

_____ **i.** very tasty with seasonings

_____ **j.** the front side of a store at street level and facing the street

SELECTION 6

Planning and Building an Office

By Corey Sandler

Vocabulary Preview

assessor: a person who determines the value of property for taxation

beam: a main horizontal support of a building

camped: settled in a temporary position

columns: vertical supporting pillars

compensate: undo the effect of

consulting: giving advice

corporate: belonging to a business organized under legal rules for a corporation

dedicated: used for a particular purpose or machine

dehumidifier: a device that removes moisture from the air

furnace: an enclosed structure in which heat is produced

niceties: attention to detail

professionals: people engaged in a particular job as a permanent career

radon: a radioactive gas

thermostat: an automatic device for regulating temperature

virgin: being used for the first time

When I decided to operate my writing and **consulting** business full-time from home, I knew I needed a fully equipped office similar to the **corporate** office I was leaving. I needed something that would be in my house—but not really part of my home. I started by making a list of my possibilities:

Option 1

I could set up in the extra bedroom on the second floor, just down the hall from my bedroom and those of my children. It's an attractive, airy room with a ceiling and plenty of closet space. It had electrical outlets, telephone wiring, heating, air conditioning, and carpeting.

But I knew right away that it was too close to the living quarters. If I needed to be pounding away at the keyboard at 5:00 in the morning, I would wake up the sleepers; if I needed silence to think and conduct my business on the telephone, the children would be **camped** outside with toy drums and pianos. And there was no possibility of expansion without someone losing a bedroom.

Option 2

I could use the unfinished attic that runs the length of the house. The attic would give me all the space I could possibly need, although it would be difficult to hang anything on the sloping walls.

This option presented a number of construction and technical barriers, though. I'd have to install a permanent set of stairs to replace the pull-down ladder in the hallway. And I'd have to deal with cooling the attic in the summer. I also realized that although the attic was sufficiently blocked off from the rest of the house to be private, any visitors to the office would have to walk by the bedrooms of the house—neither a grand nor a businesslike entrance.

Option 3

I could work down in the unfinished basement. The basement does offer plenty of space and easy access to electrical and telephone lines. But callers would have to enter through a door in the kitchen—better than walking by the bedrooms, but still not quite what I wanted. Also, the space was not clean; the ceiling was about a foot lower than upstairs (and it was covered with pipes); and there was a water meter on the wall and a bunch of **columns** and **beams** holding up the house.

When I thought it through, though, the basement was irresistible. I could "commute" from my bedroom to the office in my home *and* be isolated from the family. It was **virgin** territory, just waiting to be developed.

I did my initial planning on the back of an envelope, but soon moved onto my computer to sketch out a floor plan that included electrical outlets, switches, lighting, and furniture.

At the foot of the basement stairs, I created a mini hallway with a pair of doors: one leads left into my office suite and the other into the storage section of the basement. I made sure that any visitor to my office would be able to enter directly without seeing the cobwebbed section on the other side of the wall. The doors also serve as extra insulation from the noise upstairs. I built the office as far away from the **furnace** as possible to reduce the noise.

A large steel beam and a row of columns run down the length of the basement ceiling. Rather than work around them, I chose to divide the space into two rooms (each about 12 by 16, or 200 square feet). That way, I could lay out the furniture differently in each area, using one room as my writing area and the other as a laboratory and storage area.

◆ Making the Basement Livable

Heating and cooling were simple. To begin with, the basement's temperature is relatively stable, generally requiring just a small amount of heat to make it comfortable in winter and little or no cooling in summer.

On the basement ceiling are ducts that distribute cooled or heated air to the house. I thought about tapping into them for heat, but a heating and air-conditioning contractor quickly convinced me to drop that idea. He said that tapping into the ducts would throw off the balance of heating and cooling upstairs, and the sheet metal work would cost as much as installing electric strip heating with a separate **thermostat.** So I chose electric heat.

I purchased a large **dehumidifier** to **compensate** for dampness. It runs every night during warm months. I sealed the cement floor with a heavy enamel paint.

To test for **radon,** I bought a detector, left it in place for a week, and sent it off to a laboratory. My basement was clean during the test period.

I built the two rooms of the office in two stages. The formal writing space was completed first, with full plasterboard walls and ceiling. The laboratory and storage area was completed later. I had **professionals** do all of the work, except for the complicated ceiling in the filing area. I reserved that for myself—to have some fun swinging a hammer after sitting at a desk for 12-hour stretches and to save about $500. I boxed in the pipes with plywood and installed a higher drop ceiling in the rest of the room.

Both carpenters (one for each room) did fine jobs, and included special touches: a box with an access door around the water meter and attractive wooden frames around the tiny basement windows—the only source of natural light.

I filed for building and electrical permits, even though I was told by several contractors that such legal **niceties** weren't really necessary. However, I decided the $100 or so in fees might protect me or a future buyer from problems with the tax **assessor.**

◆ Wiring

Like most basements, mine had only a minimal number of electrical outlets and a few bare pull-string lights when work began. I had three new lines installed, each running to a separate circuit breaker.

Why so much power? Well, here's what's in my office: three computers and monitors; a laser printer; a high-speed impact printer; a facsimile machine; a recorder-transcriber; a scanner; a stereo system; an answering machine; five telephone sets; a television set; and a set of Nintendo and NEC video game machines. (It's not what you think: One of my ongoing projects is a series of books on video games for Bantam.)

Why **dedicated** circuit breakers? In theory, modern electronic devices are pretty well isolated from interference, especially if you are wise enough to install noise filters and surge protectors at each outlet. However, a few electrical systems in today's homes can cause problems for computers. Furnaces, air conditioners, refrigerators, and microwave ovens draw a lot of power when you turn them on. I didn't want to explain to a client that my four-year-old fried one of my most complex files when she melted her marshmallows onto a graham cracker in the microwave. And fluorescent bulbs emit radio frequency interference.

◆ A $5,000 Job

Construction costs for the two-room office came to about $3,000. Electrical work came to $750. I paid an additional $1,000 or so for carpeting, paint, and assorted hardware. The drop ceiling and boxed-in duct work I did cost about $400, less than half what the carpenters were asking.

I'm writing this diary in my home office early on a Monday morning. Upstairs the family is going through the regular mad dash for the school bus. Dishes are flying, my four-year-old is throwing a tantrum, and my six-year-old is arguing with a Nintendo monster. Down here in my cocoon, all is peaceful and businesslike.

Comprehension Questions

1. **This reading selection is mainly about _____.**

   a. cleaning up a basement
   b. when to work at home
   c. hiring a contractor
   d. choosing a site for a home office and constructing it

2. **Doing building work yourself _____.**

   a. is dangerous
   b. costs more
   c. is a good idea
   d. usually saves money

3. **Using an extra bedroom for a business office is not a good idea because _____.**

   a. it is in the sleeping area of the house
   b. it is not big enough
   c. it does not have enough electrical outlets
   d. the carpeting would get dirty

4. **The easiest part of making an office in a basement is** _____.

   a. closing in the ceiling pipes
   b. putting up the walls
   c. installing new wiring
   d. adjusting the heating and cooling system

5. **The best thing about making an office in your home's basement is** _____.

   a. it is in the home but separated from the family
   b. visitors will enter through the kitchen
   c. there are always plenty of electrical outlets
   d. the ceilings are low

Vocabulary Test

On each line, write the word that matches the definition.

assessor	**beam**	**camped**
columns	**compensate**	**consulting**
corporate	**dedicated**	**dehumidifier**
furnace	**niceties**	**professionals**
radon	**thermostat**	**virgin**

1. _____   vertical supporting pillars

2. _____   a radioactive gas

3. _____   an enclosed structure in which heat is produced

4. _____   being used for the first time

5. _____   giving advice

6. _____   settled in a temporary position

7. _____   a person who determines the value of property for taxation

8. _____   attention to detail

9. _____   an automatic device for regulating temperature

10. _____   used for a particular purpose or machine

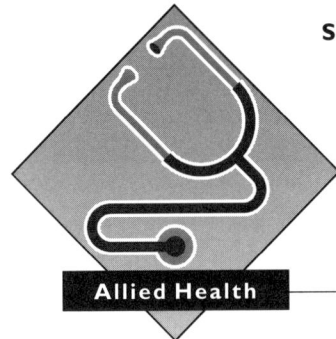

SELECTION 7

Your Elderly Patient Needs Special Attention

By Paul L. Cerrato, B.S., M.A.

Vocabulary Preview

coalition: a combination of distinct parties or persons for joint action

dentures: set of false teeth

dyspnea: difficult breathing

geriatric: relating to aged people

malnourished: undernourished; not getting adequate nutrition

neurological: relating to the nervous system

respondents: people who respond to a poll

routine: a regular course of procedure

screening: examining in order to make a separation into different groups

Many older Americans are seriously **malnourished.** By some estimates, as many as 40% of the elderly in hospitals and nursing homes are suffering from malnutrition. Of those Americans over 65 not in hospitals or nursing homes, a 1990 survey indicates that this group, too, needs help:

- 30% of **respondents** live alone and regularly skip meals.

- 45% take more than one prescription drug, which frequently cause poor appetite and vitamin deficiencies.

- 25% have incomes of less than $10,000, which makes it hard to afford adequate nutrition.

Two dozen health-care organizations—including the American Nurses Association, the National League for Nursing, and the American Academy of Family Physicians—have joined forces to tackle the problem. The **coalition** has launched a campaign called the Nutrition Screening Initiative (NSI). Its purpose is to promote **routine** assessment of elderly patients' nutritional status and better nutritional care. Toward that goal, they plan educational efforts to increase health professionals' awareness of the need to do routine nutritional **screening.**

Although the coalition has yet to offer an assessment tool, by working closely with the attending physician and staff dietitian, you can take certain steps right now. Outlined below are essential components of a screening program for older patients.

◆ Nursing History

To determine whether your patient was eating properly before admission, your interview should evaluate dental status, living conditions, and drug history.

Questions worth asking: Do poor-fitting **dentures** make it hard for you to chew? Do you frequently misplace them? Is there someone at home who can cook for you? Do arthritic pains or other health problems make it hard to prepare meals, use a knife or other eating utensils, or walk from the refrigerator to the kitchen table? How far is it to the nearest grocery store? Do you get there regularly, or have someone who shops for you?

Also inquire about a history of stroke or any **neurological** diseases that may cause difficulty swallowing. Ask whether the patient has noticed a decline in the senses of taste and smell, and whether he has any respiratory problems. Chronic **dyspnea,** for example, can make it hard to eat.

Drug-induced nutritional deficiencies are a real possibility, because so many elderly people use multiple medications on a long-term basis. Some agents reduce the amount of food taken in by causing anorexia and nausea; other agents deplete nutrient stores by triggering diarrhea or frequent urination.

Don't forget to ask patients about recent weight loss. Although there's controversy as to just how much a normal elderly person should weigh, a weight loss of 2% in a week, 5% in a month, or 7.5% over three months is reason enough for concern.

The patient's diet history, which should be available from the dietitian, can give you an idea of whether he or she is taking in enough protein, calories, and those nutrients needed in minute amounts. Of course, even someone who's eating normally can suffer from malnutrition if he's not absorbing or metabolizing food properly. To determine if the patient is utilizing what he eats, you'll need to do a physical assessment.

◆ Physical Examination

Accurate height and weight measurements are a must, and an estimate of fat reserves.

Though not generally thought of as a nutritional marker, low serum cholesterol—below about 150 mg/dl—can also indicate protein/calorie malnutrition.

Perhaps you have heard it said that 50 million Frenchmen can't be wrong. Well, perhaps 24 professional associations can't be either. Their recommendation: that all **geriatric** patients be routinely screened for malnutrition, with the emphasis on *routinely.*

Comprehension Questions

1. **Many   nursing   and   medical   organizations   agree   that** _____.

    a. too many people are in nursing homes
    b. older people do not eat enough
    c. the elderly need regular checking of nutritional status
    d. malnourishment is caused by old age

2. **According to some studies, as many as** _____ **of the elderly in hospitals or nursing homes are malnourished.**

    a. 25%   **c.** 35%
    b. 30%   **d.** 40%

3. **The writer points out that people can eat well and still be malnourished if** _____.

    a. they are not absorbing food properly   **c.** they are overweight
    b. they are over 65   **d.** they do not take vitamins

4. _____ **can point to malnutrition.**

    a. Bad teeth   **c.** High blood pressure
    b. A cholesterol count below 150   **d.** Arthritic pain

5. **To screen elderly patients for nutritional condition, you should be sure they have a physical exam and a thorough** _____.

    a. blood test   **c.** diet history
    b. interview   **d.** checkup

Vocabulary Test

On each line, write the word that matches the definition.

coalition   **dentures**   **dyspnea**
geriatric   **malnourished**   **neurological**
respondents   **routine**   **screening**

1. _____   examining in order to make a separation into different groups

2. _____   undernourished; not getting adequate nutrition

3. _____   people who respond to a poll

4. _____   relating to the nervous system

5. _____   sets of false teeth

6. _____   difficult breathing

7. _____   a combination of distinct parties or persons for joint action

8. _____   a regular course of procedure

9. _____   relating to aged people

Greater New Orleans

By Shirley Ann Grau

Hospitality and Tourism

Vocabulary Preview

climate: the average weather conditions of an area

cottage: a small, usually wooden, one-family house

Creole: a descendant of the French or Spanish people who settled around the Mississippi Delta

marsh(es): soft, wet land usually having plants like grasses or cattails growing on it

relic: object left after a civilization disappears

standard: something established by custom or general agreement as a model or example

swamp: wet spongy land saturated and sometimes covered with water

thoroughbred: horses purely bred from the best lines of horses over a long time

---

New Orleans? How do I tell you about it? . . . Where do I start?

New Orleans is an old city, as American cities go. It was founded in 1718. In the past twenty-five years it has changed more than it did in its first 200 years. It has grown so fast that although I have lived here nearly all my life, I'm constantly amazed. **Swamps** and **marshes** have been drained and filled. Suburbs stretch up and down the river and into the pines near the shore of Lake Pontchartrain. The woods where I once hunted and dug for Indian **relics** have become shopping centers and parking lots.

The new business heart of New Orleans is Poydras Street. It stretches from the Mississippi River to the Superdome. All along the street are hotels and office buildings. It reminds you of Dallas or Houston.

A short walk away is the French Quarter. It's a fascinating place of narrow streets, wonderful old buildings, historical flavor, and great beauty.

The French Quarter is the perfect introduction to the sights and sounds of New Orleans. You can take a long, slow walk, up one street and down another. You can look through iron gateways into courtyards, visit the historical museums, and visit small shops. There are many shops, ranging from very expensive art and antiques to interesting junk. You'll find lots of restaurants, famous ones as well as simple cafés, and, of course, the jazz at Preservation Hall.

A few miles above the French Quarter is the Garden District. In the 1800s, this was the American section of New Orleans. The streets here are wide. The elegant houses have an openness. This contrasts sharply with the narrow streets, plain buildings, and closed courtyards of the French Quarter.

All of the houses in the Garden District are large by today's **standards.** It's wonderful to see them sit proudly among great trees and gardens.

Also in the Garden District is a unique shopping district: Magazine Street. Dozens of small shops in converted **cottages** can be found along this busy street. There's a bit of everything: books and food, flowers and clothes, prints and art supplies and framing, and any number of antique shops.

People like to say that New Orleans has two seasons: summer and February. That's because there is no winter season, no predictable time of constant chill. New Orleans has winter in bits and pieces, with long warm stretches between. I remember only one snowfall, a light dusting that my children gathered and stored in the freezer to prove to themselves that snow had indeed fallen! New Orleans can—and does—have rainy weeks when the temperature stays around forty degrees. It's a time when everyone grows miserable and grumpy. There may also be an occasional hard frost that sends thrifty **Creole** housewives to their gardens to pick the last fruits from the vines. The banana trees turn brown. So do the ginger lilies and the top flowers of the camellias. But little else is affected by the frost.

Winter in New Orleans brings a constant stream of beautiful flowers. At Thanksgiving you'll see early sasanquas, tall bushes with camellia-like flowers. Then come the real camellias; one variety or another will be in bloom until March. By Christmas the azaleas have started, their blazing peak coming later in February or March. In April the magnolia trees bloom, followed by gardenias and jasmines. All through the year, the tall Sweet Olives have tiny, waxy flowers and fill the air with their heavy sweet smell.

Recently, New Orleans has expanded its cultural life. There are museums, art galleries, and a great zoo. There is ballet, opera, and a symphony orchestra. There are many interesting music programs at the local universities. But seriousness is not a big part of life in New Orleans. This city believes in enjoyment and good times.

There is a steady procession of sporting events in the huge Superdome. The Fair Grounds and Jefferson Downs have **thoroughbred** racing all year long. And public celebrations—how New Orleans adores them! Mardi Gras is the best-known, of course, but jazz festivals, parades, and food festivals are all a part of life here—they go on all year long.

When my grandfather visited New Orleans, he recorded his thoughts in a travel journal. "The **climate** is warm with much rain. This is a lively city in which the old take as much pleasure as the young."

It is still true today.

Comprehension Questions

1. **At the beginning of this reading selection, the writer emphasizes one main point, the idea of _____.**

   a. celebration   **c.** activities
   b. history   **d.** change

2. **The part of New Orleans marked by openness and elegance is the _____.**

   a. Fair Grounds   **c.** Garden District
   b. French Quarter   **d.** Magazine Street

3. **The _____ is a place of great historical interest as well as beauty.**

   a. Fair Grounds   **c.** Garden District
   b. French Quarter   **d.** Magazine Street

4. **The writer says winter brings a constant _____.**

   a. supply of flowers   **c.** spell of rain
   b. period of hard frost **d.** warm climate

5. **The main idea the writer presents overall is that New Orleans is a great place for _____.**

   a. nature lovers   **c.** high-technology companies
   b. enjoyment   **d.** creative activities such as painting and poetry

Vocabulary Test

On each line, write the word that completes the sentence.

climate	**Creole**	**relics**	**swamp**
cottage	**marsh**	**standard**	**thoroughbred**

1. Wet, spongy land that is saturated with water and, at times, covered with it is called a _____.

2. A _____ is something recognized as a model or example to match.

3. A person can often find _____ by digging in the area where a civilization used to be.

4. Many people like to live where there is a mild _____ all year long.

5. A small wooden house for one family is called a _____.

6. Grasses and cattails usually grow in the soft, wet land called a _____.

7. A _____ is a descendant of the French or Spanish people who settled around the Mississippi Delta.

8. _____ horses have been bred from the best lines over many years.

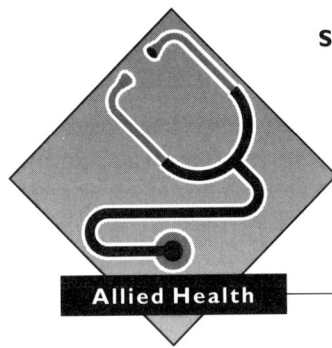

Electroencephalographic (EEG) Technician

By Craig R. Ilk

Allied Health

Vocabulary Preview

combative: marked by an eagerness to fight

convulsive seizure: a sudden and abnormal violent and involuntary series of muscle contractions throughout the body

correlated: organized in a way that shows relationships

electrodes: one of the parts that give off, collect, or control the flow of electricity in an electric device

epileptic: affected with epilepsy, a disorder marked by disturbed electrical rhythms and convulsive attacks

impulses: sudden forces transmitted through tissues and nerve fibers

neurosurgeon: a surgeon who works on the nerves, brain, or spinal cord

ongoing: actually being in process

The electroencephalographic (EEG) technician is the individual responsible for operating an instrument called an electroencephalograph. This machine records the electrical activity of the brain by producing a written tracing of the brain's electrical **impulses.** The impulses are measured in millionths of a volt after the instrument has amplified the waves many times. These tracings, or electroencephalograms, are then examined by a neurologist, who is a physician with special training in the study of the brain and nerves. The neurologist is then able to determine if there are any diseases present that may interfere with the brain's normal activity of controlling the functions of the human body.

The existence of electrical brain waves has been known for many years. Since their discovery, people have attempted to evaluate them in order to discover disease. The technicians operating the electroencephalograph were all trained on-the-job until sometime before 1972 when formal training programs began to appear. The EEG technician, however, was not recognized as a member of the allied health profession until 1972 when the American Medical Association (AMA) Council on Health Manpower identified this occupation.

The EEG technician attaches **electrodes** to specific areas of the patient's head, to measure the electrical activity of the brain. Once the electrodes are in place, the recording is begun. The process requires about one hour to complete. During the examination, the EEG technician observes the patient's behavior, making notes on a record that may be **correlated** with the tracing. The EEG technician also knows if abnormal impulses are due to poor equipment functions or to misplaced electrodes and, in many cases, is able to correct the problem. Other abnormal waves, which might indicate a physical change such as a **convulsive seizure,** must also be recognized by this technician so that proper medical attention may be immediately summoned.

The EEG technician encounters patients who have a wide variety of medical problems. Some patients have a psychiatric disease and can be **combative;** others may be unconscious. Children and adults will be seen in the EEG lab and many of them may be **epileptic.** The EEG technician, therefore, must be able to control the patient and attempt to explain away his fear and apprehension about the examination.

Minor adjustments and repairs to the equipment may be made by the EEG technician. This is not to say that the EEG technician has a thorough knowledge of the machine. Major repairs and adjustments are made only by specially trained repairmen.

Most EEG technicians acquire their training on-the-job, or in an educational program in the same institution where they are employed. Jobs for EEG technicians are found in the neurology departments of hospitals and clinics and in the private offices of neurologists and **neurosurgeons.** Regular hours, with the most work being done during the day, are a feature of this profession.

The employment outlook remains good, particularly in the larger medical centers and hospitals, where **ongoing** research on the brain and brain diseases is allowing patients to live longer and, subsequently, to require more care.

Comprehension Questions

1. **The main job of the electroencephalographic (EEG) technician is** _____.

   a. to read electroencephalograms
   b. to operate an electroencephalograph
   c. to help neurologists
   d. to make patients comfortable

2. **An electroencephalograph is a** _____.

   a. machine   **c.** tracing
   b. technician   **d.** graph

3. **An EEG technician was not recognized as a member of the allied health profession until _____.**

   a. 1968   **c.** 1979
   b. 1972   **d.** 1986

4. **An important part of an EEG technician's job is _____.**

   a. observing the patient's behavior   **c.** scheduling appointments
   b. repairing the equipment   **d.** examining the tracings

5. **The EEG technician should be comfortable working with people and with _____.**

   a. neurologists   **c.** children
   b. other EEG technicians   **d.** electrical equipment

Vocabulary Test

On each line, write the word that matches the definition.

combative	convulsive seizure	correlated
electrodes	epileptic	impulses
neurosurgeon	ongoing	

1. _____ actually being in process

2. _____ affected with epilepsy, a disorder marked by disturbed electrical rhythms and convulsive attacks

3. _____ organized in a way that shows relationships

4. _____ one of the parts that give off, collect, or control the flow of electricity in an electric device

5. _____ a sudden and abnormal violent and involuntary series of muscle contractions throughout the body

6. _____ sudden forces transmitted through tissues and nerve fibers

7. _____ a surgeon who works on the nerves, brain, or spinal cord

8. _____ marked by eagerness to fight

How to Take Care of Your Air Conditioner

By M. B. "Speed" Williams

Vocabulary Preview

carbon monoxide: a colorless, odorless, deadly gas (CO) that is formed as a product of the incomplete burning of carbon.

coil: a series of loops

condenser: an instrument in which gas or vapor is made more compact

cupped: curved in the shape of a cup

deliberation: careful discussion or thought

duct: a tube or pipe through which air or liquid can flow

duct tape: a sticky fabric tape, usually silver, that is used to wrap pipes

grille: arrangement of parallel bars or strips

obstruction: a blockage

pulley: a wheel with a grooved edge along which a rope moves as the wheel turns; used to lift or lower heavy objects

refrigerant: a substance, usually enclosed in tubes, that causes cooling

registers: a row of movable slats or bars that regulate the circulation of heated air

residential: restricted to homes, not businesses

sawhorse: an inverted V-shaped frame on which wood is laid for sawing

vent: an opening for the escape of gas

A clear air-conditioning system breathes freely and easily. With proper care, you can both cut your air-conditioning costs substantially and improve efficiency and comfort. Plus your air conditioner will last longer.

We'll explain how to care for either a central air system or a window unit. Because the central air-conditioning systems are more complex, we'll start with them.

A "split system" central air conditioner has two main units. Outside, there's a large metal box called the **condenser.** Inside the house, there's a cooling **coil** often mounted on top of the furnace. A fan forces cooled air through a system of **ducts** in the house.

1. Turn off the main power to unit. Turn thermostat to OFF.

2. Trim or remove any shrubs or **obstructions** within a 6–10-ft. radius of the condenser. This includes anything above the condenser.

3. Relocate the clothes dryer **vent** away from the condenser. When it's located near the condenser unit, the lint leaves a felt-like coating over most of the coil's face.

4. Remove the cowl, or cover, to reach the dirty (outer) side of the coil.

5. Use a bright flashlight to inspect the cooling coil with **deliberation** and care. If the coil's dirty, the coil and dirt will be the same color, making it very easy to overlook the dirt. A dirt coating only a few thousandths of an inch thick will reduce the air conditioner's efficiency by 10 to 15 percent.

6. If the coils are extremely dirty, you may want to hire a heating/cooling contractor to clean the unit. Watch what they do since you may want to do this in the future. Once the heavy dirt's been removed, you'll be able to keep it clean.

7. Brush the dirty side of the coil to remove dirt. Blow loose dirt away.

8. Make a raincoat out of plastic garbage or leaf bags to protect the compressor. Secure the bags with **duct tape.** This will protect the fan motor and any exposed wiring.

9. Use a garden hose and nozzle to clean the coils. Use the strongest solid stream of water. Direct the water into the coil in the direction opposite to the air flow. Air flow direction is into the condenser box. At first the water will dribble through the coil. Eventually, the water will flood through, indicating it's clean.

10. Check the fan motor for oil hole(s), which are usually plugged with rubber or bright metal plugs. If present, put no more than 10–20 drops of nondetergent motor oil in each hole.

11. Replace the cowl. Check that the wiring between the unit and the house is properly routed so it will not be stepped on or cut by lawn mowers.

12. Remove the fan compartment cover. Check the **cupped** side of the fan blades for dirt. If the dirt on the fan blades is 1/16th in. or more, have a qualified maintenance firm clean the fan and check the cooling coil for dirt.

13. If the fan is belt-driven, check the V-belt for breaks. Replace if worn. There should be about 1 in. total flex in belt.

14. Adjust belt flex if needed. Do *not* change the adjustable **pulley** on the motor. This changes the amount of electric current drawn by the motor and should only be done by a qualified technician.

15. Remove dirty filter and replace.

16. Install a clean filter. Make sure the arrows point toward the fan. Check the filter every month and replace if dirty.

17. If the fan motor has oil holes, use 10–20 drops of nondetergent motor oil. Oil the fan bearings if they have oil holes. Replace the fan compartment cover tightly. Make sure it is positively seated. If it's loose, combustion gases can be drawn in during the heating season and could introduce dangerous **carbon monoxide** into the house.

18. If the outdoor temperature's 60°F or above, test the system. Turn the power on, and set the thermostat to COOL. Run it for 15–20 minutes. Go outside to locate the larger of the two copper pipes. Pull the foam insulation back. The pipe should be cool to the touch (about 45–55°F). If it's not cool, there's a problem. Call a heating/cooling contractor immediately.

19. Balance the air flow **registers.** During the cooling season, open the registers on the upper floor(s). If the registers on the lower floor(s) are wide open, little or no cooled air will reach the upper floors. Minor adjustments may be needed to equalize the temperature in each room.

20. If your system has a central return rather than individual returns in each room, leave the doors slightly open or cut 3/4 to 1 in. off the door(s) bottom for air circulation.

21. When the heating season comes, you'll need to balance the system for heating. Close (partially or fully) the registers on the upper floors to force hot air into the lower floor(s).

22. Window air-conditioning units are similar, but the position of the components may vary.

23. Remove window units to perform the necessary maintenance. Don't forget to unplug the unit first.

24. Clean both coils (evaporator and condenser). Place the unit on **sawhorses** to let the water drain. Wrap all electrical components in trash bag raincoats and secure with duct tape.

25. Check the condition of the filter. It's usually a thin sheet of foam rubber located behind the plastic **grille** on the front face of the unit. Most filters can be washed with a mild, soapy detergent.

26. Replace the filter if it's worn. Many hardware stores carry sheets of foam you can cut to fit your unit.

27. Oil the fan motor(s) with 10–20 drops of nondetergent motor oil.

28. DON'T run a central or window air conditioner if the outside air temperature is below 60°F.

29. DON'T attempt to add **refrigerant** to a **residential** air conditioner. Only a professional will have the equipment and knowledge to do this properly and prevent air from getting into the system.

Comprehension Questions

1. **The subject matter here deals mainly with _____.**

   a. the differences in the methods of caring for central air conditioners and window units
   b. advantages and disadvantages of central and window air units
   c. reasons for taking proper care of air-conditioning units
   d. detailed instructions for the care of air-conditioning units

2. **One thing the homeowner should not do is _____.**

   a. change the adjustable pulley on the motor
   b. move the foam insulation
   c. oil the fan bearings
   d. use motor oil anywhere

3. **If the fan compartment cover is not replaced tightly, _____.**

   a. it may blow off and damage the fan
   b. carbon monoxide may get into the house
   c. the amount of electric current used by the fan may change
   d. the compressor will not last as long as it should

4. **Most filters can be washed with _____.**

   a. gasoline   c. detergent
   b. regular cleaning fluid   d. filter cleaner

5. **Which of these titles best expresses the main idea?**

   a. When to Call in an Expert
   b. What Not to Do When Cleaning Your Air Conditioner
   c. Do-It-Yourself Guide to Air-Conditioner Care
   d. The Home Handywoman: You Can Do This Yourself

Vocabulary Test

On each line, write the word that matches the definition.

carbon monoxide	cupped	grille	registers
coil	deliberation	obstruction	residential
duct	pulley	sawhorse	condenser
duct tape	refrigerant	vent	

1. _____ a series of loops

2. _____ curved in the shape of a cup

3. _____ a substance, usually enclosed in tubes, that causes cooling

4. _____ an opening for the escape of gas

5. _____ an instrument in which gas or vapor is made more compact

6. _____ restricted to homes, not businesses

7. _____ a sticky tape that is used to wrap pipes

8. _____ careful discussion or thought

9. _____ a blockage

10. _____ a tube or pipe through which air or liquid can flow

What Your Mouth Can Tell Your Dentist

By Laurie S. Senz

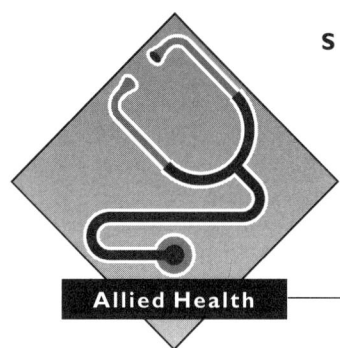

Allied Health

Vocabulary Preview

accessible: able to be reached

ailment: a bodily disorder or chronic disease

barometer: something that indicates changes

bulimia: the abnormal craving and eating of large amounts of food, usually followed by forced vomiting

diabetes: a bodily disorder characterized by insufficient production or use of insulin, leading to an excess of sugar in the blood and urine

gastrointestinal tract: the system of body parts and organs that includes the stomach and intestines

insistent: continue to be firm in a requirement

likelihood: probability; chance

malignancy: an abnormal spreading mass of tissue; a cancerous tumor

mucous membranes: a layer of tissue that lines bodily entrances and exits (like the nose) and secretes a sticky fluid

oral: involving the mouth

overall: general; as a whole

pathologist: a person who studies diseases and the changes they cause in a body

periodontist: a dentist who specializes in treating the gums and supporting structures of the teeth

reluctantly: holding back; not willingly

stethoscope: an instrument used to detect sounds made inside the body

The pain in David Rogers' lower jaw was getting worse. It was beginning to interfere with his concentration. **Reluctantly,** he took time from work to visit the nearest dentist.

The dentist made a thorough examination. He even took Rogers' blood pressure. "Your heartbeat sounds irregular to me," he said as he removed the **stethoscope.** "It may be normal for you, but I think we should check it out before we go any further."

Rogers protested. Except for his aching lower jaw, he felt fine. But the dentist was **insistent,** so Rogers finally gave in and went to see a physician in the same building. "Anything to get rid of this pain in my mouth," he muttered.

The pain, it turned out, was a lifesaver. The physician discovered that Rogers was in the early stages of a heart attack. Fortunately, he was able to stop the attack before it did serious damage. Rogers was lucky. His dentist had known that lower-jaw pain may be a symptom of a heart attack. A few months later, the grateful Rogers returned to the dentist, this time to thank him. "You probably saved my life," he told him.

Lucy Parker rarely got cavities. Nevertheless, she believed in regular dental checkups.

During one checkup, her dentist found a whitish patch. It turned out to be cancer. In her case, there was no doubt. The checkup really did save her life.

Both David's and Lucy's stories are true. They illustrate the vital importance of regular trips to the dentist. A six-month checkup can provide the first warning not only of dental disease, but of general health problems as well.

"Cancer and heart disease are the two biggies that kill people," says Dr. Michael Roberts, the chief of patient care at the National Institute of Dental Research. "But they are not the only health problems that can be spotted by a dentist." According to the American Dental Association, more than 40 serious **ailments,** including **diabetes, bulimia,** brain tumors, and AIDS, can be detected in the mouth.

"The mouth is the most visible and **accessible barometer** of the body's health," says Dr. Lawrence Cohen, chairman of the Department of Dentistry at the Illinois Masonic Medical Center. "It's a mirror of disease because it's such an easily observable area. All you need is a bright light and a dental mirror. You don't have to use tubes as you do to see into the **gastrointestinal tract.**"

The American Cancer Society estimates that this year alone 29,000 patients will be diagnosed with oral cancer. Of this number, 9,500 will die. "If you go regularly to your dentist," says Dr. Diane Stern, a Florida **oral pathologist,** "the **likelihood** is that, if you develop oral cancer, it will be spotted in an early stage. The smaller the **malignancy** is at the time of diagnosis, the more likely you are to be cured." Dr. Jerry Rosenbaum, a Florida **periodontist,** agrees: "A patient's survival rate is directly related to the time the cancer is found."

Dentists may also detect numerous health problems that are not life threatening. "One of the most common conditions people get is canker sores," Dr. Cohen says. "If you deal with the younger age group, then you see a lot of the acute infections such as herpes and trench mouth, which is due to bacteria and causes open sores between the teeth. Other symptoms may be pain and a bad taste in the mouth."

Certain blood diseases, such as anemias, can also be detected in the mouth very early, Dr. Cohen adds: "For example, a burning or sore tongue and pale gums are common symptoms of iron, folic acid, and vitamin B_{12}-

deficiency anemias, while sickle-cell anemia may present itself as an unnatural paleness of the **mucous membranes.**"

"The dentist is the doctor of the mouth," Dr. Roberts explains. "He is the expert on the head, neck, and oral cavity. He knows what normal tissue looks like, and he looks for things that are not normal. If something looks or feels unusual, then he will pursue it and, if necessary, refer the patient to a physician or a specialist for a workup and diagnosis."

"That's one of the reasons we stress regular preventive care," Cathy Penesis of the American Dental Association says. "Not only for the health of the teeth, but for the **overall** health of the individual."

Comprehension Questions

1. **A summary sentence usually expresses the main idea of an article. Which of these is the best summary sentence?**

   a. A person with pale gums should see a dentist before a doctor.
   b. About 30,000 people a year are found to have oral cancer.
   c. Cancer and heart disease are two major causes of death.
   d. Regular dental checkups can help detect many health problems.

2. **This article tells us that _____ can be a symptom of a heart attack.**

   a. a feeling of pressure in the chest   **c.** indigestion
   b. pain running down one arm   **d.** pain in the lower jaw

3. **A whitish patch in the mouth can mean _____.**

   a. trench mouth   **c.** iron-deficiency anemia
   b. cancer   **d.** herpes

4. **More than _____ serious diseases can be detected in the mouth.**

   a. two dozen   **c.** 40
   b. 100   **d.** 60

5. **This article tells mainly about _____.**

   a. people whose lives have been saved by dentists
   b. how to use good preventive care for your mouth
   c. finding signs of diseases in the mouth
   d. the danger of oral cancer

Vocabulary Test

On each line, write the word that matches the definition.

accessible	diabetes	malignancy	pathologist
ailment	gastrointestinal tract	mucous membranes	periodontist
barometer	insistent	oral	reluctantly
bulimia	likelihood	overall	stethoscope

1. _____ holding back; not willingly

2. _____ involving the mouth

3. _____ continued to be firm in a requirement

4. _____ able to be reached

5. _____ probability; chance

6. _____ an instrument used to detect sounds inside the body

7. _____ the abnormal craving and eating of large amounts of food, usually followed by forced vomiting

8. _____ an abnormal, spreading mass of tissue; cancerous tissue

9. _____ a dentist who specializes in treating the gums

10. _____ something that indicates change

Increasing Your Earning Power

By Arnold R. Deutsch

Vocabulary Preview

broker: an agent who acts as a "go-between," especially in sale of real estate, stocks, commodities, and bonds

diverse: differing from one another

exhaustive: thorough; testing all possibilities

inflation: a fast rise in the cost of living

municipality: a city, town, or other district having local self-government

options: choices; alternative courses of action

perennial: continual; persistent

prospect: chance; outlook

stagnant: not developing; inactive

sufficient: as much as is needed; enough

You don't need to read any more about **inflation**—you are already an expert. You know your paycheck isn't **sufficient** to buy the things you or your family would like to have. But before you work up the courage to see the boss and ask for a raise, ask yourself these questions: "Am I stuck in a low-paying job because I'm not ambitious, intelligent, hardworking, or reliable? Or is it really something else which keeps me in a salary rut?"

Maybe you are a recent high school graduate, college graduate, or housewife returning to work. You find yourself looking longingly at the want ads for those high-paying jobs. You might ask yourself: "Do I have what it takes to earn a high salary?"

Too many workers today find themselves either stuck in low-paying jobs, possessing skills which are no longer in demand, trained for jobs with no real future, or living in an area where there are few opportunities. If you are interested in higher earnings, increased job satisfaction, and brighter **prospects** for the future, here are some significant factors which influence your job, pay and status.

◆ Education

This is a major factor in determining your pay and your job. Although college degrees are no longer absolute guarantees of an income higher than the recent national average, there are still incentives to earn that degree. Specific college degrees, including career-oriented associate degrees from two-year or community colleges, will net the most desirable jobs. Business degrees give a person the most flexibility in following different career **options.** With a grasp of math, finance, and business administration, graduates can become systems analysts, actuaries, bank officers, managers, accountants—all highly promotable occupations. People with degrees in many technical fields (physics, chemistry, psychology, economics) command excellent starting salaries and have a choice of positions in industry, business, civil service, and academic areas.

However, a college education is not a requirement for many well-paying careers. Apprenticeships, aptitude tests, and on-the-job training can also lead to a better job. The following jobs depend on a combination of formal training and aptitude and will be growing fast in the future: dental laboratory technician, plumbers, electricians, and business-machine repair.

◆ Skills and Talent

This is another major factor in determining your earning power. Many skills that command top pay simply cannot be learned in school. For example, people who have good selling ability may make a good salary as real estate salespersons. Cosmetologists who have topnotch skills at helping people look attractive are well paid. If you have artistic talent or a knack with words, it may pay to develop those skills, because they are the key to high earnings in the advertising field, although a college degree is often the minimum requirement for a starting position. If you have mechanical skills, a career in that area may pay off better for you than a conventional white-collar job.

◆ Location

Career counselors now point out that where you work is almost as important as how much education you have or what you do. People who work in cities often earn more than those in suburban areas. (An exception to this may be lawyers working in the suburbs—they often earn as much as their city counterparts.) Both suburban and city workers earn more than those working in rural areas. Furthermore, the types of occupations and number of jobs are often severely limited by the size and affluence of the local population. For example, veterinarians have a wide salary range—those who practice in rural areas are usually earning salaries at the low end of the scale.

◆ State of the Economy

Economic and social problems, such as high unemployment, inflation, and falling birth rates, can drastically affect an entire nation's job structure—or just a small **municipality**'s job outlook. When new automobile prices rise rapidly, auto-body repair workers and mechanics enjoy increased earnings because many people decide to fix up their old cars rather than buy new ones. Stiff competition and **stagnant** salaries in such occupations as elementary school teaching and day-care work reflect the current low birth rate plus an oversupply of recently graduated teachers. Even professionals with technical degrees—civil engineers and architects, for example—can find themselves with stagnant earnings and poor prospects. This was the case during the building boom/bust of the early 1970s and the withdrawal of federal funds for public works projects during the same period. While there is now a rising demand for civil engineers and architects, their future job prospects are closely tied to the economy.

◆ Experience

This factor can make a big difference in your earnings. Although there are many jobs in which experience doesn't add income, for workers as **diverse** as travel agents, technical writers, chemists, and welders, experience is the key factor in raising income and opening up future possibilities.

◆ Independence

Some well-paid occupations can bring in even more earnings if done on an independent, self-employed basis. Engineers, psychologists, insurance agents, carpenters, managers, and auto mechanics can often boost their earnings by striking out on their own as consultants, **brokers,** or small-business owners.

◆ Sex

This may be affecting your earnings potential. Salary differentials based on sex are narrowing, but still exist. If you are a woman, consider breaking into nontraditional jobs (those formerly held primarily by men) such as a machinist or telephone installer.

◆ Field

One problem may be that you are in a field in which there is a continuing oversupply of job applicants. Teaching, as mentioned above, is one of several areas—others are social work, psychology, law, and photography—in which more people are being graduated than there are jobs available. The "glamour" fields of entertainment, advertising, and publishing attract so many people that basic salaries are not high, and moving up is very difficult. Also avoid fields that are declining because of technological or economic change.

This is not an **exhaustive** list of factors which will influence your earnings. There are others—such as race, age, and the size of the company you work for—which may have particular reference to your situation. One way to avoid being held back by factors which you may not be able to change is to pick one of the fast-growing occupations such as physician's assistant, nurse practitioner, dental-lab technician, computer programmer, or bank officer, where your drawbacks can be minimized. Or move into craft jobs such as tool-and-die making or welding, where shortages are **perennial.** You can research better paying careers, occupations that lead to promotions, and training possibilities by consulting the occupation or employment section of your local library.

Comprehension Questions

1. **The main thought in this selection is that _____.**

   a. you have to have a college degree to earn a lot of money
   b. experience is the only thing that counts
   c. men earn more than women
   d. there are many factors that affect earning power, most of which you can control

2. **City and suburban workers _____ earn more than rural workers.**

   a. usually
   b. sometimes
   c. do not
   d. never

3. **The two major factors that determine salary are _____.**

   a. age and sex
   b. the size of a company and its location
   c. education and skills or talent
   d. inflation and the economy

4. **Which is probably not a job for the future?**

   a. business-machine repair
   b. dental-laboratory technician
   c. plumber
   d. architect

5. **The main thing the author wants to tell the reader is that** _____ **.**

   a. good jobs are easy to find
   b. a person does not have to be stuck in a low-paying job
   c. job markets are changing
   d. a raise is the only way to a higher salary

Vocabulary Test

On each line, write the number of the word that matches the definition.

1. **options**
2. **diverse**
3. **stagnant**
4. **inflation**
5. **sufficient**
6. **broker**
7. **prospect**
8. **exhaustive**
9. **perennial**
10. **municipality**

_____ a. a fast rise in the cost of living

_____ b. as much as is needed; enough

_____ c. chance; outlook

_____ d. continual; persistent

_____ e. thorough; testing all possibilities

_____ f. differing from one another

_____ g. a city, town, or other district having local self-government

_____ h. not developing; inactive

_____ i. choices; alternative courses of action

_____ j. an agent who acts as a "go-between," especially in sale of real estate, commodities, stocks, and bonds

Electronics Technician

Trade and Technical

Vocabulary Preview

calibrate: to adjust by matching to a standard of correctness for best operation

circuitry: closed paths through which electricity can flow

components: parts of an electronics system (tape decks, receivers, speakers, etc.)

consumer: made to directly satisfy regular buyers, as opposed to industrial or business buyers

crude: simple; not sophisticated

electron: one of the smallest possible pieces of matter; usually found outside the nucleus of an atom

transistor: a small device that controls the flow of electricity (used in radios, televisions, computers, etc.)

vacuum: a space that is so empty that it has nothing in it, not even air

Electronic equipment includes **consumer** products such as radios, televisions, stereos, and calculators and industrial and office equipment such as computers and radio and television broadcasting equipment.

Electronics technicians assemble, install, repair, maintain, **calibrate,** and modify electronic **circuitry, components,** and systems. Electronics technicians involved with the development of new electronic equipment work closely with electronics engineers and recommend changes or modifications in circuitry or other design elements. Other electronics technicians are concerned principally with checking out newly installed equipment or with instructing and supervising lower-grade technicians in installation, assembly, or repair activities. All technicians working in the field of electronics technology may be called upon to set up test apparatus, conduct tests, analyze test results, and prepare reports, sketches, graphs, and drawings to describe electronics systems and their characteristics. Electronics technicians operate bench lathes, drills, and other machines and handtools.

Although the field of electronics has had its most significant growth and spectacular development during the twentieth century, it is actually the product of more than 200 years of study and experiment. One of the important early experimenters in this field was Benjamin Franklin. His experiments with lightning and his theory that electrical charges are present in all matter influenced the thinking and established much of the vocabulary of the researchers who came after him.

The invention of the electric battery by the Italian scientist Alessandro Volta in 1800 began a century of significant discoveries in the field of electricity and magnetism. Researchers working throughout Europe and the United States made important breakthroughs in understanding how to strengthen, control, and measure the flow of electricity moving through **vacuums.**

During the early years of the twentieth century, further discoveries concerning the flow of **electrons** in vacuums were made by experimenters such as Lee De Forest and Vladimir Zworykin. These discoveries led the way to developing equipment and techniques for long-distance broadcasting of radio and television signals. It was the outbreak of World War II, however, with its needs for long-distance communication equipment, and ultimately missile-guidance systems, that brought about the rapid expansion of electronics technology and the creation of the electronics industry.

As the field of electronics technology turned to the creation of consumer and industrial products following the end of World War II, its growth was spurred by two new technological developments. The first was the completion in 1946 of the first all-purpose, all-electronic digital computer. This machine, **crude** as it was, could handle mathematical calculations a thousand times faster than the electromechanical calculating machines of its day. Since 1946, there has been a steady growth in the speed, sophistication, and versatility of computers.

The second important development was the invention of the **transistor** in 1948. The transistor provided an inexpensive and compact replacement for the vacuum tubes used in nearly all electronic equipment up until then. Transistors allowed for the miniaturization of electronic circuits and were especially crucial in the development of the computer and in opening new possibilities in industrial automation.

Discoveries during the 1960s in the fields of microcircuitry and integrated circuitry led to the development of such products as pocket calculators, digital watches, microwave ovens, high-speed computers, and the long-range guidance systems used in space flights.

By the 1970s, electronics had become one of the largest industries and most important areas of technology in the industrialized world, a world which has, in turn, come to rely on the instantaneous worldwide communications, the computer-controlled or computer-assisted industrial operations, and the wide-ranging forms of electronic data processing that are made possible by electronics technology.

Working in partnership with scientists and engineers, today's electronics technicians belong to one of the fastest-growing occupational groups in the United States. Their importance, already widely acknowledged, will continue to be increasingly recognized in coming years.

Comprehension Questions

1. **An electronics technician will _____.**

    a. have a hard time finding a job
    b. be part of one of the fastest-growing industries, vital to the computer-oriented world
    c. repair all kinds of electrical appliances, like toasters and vacuum cleaners
    d. not need to know anything about transistors and electronic circuits

2. **The most rapid expansion of electronics technology occurred after _____.**

    a. Benjamin Franklin's experiments
    b. the invention of the battery
    c. the invention of television
    d. the outbreak of World War II

3. **The transistor replaced _____.**

    a. vacuum tubes
    b. computers
    c. batteries
    d. wires

4. **An electronics technician would probably *not* work on _____.**

    a. computers
    b. broadcasting equipment
    c. microwave ovens
    d. lamps

5. **Another title for this article could be _____.**

    a. Electricity and Magnetism
    b. Discoveries in Electricity
    c. Electronics: From Lightning to Modern Technology
    d. Modern Computers

Vocabulary Test

On each line, write the word that matches the definition.

calibrate   **circuitry**   **components**

consumer   **crude**   **electron**

transistor   **vacuum**

1. _____   simple; not sophisticated

2. _____   a small device that controls the flow of electricity

3. _____   closed paths through which electricity can flow

4. _____   one of the smallest pieces of matter; usually found outside the nucleus of an atom

5. _____   parts of an electronics system (tape decks, receivers, speakers, etc.)

6. _____   to adjust by matching a standard of correctness for best operation

7. _____   made to directly satisfy regular buyers

8. _____   a space that is so empty that it has nothing in it, not even air

Everybody Happy?

By Wendy Jordan

Business and Computers

Vocabulary Preview

caulk: material used to fill cracks and seams in order for an item to be watertight

declines: goes down

employee: a person who is paid for working for another person

executives: people who help to manage and make decisions for a company or organization

merchandise: things to be bought and sold

on budget: keeping to a plan for spending money

productivity: the yield of results, benefits, or profits

view: see or regard

You have a problem if your **employees** can't figure out whom to please—you or your customer. It may seem clear to you that no choice is necessary. If your employees do good work that makes the customer happy, you are happy, too. If your employees perform as well as you hope they will, the customer is guaranteed to be satisfied.

But while that is clear to you, it is not clear to many employees. Here are three recent examples.

A large home-center chain opened a new store and a remodeler friend of mine decided to give it a try. He needed three items. The first, an advertised item, was not on the shelf. The second was missing some pieces. The third, a small part for a shower rod, was nowhere to be found. The manager of this new store called for a salesperson to solve these problems, then went back to the task of straightening tubes of **caulk** on a shelf. The remodeler waited, the salesperson never came, and the manager continued straightening tubes of caulk. Finally, the remodeler left. He won't be back.

The **executives** of this home-center chain would be sick if they knew how the store manager handled the customer. But the manager probably thought he was doing the right thing. He probably thought his boss would be pleased to see such well-displayed **merchandise.**

Last year a family used a highly respected remodeler to enclose their porch. This year they are remodeling their kitchen—but using a different remodeler. When I asked if they were pleased with the porch remodeler, they

123

replied, "Yes and no." Everything was fine when the head of the firm was on the job. When he wasn't, problems arose.

Another first-rate remodeler admitted that when he is at a job site the workers snap to it, but **productivity declines** after he leaves.

What's the problem? My guess is that all these employees—the store manager and the two remodeling crews—believe that success lies in pleasing the boss. They have the wrong idea of how to do so.

The not-so-successful employee is the one who **views** himself or herself as an order taker. This person does exactly what the boss says, no more. He or she does it when the boss is watching. This employee doesn't see the big picture.

It is a two-sided problem. Both boss and worker must communicate well. The successful boss explains the company's goal—for example, to satisfy the customer—and guidelines for achieving it—for example, doing good work on schedule and **on budget.** The successful worker listens to what his or her boss says, accepts it, and makes it happen.

A successful company operates as a team. Everyone in the company understands the goal and how to achieve it. Everyone gets the training necessary to do well. Everyone helps solve problems. And everyone shares the glory when a job is well done. With a company like that, everybody is happy: customer, boss, and employee.

Comprehension Questions

1. **The main point being made here is that _____.**

   a. workers often slack off when the boss isn't around
   b. bosses aren't always paying attention
   c. the customer is always right
   d. success is related to communication and teamwork

2. **The not-so-successful employee sees himself or herself as _____.**

   a. just someone who takes orders
   b. part of the management-employee team
   c. someone who understands the company's goals
   d. underpaid

3. **In the example given, the manager of the home center _____.**

   a. fired the employee who didn't help the customer
   b. ignored the customer completely
   c. continued to straighten shelves while the customer waited
   d. couldn't find what the customer wanted and didn't offer any other suggestions

4. **In the two remodeling examples, problems arose when** _____.

    a. customers interfered with the work
    b. the boss was away from the job
    c. customers kept changing their minds about what they wanted
    d. the boss did not tell the workers exactly what to do

5. **This reading selection mainly** _____.

    a. gives advice to customers of remodeling and home-service companies
    b. tells bosses how to improve workers' performance and make customers happy at the same time
    c. advises bosses to pay more attention to what their employees are doing
    d. gives examples of mistakes in handling customers

Vocabulary Test

On each line, write the number of the word that matches the definition.

1. **merchandise**   _____   **a.** a person paid to work for another person
2. **view**
3. **declines**   _____   **b.** material used to fill cracks and seams
4. **productivity**   _____   **c.** the yield of results, benefits, or profits
5. **executives**   _____   **d.** keeping to a plan for spending money
6. **on budget**   _____   **e.** see or regard
7. **caulk**   _____   **f.** goes down
8. **employee**   _____   **g.** things to be bought or sold
              _____   **h.** people who help to manage and make decisions for a company or organization

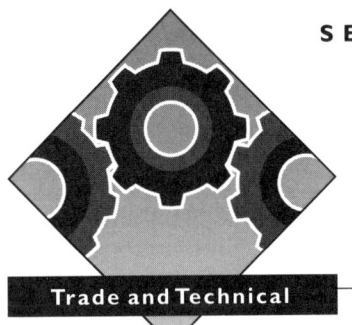

Tire Maintenance and Safety

From Firestone Tire Maintenance Warranty and Safety Manual

Trade and Technical

Vocabulary Preview

accurate: free from error; exact

adequate: enough for a certain requirement

certification: the act of stating that something is true as represented

diameter: the distance across a circle, through the center

fabric: cloth

gauge: a measuring instrument

impact: the action of one object hitting against another

puncture: a hole made with something sharp

rotation: changing position in a regular pattern

sidewall: the side of a tire that is not the tread

tread: the part of a tire that makes contact with the road

Any tire, no matter how well made, may fail. It could fail because of **punctures, impact** damage, improper inflation, overloading, or misuse. Tire failure may mean a risk of serious personal injury or property damage. To reduce the chance of tire failure, read and follow all the safety information below.

◆ Tire Inflation

Always keep the recommended tire pressure in all your tires, including the spare. On some vehicles, the recommended front and rear tire pressure will be different. A sticker on the tire or your car's owner's manual will tell you the recommended air pressure.

Underinflation can cause tires to overheat, damaging the tire. It can also reduce tire life, cause the car to handle poorly, and reduce gas mileage.

Overinflation affects tire wear and makes the tire more likely to be cut, punctured, or broken by sudden impact. Note: Never inflate a tire unless it is on the car or secured to a tire mounting machine.

◆ Tips for Safe Tire Inflation

- Check your tire air pressure, including your spare tire, at least once a month and before long trips. Be sure to use an **accurate** pressure **gauge.**

- Check your air pressure when the tires are "cold." The tires are "cold" when your vehicle has been driven less than a mile at moderate speed after being stopped for three or more hours. If you check tires that are not "cold," the correct pressure should be four pounds per square inch higher than "cold" pressure.

- If you must add air when your tires are hot, add four pounds per square inch above the recommended cold air pressure. Recheck the inflation pressure when the air is cold.

◆ Safe Loading

Never exceed the maximum load rating stamped on the **sidewall** of your tire or the maximum vehicle load rating, whichever is less. The maximum vehicle load rating (GVWR) is found on the **certification** label on the driver's door.

Your car's owner's manual will tell you load limits and any special trailer-towing instructions. Driving your vehicle in an overloaded condition could cause high heat to build up in your tires. This can lead to sudden tire failure then or at some later date.

◆ Spotting Damaged Tires

- After striking anything unusual in the roadway, have the tires checked.

- Inspect your tires for cuts, cracks, splits, or bruises in the **tread** and sidewall areas. Bumps or bulges may indicate a separation within the tire body.

- Inspect your tires for uneven wear. Wear on one side of the tread or flat spots in the tread may indicate a problem with the tire or vehicle.

- Inspect your tires for **adequate** tread depth. When the tire is worn to 1/16 inch or less tread-groove depth or the tire cord or **fabric** is exposed, the tire is dangerously worn and must be replaced immediately.

- Inspect your tire rims also. If you have a bent or cracked rim, it must be replaced.

◆ Tire Repairs

- Never repair a tire with less than 1/16 inch (1.6 millimeters) tread remaining. At this tread depth, the tire is worn out and must be replaced.

- Never repair a tire with a puncture larger than 1/4 inch (6.4 millimeters) in **diameter.**
- Repairs of all tires (radial and nonradial) must be of the plug and inside patch type unless the hole is too small to insert a plug. Using plugs alone on any type of tire is not a safe repair.
- Never repair a tire with a puncture or other damage outside the tread area.
- Any tire repair done without removing the tire from the rim is improper.
- Tubes, like tires, should be repaired only by a qualified tire service person.
- Never use a tube as a substitute for a proper repair.

◆ Tire Storage

Tires should be stored indoors in a cool dry place where water cannot collect inside the tires. The tires should be placed away from electric generators and motors and sources of heat such as hot pipes. Storage surfaces should be clean and free of grease, gasoline, or anything else that could decay the rubber. Improper storage can damage your tires in ways that may not be visible and can lead to serious personal injury.

◆ Tire Rotation

The purpose of tire **rotation** is to minimize irregular or uneven wear caused by maintaining a tire in one rotation direction and one position over an extended period. Check your car's owner's manual for recommended tire rotation patterns. Tires should usually be rotated every 6,000 to 8,000 miles.

Comprehension Questions

1. **This article points out that any tire may fail, but _____.**
   - **a.** expensive tires run better
   - **b.** new tires are safer
   - **c.** knowing and following tire safety rules reduces the chances of tire failure
   - **d.** only if you do not use the right tire

2. **Overinflation of a tire may _____.**
   - **a.** cause it to overheat
   - **b.** make it more likely to be cut, punctured, or broken by sudden impact
   - **c.** reduce gas mileage
   - **d.** cause it to skid

3. A good tire would show _____.

    a. splits in the sidewall
    b. uneven wear
    c. cuts and cracks in the tread
    d. adequate tread depth

4. When not being used, tires should be stored _____.

    a. indoors in a cool, dry, clean place
    b. outside your garage
    c. in a warm place
    d. with the extra oil and gasoline

5. Tire safety is important because _____.

    a. safe tires protect you and your car from the risk of injury or damage
    b. tires are expensive
    c. it makes you a good driver
    d. the tires might last longer

Vocabulary Test

On each line, write the word that completes the sentence.

accurate   adequate   gauge   impact   punctures   rotation   tread

The life of tires can be extended if you care for them properly. Check the pressure often with an _____ pressure _____. Regular tire _____ will help the _____ to wear evenly. Have _____ fixed by a professional. Check tires for cracks or leaks after any sudden _____. Even if a tire has tread depth _____ enough to pass a state inspection, if the tire has 40,000 or 50,000 miles on it, it should be changed.

Quality-Control Technician

Vocabulary Preview

abrasion: a wearing, grinding, or rubbing away of

compile: to collect and edit

confer: to compare views; to consult

conformance: the act of agreeing to a specified standard or authority

inventories: counting and listing of goods on hand

mechanized: conducted by machinery

visual: performed by sight

Quality-control technicians test and inspect industrial products, parts of products, and materials that go into products to be sure of the quality and reliability of products and to determine their mechanical, electrical, chemical, or other material characteristics. They also record, **compile,** and evaluate statistical data and make suggestions to engineering personnel concerning modifications in materials, equipment, or processes. Quality-control technicians are at work in nearly all manufacturing industries.

Quality-control technology is an outgrowth of the Industrial Revolution. One of the principal features of the Industrial Revolution as it began in England in the eighteenth century was that each person involved in the manufacturing process was responsible for a particular part of the process. The worker's responsibility was further specialized by the introduction of the concept of interchangeable parts by Eli Whitney in the late eighteenth and early nineteenth centuries. In a manufacturing process using the concept of interchangeable parts, a worker could concentrate on making just one part, while other workers concentrated on creating other parts. Such specialization led to increased production efficiency, especially as manufacturing processes became increasingly **mechanized** during the early part of the twentieth century. It also meant, however, that no one worker was responsible for the overall quality of the product. This led to the need for another kind of specialized production worker, a worker whose primary concern was not in a particular aspect of assembling the product but in the product's overall quality.

At first, this kind of responsibility belonged to the mechanical engineers and mechanical technicians who developed the manufacturing systems, equipment, and procedures. However, quality control soon became a separate field of industrial technology.

As quality-control technology became more complex, so did the work of quality-control technicians. No longer is their job simply periodically to remove finished or semifinished products from the assembly line for **visual** inspection and testing to see if the item works as it should. Today's technician operates sophisticated instrumentation devices, helps develop testing programs according to advanced statistical sampling theories, and **confers** with engineers regarding materials, equipment, and procedures.

There is a wide variety of activities involved with quality-control technology in addition to the basic inspecting and testing of products and parts. For example, to arrive at the quality and reliability standards used in testing programs, quality-control technicians interpret drawings, diagrams, and chemical, mathematical, and physical formulas. They select products for testing at certain stages of production and set up and perform destructive and nondestructive tests on materials, parts, and products. (In destructive tests, the part being tested is effectively destroyed as part of the testing; in nondestructive testing, the object of the testing is left intact.)

Another important area of quality-control technology involves the recording and evaluation of test data. Technicians prepare data in chart form and write summaries about a product's **conformance** to or departure from existing standards. Most importantly, they offer suggestions in written or oral form to engineers regarding ways of modifying existing quality standards and manufacturing procedures in order to achieve the best product quality from existing or proposed new equipment.

Here are two examples of the specific work a quality-control technician might do. Quality-control technicians involved with the packaging of beer perform a variety of physical-measuring and chemical-analysis tests of the packaged beer and of the materials used in the packaging. They select samples of crowns, cans, lids, bottles, labels, and cartons from the packaging lines, following established procedures concerning the time, place, and frequency of sampling. They measure the dimensions of the crowns, cans, bottles, lids, and labels, and they conduct abrasion tests on these items with an **abrasion** machine. They also measure the hardness of these items using a hardness tester and the bursting strength of bottles using an hydraulic bursting machine. They test the wet and dry tearing strength of labels and cartons, and they weigh filled cans and bottles to measure the volume of beer. Finally, they record the results of all of these tests and, when necessary, prepare graphs and charts to explain or present their findings.

Quality-control technicians working with coin-operated machines test and adjust vending, amusement, or other coin-operated machines. They use a variety of different handtools, including light bulbs, to verify electronic circuit continuity and electrical timers to test operating cycles of machines. They examine the paint and finish on manufactured units for blemishes, chips, or other flaws and may reject units requiring extensive mechanical or electrical repairs or refinishing.

Quality-control technicians should have an aptitude for and an interest in mathematics, science, and other technical subjects and should feel comfortable using the language and symbols of mathematics and science. They should have good eyesight and good manual skills, including the ability to use handtools. They should be able to follow technical instructions and to make sound judgments about technical matters. Finally, they should have orderly minds and be able to maintain records, to conduct **inventories,** and to estimate quantities.

Comprehension Questions

1. **The main job of a quality-control technician is _____.**

    a. evaluating data
    b. making suggestions to engineers
    c. determining a product's use
    d. testing and inspecting industrial products

2. **The need for quality control is a result of the _____.**

    a. American Revolution
    b. Industrial Revolution
    c. French Revolution
    d. Russian Revolution

3. **The two most important subjects for a quality-control technician to be comfortable with are _____.**

    a. English and history
    b. shop and science
    c. math and science
    d. math and typing

4. **The responsibility for quality control at first belonged to _____.**

    a. the mechanical engineers and technicians
    b. Eli Whitney
    c. the assembly-line worker
    d. the boss

5. **The Industrial Revolution introduced large factories and assembly-line work. As a result, workers are only responsible for _____.**

    a. themselves
    b. a day's work
    c. the part of a product that they make
    d. the final product

Vocabulary Test

On each line, write the number of the word that matches the definition.

1. **mechanized**   _____   **a.**   the act of agreeing to a specified standard or authority

2. **confer**   **b.**   counting and listing of goods on hand

3. **abrasion**   _____   **c.**   to compare views; to consult

4. **inventories**   _____   **d.**   conducted by machinery

5. **conformance**   _____   **e.**   performed by sight

6. **visual**   _____   **f.**   to collect and edit

7. **compile**   _____   **g.**   a wearing, grinding, or rubbing away of something

The Professional Image Report: How Relevant Is the Serious Suit?

By Leah Rosch

Vocabulary Preview

authority: power to decide and enforce rules

conservative: cautious; careful; unchanging

contingent: a representative group

ditched: gotten rid of

overwhelming: overpowering; extreme

prevail: be greater in influence

significant: important

standard: an accepted model against which other things are judged

uniform: always the same

version: a description from one point of view

The ground rules for women's office wear have been determined, to a great extent, by following the lines of what men wear. Of course, men, too, have rules of dress to follow. But because of the **uniform** nature of men's suits, clothing mistakes typically are not dramatic. They dress dull, but safe.

Are women following in their shoes by creating a professional uniform of their own? Yes, but not exactly. The career woman's dress code for the 1990s is still being written. Winning for the moment is the low-risk **conservative** business suit—the feminine **version** of what has worked for men. And rising fast is a newer and more stylish symbol of women's new confidence in themselves and their professionalism.

Which **standard** will **prevail** for career women: the classy but safe suit or the more individual way of dressing that usually has been a woman's choice?

Half of all women report they are most likely to wear the low-risk, conservative suit to work. The appeal of the suit is understandable, especially for women in fields with mostly men. Perhaps it's still a case of "fitting in" with the male mold. As a banker from South Dakota observes, "A man has a difficult time referring to a woman in a blue pin-striped suit as 'one of the girls.'"

There is, in fact, a small but **significant contingent** (29%) who wish they could dress more like men: throw on a suit and be done with it. "Yes, I secretly wish I could just put on a pair of trousers, shirt, and tie each day without the extra time, effort, and expense I must invest in a 'career woman' image," says an assistant vice president from California. And an insurance manager in New York says: "I envy the fact that a man can wear the same suit two days in a row. In fact, as long as he changes his shirt and tie, no one even realizes it's the same suit. But if a woman wears the same outfit two days in a row, people might wonder why."

But the suit a woman wears is unlikely to resemble the original navy-blue-suit-and-floppy-bow-tie uniform. "I wear real business-type suits," says a marketing coordinator from New Jersey. "But even to an important industry luncheon, I'll wear a red suit as opposed to navy or gray."

Many of today's career women have **ditched** the safe uniform altogether. "Good news!" says an insurance-marketing representative from Tennessee. "There's a strong movement toward very classy, elegant dresses that may be worn in almost any business situation." A personnel-management consultant in Washington says she's tired of looking like a "mini man": "For the past two years, when I added to my work wardrobe, I bought strong, professional dresses."

Not that this new way of dressing is without rules of its own. For one thing, the dress is definitely not sleeveless. And an **overwhelming** majority agree that wearing a jacket as part of any outfit—including the classy business dress—adds **authority.**

Comprehension Questions

1. **The main idea here is _____.**

    a. how a woman's suit compares with a man's suit
    b. why a suit is good for work
    c. why career people like suits
    d. whether or not the suit will remain the main outfit of career women

2. **The business suit has been standard dress for career women mostly because _____.**

    a. it is easy to wear
    b. it is comfortable
    c. it worked for men
    d. it makes you look important

3. **Most women agree that wearing a jacket with any outfit _____.**

    a. adds variety   c. makes it warmer
    b. adds authority   d. makes it look like a suit

4. One woman envies the fact that a man _____.

   a. does not have to be as colorful
   b. can wear the same suit two days in a row
   c. can spend less time getting dressed
   d. has a professional uniform

5. From this article we learn that _____.

   a. most businesswomen want to look professional and still feminine
   b. women like only business suits
   c. men think businesswomen should wear suits
   d. women may not wear suits at all in the 1990s

Vocabulary Test

On each line, write the number of the word that matches the definition.

1. **ditched**	_____	**a.**	be greater in influence
2. **prevail**	_____	**b.**	cautious; careful; unchanging
3. **standard**	_____	**c.**	important
4. **authority**	_____	**d.**	always the same
5. **significant**	_____	**e.**	a representative group
6. **conservative**	_____	**f.**	overpowering; extreme
7. **uniform**	_____	**g.**	power to decide and enforce rules
8. **contingent**	_____	**h.**	gotten rid of
9. **version**	_____	**i.**	a description from one point of view
10. **overwhelming**	_____	**j.**	an accepted model against which other things are judged

Catch the 'Wave

By Donna Haverstock

Trade and Technical

Vocabulary Preview

commercial: having to do with business or trade

convenient: easy to reach and use

foodservice: the business of preparing and serving things to eat

nutrient: a substance that provides what is needed to grow and develop

restaurateur: the owner or operator of a public eating place

skillet: a shallow frying pan with a long handle

vendor: a person who sells things

Microwave-oven use shows no signs of slowing down. Across the United States, more homes have microwave ovens than VCRs, toasters, or dishwashers. Microwaves are expected to be in 80 percent of homes by the year 2000. **Restaurateurs** also have good reason to take another look at how they can use a microwave to its full potential.

Most of us, at home or in a **commercial** kitchen, use microwaves mostly for defrosting and reheating. It's quick and **convenient.** But these ovens' other benefits—keeping **nutrients,** reducing energy costs, and, most importantly, turning out good-tasting, high-quality food—should also be considered.

Being able to adjust the power allows greater control of the heating rate and aids in keeping nutrients. Research shows that with the use of low power, microwave-prepared foods have the same as or more B vitamins, thiamine, riboflavin, pyridoxine, folacin, and vitamin C than foods prepared in usual ways. Because microwave cooking requires less time, vitamins and minerals are spared some of the destruction that normally occurs in baking and roasting.

Microwaving also has a positive effect on the protein value in breads. Compared to oven-baked breads, microwave-baked breads have a higher nutritional value. And because of reduced cooking times, bacon cooked in a microwave has fewer of the harmful chemicals produced when cooked in a **skillet.**

Consumers consider vegetables their favorite microwave-prepared food. It's easy to cook crisp but tender vegetables, while keeping all those nutrients in the vegetables where they belong, not lost in the cooking water.

Although short cooking time improves nutrition and convenience, it could create a problem. If the time is too short, harmful bacteria might not be killed as they are in regular cooking. Microwaves cook food from the inside out, and often do not evenly heat foods. So cover and stir foods for more even heating and follow manufacturers' suggestions for time and temperature.

Are there any other benefits we can look forward to in the microwave world? In the future, it's possible that microwaves might aid in preservation. For example, a little microwave energy could extend the shelf life of fresh poultry either before or after it is purchased from **vendors.** Bacteria could be reduced enough so that a fresh product would remain "fresh" for a longer period. This method would have many, many applications in **food-service.**

Comprehension Questions

1. **The main idea of this selection is that _____.**

   a. more people have microwave ovens than VCRs
   b. microwave ovens are quick and convenient
   c. microwave ovens turn out good-tasting, nutritious food quickly
   d. microwaves might someday aid in food preservation

2. **At this time, most people use microwaves for _____.**

   a. baking bread
   b. roasting meat
   c. boiling water
   d. defrosting and reheating

3. **Vitamins and minerals are spared some of the destruction that normally occurs in baking and roasting because _____.**

   a. you use less water
   b. microwave cooking requires less time
   c. the food does not get as hot
   d. the food cooks from the inside out

4. **To be sure that harmful bacteria are killed in microwaved food, you should _____.**

   a. cover foods and stir occasionally for more even heating and follow manufacturers' directions
   b. cook it longer
   c. boil it first
   d. make sure the food is clean

5. **This article emphasizes _____ as a benefit of microwave-cooked food.**

   a. convenience
   b. nutrition and food quality
   c. cost
   d. time-saving

Vocabulary Test

Draw a line from each word to its correct definition.

1. **convenient**
2. **restaurateur**
3. **nutrient**
4. **commercial**
5. **vendor**
6. **skillet**
7. **foodservice**

   a. the business of preparing and serving food
   b. a shallow frying pan with a long handle
   c. a person who sells things
   d. the owner or operator of a public eating place
   e. easy to reach and use
   f. having to do with business or trade
   g. a substance that provides what the body needs to grow and develop

A Computer Is Just a Tool

Vocabulary Preview

democratic: favoring social equality
digital: working directly with numbers rather than quantities of electric currents
glitter: attractiveness; superficial excitement
maddening: strongly irritating
microelectronic: miniature electronic circuits and parts
misperception: incorrect understanding or knowing
update: current information or report
white lie: an unimportant lie

The three biggest lies in America are: (1) "The check is in the mail." (2) "Of course I'll respect you in the morning." (3) "It was computer error." Of these three little **white lies,** the worst of the lot by far is the third. It's the only one that can never be true. The first two could be true. But if the term is properly used, there can never be any such thing as "computer error."

A basic truth that tends to get lost in the **glitter** surrounding the **microelectronic** revolution is that **digital** devices—clocks, calculators, computers, etc.—are nothing more than tools to help people do a job. The pencil is a useful tool; the screwdriver is a useful tool; the computer is a useful tool. Nothing more.

Years ago, you might have seen a bank clerk accidentally write down your $1,000 deposit as $100. Did anybody then call this "pencil error"? No. The responsibility belonged to the teller, not the tool.

Today, if a bank statement cheats you out of $900 that way, you know what the clerk is sure to say: "It was computer error." Nonsense. The computer is reporting nothing more than what the clerk typed into it.

If a mechanic installs a new muffler that falls off as soon as you drive off the lot, would you stand by quietly when the dealer blamed the problem on "screwdriver error"? When the bill for that job turns out to be too high, why, then, do we let the same people get away with the excuse "that it was computer error"?

The most irritating case of all is when the computerized cash register in the grocery store shows that an item costs more than it actually does. If the innocent buyer points out the mistake, the checker, bagger, and manager all come together and offer the familiar explanation: "It was computer error."

It wasn't, of course. That high-tech cash register is really nothing more than an electric eye. The eye reads the Universal Product Code—that ribbon of black and white lines in a corner of the package—and then checks the code against a price list stored in memory. If the price list is right, you'll be charged accurately.

Grocery stores **update** the price list each day—that is, somebody sits at a keyboard and types in the prices. If the price they type in is too high, there are only two explanations: carelessness or dishonesty. But somehow "computer error" is supposed to excuse everything.

One reason we let people hide behind a computer is the common **misperception** that huge, modern computers are "electric brains" with "artificial intelligence." At some point there might be a machine with intelligence, but none exists today. The smartest computer on Earth right now is no more "intelligent" than your average screwdriver. At this point in the development of computers, the only thing any machine can do is what a human has instructed it to do.

Anybody who has tried to write a simple program on a computer—and if you haven't done so, you ought to give it a try—is aware of that. The really **maddening** thing about computers is that they do exactly what you tell them to do. The stupidest typing error you make when entering the program will come back to haunt you, because the computer is too dumb to correct it. This explains why some of the programs we buy for our personal computers produce "computer errors" that seem really ridiculous.

The nice thing about the computer revolution we are living in is that computers are becoming **democratic.** Anybody can have one. Over time, as more people get their hands on computers and learn how they work, we will all understand that the excuse "It was a computer error" is always a little white lie.

Comprehension Questions

1. **The writer's main point is that _____.**

   a. computers are really stupid
   b. supermarket price errors are often made through dishonesty
   c. a faulty muffler job is not a screwdriver error
   d. computer errors are basically human errors

2. **A high-tech cash register is really just _____.**

   a. an expensive piece of window dressing
   b. an electric eye
   c. a way to keep employees honest
   d. a simple adding machine

3. **Grocery stores update their price lists by means of _____.**

   a. a telephone hookup
   b. a scanner
   c. an employee at a keyboard
   d. a VDT

4. **According to the writer, one of the three biggest lies is _____.**

   a. "There'll be no tax increase this year."
   b. "The check is in the mail."
   c. "I promise not to tell anyone."
   d. "You'll get a raise soon."

5. **Another way of expressing the main idea of this selection is _____.**

   a. a computer is only as smart as the person telling it what to do
   b. at some point there may be a computer with artificial intelligence
   c. computers are becoming democratic—anyone can have one
   d. computers only make errors that people program them to make

Vocabulary Test

Draw a line from each word to its correct definition.

1. **maddening**
2. **microelectronic**
3. **update**
4. **digital**
5. **white lie**
6. **democratic**
7. **misperception**
8. **glitter**

a. an unimportant lie
b. incorrect knowing or understanding
c. favoring social equality
d. strongly irritating
e. working by means of numbers, not quantities of electricity
f. attractiveness; superficial excitement
g. miniature electronic circuits and parts
h. current information or report

New Cook-Chill System Earns High Grades

By Susie Stephenson

Trade and Technical

Vocabulary Preview

à la carte: according to a menu that prices each item separately

batch: the quantity cooked or baked at one time

bulk: of or relating to materials stored in large quantities

contamination: a state of being soiled, infected, or unfit for use

cook-chill: cooked first and then quickly chilled

cost-effective: good value for the money spent

minimize: to reduce to the least quantity possible

parochial: of or relating to a church parish

The foodservice department for the Olathe (Kan.) Schools, the fastest growing school district in the Midwest, provides foodservice to 32 public schools and a **parochial** school—9,000 Type A meals plus 6,000 **à la carte** items each day from a new central food production facility with a **cook-chill** system for a base.

Director of Foodservice Cynthia Ross and a design team visited other foodservice production centers with cook-chill systems before they decided that one would be right for them. The benefits, the group determined, were many: Cook-chill would **minimize** the possibilities of food **contamination** and overcooking and would provide uniform product throughout the district. The system also would offer the opportunity to inventory meal components with a shelf life of five to six days, rather than to meet each meal on an as-needed basis, as was being done. In addition, the new system would enable the department to schedule work at more "normal" hours, making it easier to find and retain employees.

◆ Transportation Problems

"Although we had a central production facility and we were **cost-effective,** there were problems," says Ross. "We cooked in one location but we transported the food out hot. Sometimes the food got cold or it was spilled. And many of the employees had to come in at 5:30 in the morning. If a cook didn't show up, we didn't have a sub and we sometimes had to change the menu.

"The process was slow, and I worried about it," Ross continues. "We had only 60- and 80-gallon kettles. So if we were making chili, for example, we'd have to cook the beans and refrigerate them. Then cook the meat. Then put them together. Next we'd have to scoop the mixture into pans, load the pans into hot carts and truck them to our satellites. We could only use short carts because it was hot food. With the new system we can use tall carts so we need fewer trucks. But more importantly, we cook to inventory. Everything is shipped out cold. We heat to the actual menu count. Food waste is less."

Although one might expect recipe conversion to cause problems in the changeover, that wasn't the case. Ross solicited recipes from other schools with cook-chill systems, but found most of them were spicier than her students liked. So Ross simply adapted the recipes that had been used in the previous system. "I'm not sure exactly why, but I'm pretty good at that," she says.

◆ Overall Design Concerns

The new 42,903-square-foot Olathe, Kan., food production center with its cook-chill base system is a model of product-flow efficiency as it moves from receiving through the kitchen to be shipped to satellite schools. The designers, Frank Clements Associates, Houston, paid particular attention to **bulk** storage, product handling and construction materials.

Building materials were selected with longevity and minimal maintenance in mind. Corner guards and continuous vinyl wall bumpers protect the glazed block interior, which incorporated a coved base at the floor and ceiling. Skylights in the ceiling reduce lighting costs. Custom fabrication and installation was done by Smith St. John, North Kansas City, Mo.

Each cold-storage room has a dual refrigeration system to eliminate shutdowns resulting from a single-system failure.

Food production starts at the ingredient issue and assembly area. Standard recipes are maintained on computer and can be increased or decreased to the desired batch sizes. All ingredients are weighed, measured, and stored according to **batch** size prior to being sent to the cook-chill area.

All ingredients then move to the various production areas. Hot food is cooked in steam-jacketed kettles. When the cooking cycle is completed, the product is pumped into plastic casings of various sizes, sealed with stainless-steel clips and labeled. The product is then placed in an agitated bath of cold water and chilled to 34°F to 35°F. Next, the product is put in plastic shipping containers and held in refrigerated product inventory storage.

The shipping dock is the final point for hot foods (and other items produced in the facility) along the product flow line. Carts scheduled for the various schools are loaded into distribution trucks for transport to their destinations. Soiled empty carts are returned in the same vehicles to the food production center.

Special attention was given each item of equipment to reduce the standard industrial look of a large production unit and to ensure cleanliness.

Comprehension Questions

1. **This article describes the cook-chill process and _____.**

   a. tells how it saves money
   b. the colors of the work area
   c. how the food is served
   d. proves it is a good system

2. **One thing workers like about the system is that _____.**

   a. they do not have to start work at 5:30 A.M.
   b. they get more holidays
   c. the food is cold
   d. the recipes are easy

3. **Food waste is less because _____.**

   a. the students eat more
   b. they just heat what they need
   c. the menu is shorter
   d. the food is chilled quickly

4. **The Olathe School System foodservice prepares _____ Type A meals each day.**

   a. 32
   b. 3,000
   c. 6,000
   d. 9,000

5. **A cook-chill system means that _____.**

   a. cold food is cooked
   b. food is cooked, then quickly chilled, and shipped cold
   c. the kitchen is kept cold
   d. some food is cooked, and some is chilled

Vocabulary Test

On each line, write the number of the word that matches the definition.

1. **contamination** _____
2. **minimize** _____
3. **batch** _____
4. **parochial** _____
5. **à la carte** _____
6. **bulk** _____
7. **cost-effective** _____
8. **cook-chill** _____

a. of or relating to a church parish

b. good value for the money spent

c. a state of being soiled, infected, or unfit for use

d. of or relating to materials stored in large quantities

e. to reduce to the least quantity possible

f. cooked first and then quickly chilled

g. according to a menu that prices each item separately

h. the quantity cooked or baked at one time

Trade and Technical

The Whys and Hows of Freezers

Vocabulary Preview

accessible: able to be reached

accumulate: pile up; collect

bulk: large quantity

capacity: ability to hold

compressor: a machine that compacts the gases that cool a refrigerator

cubic foot: a unit for measuring volume; the amount of space that would be 1 foot in length, width, and height

duct: a tube or pipe through which air or liquid can flow

energy-efficient: making the best use of energy

frost: frozen water vapor

grounded: attached to a conducting body that returns electric current to the ground

humidity: water vapor in the air

initial: first; at the beginning

preset: built into the machine

upright: being taller than wide

A freezer is like any other sensible investment. After the **initial** cost, it provides regular benefits over an extended period of time. Freezers pay off in several different ways. They can save time and money. They also improve meals by providing storage space for a great variety of foods and prepared dishes.

Freezers have extremely cold temperatures, usually zero degrees Fahrenheit. They are designed to preserve food flavor, color, texture, and nutritive qualities for up to a year. As a result, fewer shopping trips are necessary. To save money, the freezer's storage space can be used for **bulk** purchases and items from food specials or sales.

Freezers should not be confused with your refrigerator's freezer compartment. The compartment is best used for quick-in, quick-out items. Unless the compartment is sealed off from the regular section, frequent door opening makes it difficult to store frozen foods there for very long. Refrigerator freezer compartments are comparatively small and don't hold much.

◆ Which Freezer Is Best?

When you choose a freezer, remember it's probably going to be with you for a long time. No single style or size is best, so it's important to know which freezer is right for your needs.

First, decide if you want an **upright** or chest model. Uprights are more convenient. Their storage space is more **accessible** and they take up less floor area. However, chest models are more **energy-efficient** because less cold air escapes when they are open.

What size freezer is best for you? In general, there should be five to six **cubic feet** of storage **capacity** per person. However, if you're not planning to make bulk purchases, you can get by with less. Many sizes are available.

If you're buying an upright, you'll have to choose between frostless or manual defrost. Chest freezers are always manual. Frostless freezers automatically defrost at **preset** intervals and remove the water. Manual models must be defrosted by hand every few months or whenever **frost accumulates** to about a quarter of an inch. Manual-defrost freezers generally are priced lower than frostless models. They use less energy than a frostless freezer, but will cost as much to operate if they are not defrosted properly.

All freezers are not created equal when it comes to features. Some offer little more than freezing ability. Others have a variety of conveniences, such as adjustable cold control, power signal light, clean-back design so the freezer can be placed close to the wall, key-lock door, and "flash" defrost for manual defrosting up to five times faster than with conventional models.

◆ What to Look For in a Freezer Location

Convenience isn't necessarily the number-one factor in picking the best place for your freezer.

To help it reach a ripe old age, try to find a spot that's cool, dry, and away from drafts. Drafts and heat (direct sunlight, a dryer, furnace or air **ducts**) will raise the freezer's cabinet temperature and make it work harder to keep cool. That means wasted energy and a shortened **compressor** life.

Freezers are designed to work most efficiently within specific air temperature limits, usually between 65 and 110 degrees Fahrenheit.

Dry air is important because high **humidity** can cause the freezer to rust outside and frost up inside. Garages, for example, are not good places for freezers because of potential humidity and extreme temperatures. Don't overlook the freezer's weight. Fully loaded, it may exceed 1,500 pounds. Make sure your home's structure can support the freezer if it's not on ground level.

Leave space behind, around, and above your freezer for air circulation and easier cleaning. There should be three to four inches above it and three inches on all sides. Always make sure the freezer can be **grounded** electrically before you settle on its location. Consult your owner's manual for more information about your model.

◆ Taking Care of Your Freezer

With proper care, a freezer can serve you for 15 years or more. Regular cleaning and simple maintenance will help it maintain a zero-degree temperature and keep it smelling fresh and looking almost new.

Frostless models require less care than manual defrost freezers. The interior of a frostless unit should be washed periodically with warm water and baking soda or a mild soap, rinsed, and dried.

Coils on the back of frostless and manual units should be gently vacuumed or brushed about twice a year. When manual freezers are not defrosted regularly, the frost gets thicker, energy is wasted, and the freezer gradually loses its cooling ability.

Before defrosting, turn the cold control off and unplug the power cord. Take out all food and wrap it in newspapers and blankets. It will stay frozen for several hours.

You can use air from a conventional fan to help speed up melting. A plastic scraper is good for removing frost. The defrost water should be completely drained.

Wash the interior, shelves, and baskets with a solution of two tablespoons of baking soda in one quart of warm water. For stubborn stains, use mild soap and warm water. After rinsing and drying the compartment, plug in the freezer and reset it.

◆ Freezer Operating Tips

Good habits go a long way toward a freezer that runs efficiently. To get the most from your freezer, check regularly to make sure it's providing a true zero-degree temperature.

Place a freezer thermometer inside overnight at the top and front. Don't open the door. If the temperature is above zero degrees, adjust the cold control and take another reading until the freezer is set properly.

Keep the freezer at least three-quarters full. The emptier it gets, the more energy is wasted. If more than three pounds of food per cubic foot of storage space is added every 24 hours, the resulting high or low temperatures can damage the food.

Open the door as rarely as possible to minimize cold air loss and interior frosting. Check the door seals frequently. Keep them clean and replace them if they're deteriorated.

Comprehension Questions

1. **This selection mainly _____.**

   a. discusses the advantages and disadvantages of upright and chest freezers
   b. gives advice about choosing and caring for a freezer
   c. explains how to defrost a manual-defrost freezer
   d. tells the most economical ways to use a freezer

2. **For best results, _____.**

   a. you should add three pounds of food every 24 hours
   b. use bleach on stubborn stains
   c. keep the freezer at least three-quarters full
   d. put your freezer in a garage because of the strong floor

3. **To get the most from your freezer, be sure the temperature _____.**

   a. stays at zero degrees Fahrenheit
   b. doesn't go down when you defrost
   c. stays at least below 30 degrees
   d. never varies more than 10 degrees from zero

4. **Choosing the best place for your freezer means _____.**

   a. locating it as close as possible to either the kitchen or the back door
   b. putting it in an unheated garage if possible
   c. locating it near a sink or drain if it is a manual-defrost model
   d. trying to keep it away from heat, drafts, and humidity

5. **Each of these ideas is found in the selection. Only one expresses the basic idea. Which one?**

   a. Choose the freezer that's right for your needs and then take proper care of it.
   b. If you want an upright, you'll have to decide whether to get a frostless or a manual defrost.
   c. The wrong location can mean wasted energy and a shorter life for your freezer.
   d. A freezer can save you money and time.

Vocabulary Test

On each line, write the word that matches the definition.

accessible	compressor	frost	initial
accumulate	duct	grounded	preset
capacity	energy-efficient	humidity	upright

1. _____ a machine that compacts the gases that cool a refrigerator

2. _____ first; at the beginning

3. _____ tube or pipe through which air or liquid can flow

4. _____ able to be reached

5. _____ ability to hold

6. _____ making the best use of energy

7. _____ water vapor in the air

8. _____ pile up; collect

9. _____ frozen water vapor

10. _____ attached to a conducting body that returns electric current to the ground

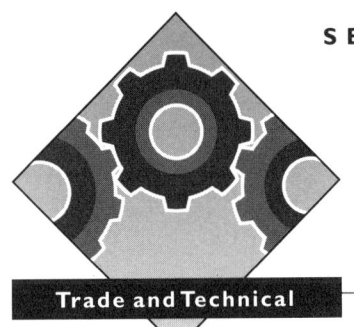

Should You Consider a Welding Career?

By Arnold R. Deutsch

Vocabulary Preview

brazing: uniting metals at high temperatures

craftsworker: a person who practices a trade or handicraft

dexterity: skill and ease in physical activity

drafting: drawing done with aid of rulers, scales, compasses, and so on

fused: joined by being melted together

metallurgical: having to do with the science or technology of metals

welding: joining metal parts by heating the parts and allowing the metals to flow together

The demand for skilled **craftsworkers** of all kinds remains high. The American Welding Society has announced that the field is wide open for welders, **welding** technicians and engineers, and **metallurgical** and research employees. There are also jobs for sales and service representatives, instructors, teachers, professors, technical writers, and editors. The list of jobs goes on and on.

Not many of us are aware of the influence welding has upon our lives. There are few things that you touch or depend upon during the day that haven't been fabricated by welding. Wherever two pieces of metal have been **fused,** a welder has been there. Be it a coffee pot, an automobile, a bicycle, or a spacecraft, all depend upon welding or **brazing** for their strength and efficiency. In construction, manufacturing, electronics, aviation, the nuclear energy field, and shipbuilding, skilled welders and welding craftsworkers are there to build and maintain the machines. Therefore, the welding field is well worth looking into.

◆ Why Consider Welding?

It is a valuable lifetime skill. Welders earn good wages and are in demand by many industries throughout the world. Welding is demanding, and there are a few basic requirements that apply to all areas of the craft. According to the American Welding Society, you should honestly ask yourself a few simple questions before considering a career as a welder.

- Are you in good physical condition? Good health determines your degree of manual **dexterity,** which is directly related to good eye-hand coordination. Good health also determines your ability to withstand heat, as well as your ability to concentrate. Good vision is a must, though you can wear eyeglasses.

- Are you disciplined? Do you have what it takes to stick with a task until it is completed? Do you want to learn?

- What about basic mechanical ability, intelligence, and common sense? By mechanical ability we mean an appreciation of the "mechanics" of things. As far as intelligence goes, you must have a basic knowledge of math and metals. Some knowledge of **drafting** would be a help.

Other attributes that will help you succeed:

- Imagination, not only in the mechanical "tinkering" sense, but in the ability to visualize what projects will look like when you're constructing them from plans. Also, imagination is needed in dealing with problems that occur from day to day.

- A positive work attitude. This is necessary for succeeding in a field that involves people working together. You must be willing to learn and be able to accept criticism. Working under stress and under pressure of time, you must be able to stay alert.

- A sense of responsibility. You must have respect for equipment and for the details of the work, respect for the safety and lives of those you are working with, and for the power you are working with. Also, one must be responsible for keeping one's skills up-to-date.

- A love of manual work. Welding is an art, almost like sculpturing. There can be joy in working with one's hands, and if you can get "in touch" with this feeling, you're in luck. Welding might be just what you're looking for.

◆ How to Get into This Field

Broadly speaking, there are three general levels for entry into the profession. They are welder, technician, and engineer.

Education can be divided into high school and vocational school, high school and technical institute, and college, with an engineering degree.

Here are a few job descriptions for the welding field.

Welding Machine Operator

This welder operates a machine or automatic welding equipment. The skill required is quite different from what is necessary for manual or semiautomatic welding. A welding machine operator is usually trained by the company in machine operation. The machine is set to produce a desired type of weld, and it is the welding operator's job to tend the machine and report any change in operating efficiency. Machine welding is used in the aircraft, automotive, and many other major industries.

Welder (Arc, Gas, Flamecutter)

Manual welding includes arc, gas, and flamecutting, and is for the person who likes to work with his or her hands to build things. There's plenty of variety involved in this area. You can work at the bottom of a mine, or at the top of a high-rise building. Whenever metals are joined, a welder is needed. Pipelines, for example, whether in Alaska, Minnesota, or the Middle East, are all made possible by welding.

Welding Technician

The welding technician stands between the welding engineer, who originates the work, and those who are concerned with completing the work. He or she adapts theory to production. Drafting ability may be needed by the technician, who may have to complete a series of tests, mount samples, analyze the work, and produce a report. A high degree of creative and technical talent is required. The technician uses drawing instruments and gauges, collects data, performs laboratory tests, builds, supervises, and controls machinery and testing equipment.

Welding Inspector

Inspection is the means by which quality is maintained. A certain standard of quality is determined, and it's the duty of the inspector to examine the work and reject any which falls below standard. This is a position of responsibility that extends beyond the range of physical work.

Welding Engineer

Wherever welding design is used, a welding engineer is needed. The growing use of welding increases the need for engineers. A chief welding engineer is part metallurgist and part design engineer, and has a working knowledge of electrical engineering, is familiar with mechanical engineering, and, of course, understands welding and its effects on metals. College will provide you with the fundamentals you need to understand elements of design and to be able to calculate stresses and to test welded parts.

Comprehension Questions

1. **This article mainly tells about _____.**

   a. jobs for welders
   b. what a welder does and why someone might want to enter the welding field
   c. how someone becomes a welder
   d. what welding is

2. **You know something has been welded if _____.**

   a. metal parts have been joined
   b. the metal melts
   c. it is labeled
   d. it is stamped by the American Welding Society

3. **The only object that would not have been welded is _____.**

   a. a bicycle
   b. a coffee pot
   c. an airplane
   d. a wooden chair

4. **Manual welding means _____.**

   a. operating a welding machine
   b. working with your hands
   c. inspecting welded parts
   d. helping a welding engineer

5. **The writer believes that "the welding field is well worth looking into" because _____.**

   a. the pay is good
   b. there are not too many welders
   c. in many industries, welders and welding craftsworkers are there to make products and maintain machines
   d. you might like welding

Vocabulary Test

On each line, write the word that completes the sentence.

brazing	drafting	metallurgical
craftsworker	fused	welding
dexterity		

1. Drawing done with the aid of rulers, scales, compasses, and so on, is called _____.

2. A person who practices a trade or handicraft is called a

    _____.

3. Things that have been joined by being melted together have been

    _____.

4. A person who has a skill and ease in physical activity has much

    _____.

5. Uniting metals at high temperatures is called _____.

6. A _____ worker is one who deals with the science or technology of metals.

7. Joining metal parts by heating the parts and allowing the metal to flow together is called _____.

Inn-vited to Vermont

By Alan Rosenthal

Hospitality and Tourism

Vocabulary Preview

clapboard: a narrow board used for siding, which is thicker at one edge than the other

green: a common grassy area in the center of a town or village (also known as a *common*)

haying: cutting grass and other green plants for animal feed

overstuffed: thickly upholstered

paddock: an enclosed area used for pasturing or exercising animals

parlor: a room used for entertaining guests

primary: first in importance, order, or value

soapstone: a type of rock having a soapy feel

For ages, Americans have treasured a certain image of Vermont. They picture a land of rolling pastures, of villages with old homes and white churches, of brooks filled with trout and crossed by covered bridges, and of forests covering the slopes of the Green Mountains. People imagine themselves looking through antique shops and country stores, picnicking on town **greens,** bicycling, hiking, watching farmers **haying,** paddling a canoe across a lake, or jumping into a swimming hole.

But perhaps more than anything, visitors fantasize about Vermont country inns and they have good reason. Vermont's country inns offer special, high-quality lodging and food. As vacationers travel along quiet back roads, they see their vision of Vermont come to life. When they stop at small inns along the way, they sample the best of the state's country-style hospitality.

As Bob McElwain, operator of Bike Vermont, an inn-to-inn bicycle touring service, explains, "Each inn is unique and has its own special personality. The innkeepers' friendliness and food are main reasons many visitors keep coming back."

Most Vermont inns were built a century or more ago. They usually have only about 10 guest rooms, often furnished with antiques and quilts but almost never with phones or TVs. These are places where travelers can escape everyday cares. Sharing dining tables and bathrooms creates the feeling of being guests in a home, not customers in a business establishment.

Books and scattered magazines point out the interests of the innkeepers, who are often pleased to direct you to the best local attractions.

"Vermont has a history of hospitality," observes Kirsten Murphy, who, with partner Marcel Perret, operates The Golden Stage Inn in Proctorsville, in southern Vermont. The inn is one of hundreds found in a relatively small state.

Like most innkeepers, Murphy and Perret are proud of the warm, friendly atmosphere they've created at their inn. "The most rewarding part of this business is spending time with people of different backgrounds, from all around the continent, who often come back with people they've met here," Murphy says. "They feel this is another home; they're comfortable here. Staying at an inn is a pleasant experience."

Guests at The Golden Stage talk on the porch or by the swimming pool, or stroll among the many flower, herb, vegetable, and berry gardens that supply the house and kitchen all summer long. Guests also look for antiques among the galleries and shops of nearby Woodstock, hike the Appalachian Trail that passes within about 20 miles of the inn, or golf in Ludlow.

Less than a mile down the road from The Golden Stage, guests at the Okemo Lantern Lodge enjoy the same types of things. Built in the early 1800s, the Okemo was later remodeled during the 1880s into the Victorian home of a wealthy mill owner. It was converted into a hostelry (an inn or hotel) in 1943. A wraparound porch leads to an inviting interior of butternut woodwork and stained-glass windows. Guest rooms are decorated with flowered wallpaper and canopy beds.

"It's just like you've always imagined your grandmother's house should be," says Dody Button, who with her husband, Pete, moved from near Saratoga Springs, New York, to take over the 10-bedroom inn. "People can relax and mingle here."

About 10 miles east of Proctorsville in Vermont's prime horse country stands the Inn at Weathersfield, which includes three **paddocks** and a stable that can house 26 horses. "Because there are no major population centers in the state, motel chains never got a start here," explains Ron Thorburn, who moved from Ohio in 1980 to run the Revolutionary War-era inn. "Even in our biggest cities—Burlington, with about 38,000 residents, and Rutland, with about 18,000—there are very few sizable hotels or motels. So the hospitality business was left in the hands of the old establishments."

Thorburn's wife, Mary Louise, adds: "Inns add to the character of the state. There's a special feeling here—a sense of history, of community. Our strong laws against litter and billboards help maintain a scenic beauty that makes country inns seem appropriate."

The Inn at Weathersfield, with 12 guest rooms, began life in the 1790s as a 4-room farmhouse. Over the years, owners added a veranda and wings on both sides, including a two-story porch with pillars added around 1900 by an owner who was homesick for the South. Today the first thing they see is this wing, which gives the false impression of a Southern plantation house as visitors come up the long, maple-lined drive.

The establishment now has a sauna and solarium as well as an old-fashioned **parlor.** Its owners boast that theirs is Vermont's only solar-powered inn. "Occasionally in Vermont, our old-fashioned electric system gives way," Mary Louise says, "but we can rely on the sun to heat our water."

In summer, guests at the Inn at Weathersfield enjoy rides in a carriage pulled by Dick, the Thorburns' horse. The ride takes them through Perkinsville, past the village green, church, and general store over one of the area's three covered bridges, and out for a tour of a **soapstone** factory. That's where griddles and muffin and boot warmers are produced. Finally, Dick drops guests off at nearby Stoughton Pond for an inn-packed picnic and a bit of swimming.

Further upstate near Middlebury, a picture-perfect town in west central Vermont, the Waybury Inn was built as a stagecoach stop in 1810. Its 14 guest rooms have hosted travelers ever since. For the past few years, however, the inn has received unusual publicity: Its Colonial-style exterior was shown at the opening of each episode of the popular weekly TV comedy "Newhart."

October Country Inn is in Bridgewater Corners, south central Vermont. Guests there sit on rocking chairs on the screened porch and watch the night sky. Indoors, some guests settle into **overstuffed** chairs to read some of the many favorites from the inn's impressive library. Other guests write letters or play Pictionary.

The proprietors, Richard Sims and Patrick Runkel, bought the inn in 1987. They have furnished the approximately 135-year-old red **clapboard** farmhouse with a mix of old and sturdy furniture. They are pleased with the inn's low-key, lived-in atmosphere. "We don't have fancy, formal antiques," says Sims. "There's nothing intimidating or fragile at our place. You can kick off your shoes here."

No matter how charming its atmosphere or its nearby points of interest, inns are often best remembered for their food. Innkeepers know well that when their guests return from their daily outings, their appetites will be hearty. At most country inns, dinner and breakfast are included in the standard room rate, and innkeepers delight in coming up with flavorful meals.

At The Golden Stage, for example, the five-course dinner menu includes many homemade items. "I make real killer desserts, which is how I think desserts should be," says Kirsten Murphy. She welcomes guests to watch her at work in the kitchen, where she bakes coffee cakes and croissants "from scratch."

Like The Golden Stage, Okemo Lantern Lodge is noted for the delicacies that come from its kitchen. Chef Dody Button grows her own herbs and makes her own applesauce.

For the past eight years, Mary Louise Thorburn has thrilled diners at the

Inn at Weathersfield with her six-course American dinners. Her summer guests also enjoy tea every afternoon.

Kimberly Smith is most proud of the Waybury Inn's blueberry waffles and "all types" of fresh muffins at breakfast. Because the inn opens its dining room to the public for dinner and Sunday brunch, Smith employs two cooks.

At October Country Inn, co-owner and chef Patrick Runkel prepares imaginative meals that feature a different ethnic specialty every night. Entrees range from French, Italian, and Mexican to Chinese, Greek, and Russian.

Most travelers agree that Vermont country inns such as these can serve as **primary** vacation destinations. Lodgers can enjoy two fine meals a day, learn about the best local sights, and share the company of friendly hosts and a few fellow travelers. They also can sleep in beautifully furnished bedrooms where the only sounds are of crickets and cows.

Comprehension Questions

1. **The main idea here is that _____.**

   a. each inn has its own personality
   b. staying at a Vermont country inn can be a vacation in itself
   c. Vermont inns are pleasant and convenient stopping places on the way to Canada
   d. most Vermont inns are near good hiking trails

2. **The writer says an inn's greatest appeal lies in its _____.**

   a. charm   **c.** innkeepers and meals
   b. nearby activities   **d.** location

3. **The inn with particular interest for horse lovers is _____.**

   a. the Golden Stage   **c.** the October Country Inn
   b. the Inn at Weathersfield **d.** the Waybury Inn

4. **The inn used in the opening credits of the Bob Newhart show is _____.**

   a. the Golden Stage   **c.** the October Country Inn
   b. the Inn at Weathersfield **d.** the Waybury Inn

5. **Before the writer begins to describe Vermont inns, he gives an introductory paragraph. The main topic of his introductory paragraph is _____.**

   a. the pleasures of a New England vacation
   b. the attraction of Vermont inns in general
   c. scenery and activities in Vermont
   d. reasons for staying at small Vermont inns

Vocabulary Test

On each line, write the number of the word that matches the definition.

1. **paddock**   _____   **a.** first in importance, order, or value

2. **soapstone**   _____   **b.** thickly upholstered

3. **parlor**   _____   **c.** cutting grass and other green plants for animal feed

4. **clapboard**

5. **green**   _____   **d.** an enclosed area used for pasturing or exercising animals

6. **primary**

7. **haying**   _____   **e.** a room used for entertaining guests

8. **overstuffed**   _____   **f.** a type of rock having a soapy feel

    _____   **g.** a common grassy area in the center of a town or village (also known as a _common_)

    _____   **h.** a narrow board used for siding, which is thicker at one edge than the other

Let Your Fingers Do the Shopping

By Lorraine Calvacca

Vocabulary Preview

database: a collection of information organized for rapid search and retrieval by a computer

explanatory: helping to make known or understood

hype: excessive promotion or advertising

in-depth: thorough

journal: a periodical that deals with matters of current interest to people in a certain occupation and that is written by people in that occupation

modem: a device used to transmit computer information over telephone lines

mouse: a small device that controls movement of the cursor on a computer display

on-line: available through a computer system

revolutionary: bringing about major change

upgrade: an improvement

users' group: an association of people who use a particular kind of computer and who share information

user-friendly: designed to be easily used and understood by a computer operator

vendor: a person who sells

window: an area on a computer monitor screen through which the directory of a disk or folder can be viewed

Whether you're self-employed or work for a big company, shopping for new office equipment can be a nightmare. There are countless models of so-called **revolutionary** new hardware, software, and computer systems on the market. Decisions are further complicated by the fact that you can get the exact same task done several different ways. For example, you can buy a stand-alone fax machine, a fax/telephone combination, or a fax chip card, which is installed inside your personal computer.

If you're in the market for new office equipment or an **upgrade** but can't figure out what to buy, here are some suggestions to help you through the **hype** without running all over town.

◆ Phone a Few Users' Groups

Industry experts regard **users' groups** as one of the best sources of reliable information. You don't have to be a member to call and ask a question or two before buying equipment. These clubs are particularly helpful because members are constantly discussing the equipment they own and how they've solved technical problems. "Users' groups are great educators," says a contributing editor of *PC World* magazine. "They work because no one's trying to sell you anything."

There are about 3,000 users' groups nationwide. Joining one after you make your purchase makes sense, especially if you work at home and constantly need advice on shortcuts or quick solutions. Many groups publish newsletters that include equipment tips, industry news, and product reviews. Larger ones also have manufacturer discounts and electronic bulletin boards, where members using a **modem**-equipped computer can correspond with one another. Local computer dealers should be able to put you in touch with a group in your area; otherwise, consult magazines that periodically print a list of users' groups.

◆ Link Up with On-Line Guides

If you already own a modem-equipped personal computer, you can research your next shopping spree without leaving your desk. Several **on-line** reference services provide summaries of articles, product reviews and consumer reports that have appeared in computer and office-products magazines. Subscribers to **CompuServe** (800-848-8199) who have queries on specific brands of hardware and software can store their questions in any of the service's 200 computer-related forums. Responses from other CompuServe customers and from manufacturers will appear the next day. CompuServe also offers an "Electronic Mall," through which users can shop and purchase equipment at the push of a button. There is a membership fee and an hourly fee for on-line time. But it's cost-effective when compared with subscribing to dozens of magazines or spending hours at the library doing research. It also gives you access to ZiffNet and InfoWorld On-Line.

ZiffNet (212-503-4485) offers a **database** of article summaries from more than 100 professional computer **journals** and magazines, including *PC World, Byte,* and *Macworld,* as well as product reviews from *PC Week, MacWeek, PC/Computing,* and *MacUsers.* To compare product features and functions, on-line users may want to consult the Computer Directory, ZiffNet's listing of more than 68,000 computer-related products made by

11,000 manufacturers. On-line bulletin boards enable users to log onto on-going question-and-answer sessions.

InfoWorld On-Line (415-572-7341) allows you to research and print out hardware and software product reviews that are produced weekly by *InfoWorld* magazine's in-house testing lab. The reviews assess the features, performance, ease of learning, ease of use, technical support, and service-ability of various equipment.

America Online (800-827-6364) offers a similar service, but with a twist. It sends out **user-friendly** software that's based on the **windows** application. You simply answer a series of questions on the screen, punch in your credit-card number and you're on-line, provided you have a modem and a computer with a **mouse.** Subscribers can access a number of magazines, including *Home-Office Computing, Macworld,* and *Compute.*

◆ Ask the Pros

If you're the type who likes to know every detail about a product before you set foot in a store, or if you make the major technology-purchasing decisions for your company, consider reading a specialized publication before you buy. In addition to **in-depth** articles, these publications are filled with lab-test reports.

Sometimes referred to as the Consumers Union of the office-products world, **Buyers Laboratory Inc.** (201-488-0404) routinely—and merciless-ly—tests all types of shredders, faxes, printers, copiers, electronic typewriters, and office furniture.

Datapro Information Services Group (800-328-2776), a division of McGraw-Hill, annually publishes more than 40 loose-leaf binders that examine products, services, and **vendors** in a variety of information-technology markets, including microcomputers, office automation, and software.

Despite its name, **National Software Testing Laboratories** (800-223-7093) tests both software and hardware. The Datapro subsidiary tests an average of 10 products per issue and publishes the results between 12 and 24 times a year. Its three titles are *Software Digest, PC Digest,* and *Macintosh Ratings Report.* NSTL also hires real-life users to evaluate a product's performance and reports the results in chart form.

What to Buy for Business Inc. (800-247-2185) produces 10 issues a year on copiers, computers, printers, fax machines, and more. Each publication evaluates a specific type of equipment in grid-chart format, based on user surveys and manufacturers' specifications. Issues include an **explanatory** overview of features that appear in the charts, as well as comparative prices. Some libraries subscribe to the company's publications.

Comprehension Questions

1. **The author's main purpose in this article is to _____.**

    a. tell people where to buy computers
    b. let people know about users' groups
    c. show people how to find out about computers and computer equip-
        ment by using the phone and computer services
    d. help people subscribe to computer services

2. **There are about _____ users' groups in the nation.**

    a. 1,000   **c.** 13,000
    b. 3,000   **d.** 300

3. **Users' group members who have a modem-equipped computer can
    correspond with one another through a(n) _____.**

    a. computer service   **c.** fax machine
    b. database   **d.** electronic bulletin board

4. **The company that hires real computer users to test products is
    _____.**

    a. National Software Testing Laboratories
    b. America Online
    c. Buyers Laboratory Inc.
    d. CompuServe

5. **This article points out that _____.**

    a. it is better to buy new equipment than used
    b. it is possible to find out all about computer equipment without leav-
        ing your computer
    c. it is handy to have a modem
    d. users' groups are difficult to find

Vocabulary Test

On each line, write the word that matches the definition.

database	**journal**	**revolutionary**
explanatory	**modem**	**upgrade**
hype	**mouse**	**users' group**
in-depth	**on-line**	**vendor**

1. _____   bring about major change

2. _____   an improvement

3. _____   excessive promotion or advertising

4. _____   thorough

5. _____   a small device that controls movement of the cursor on a computer display

6. _____   helping to make known or understood

7. _____   a collection of information organized for rapid search and retrieval by a computer

8. _____   a person who sells

9. _____   a device used to transmit computer information over telephone lines

10. _____   available through a computer system

Paddlewheeler Cruises

By Ruth Heimbuecher

Hospitality and Tourism

Vocabulary Preview

abolitionist: a person who believes in stopping slavery

blared: sounded loudly and harshly

brimming: filled to overflowing

dramatic: striking in appearance

isolated: alone; removed from other society

locals: people native to a particular place

luxurious: extravagantly rich and comfortable

paddlewheeler: a steamboat moved by a wheel that has paddles (or boards) around its outside edge

saloon: an elaborately decorated hall or dining room

supplemented: added to

wooded: covered with growing trees

Sailing on the *Mississippi Queen* combines a Huck Finn feeling of adventure with the comforts of an ocean cruise.

Instead of a raft, we were on seven **luxurious** decks aboard a steamboat longer than a football field. We cruised up the Ohio River at a leisurely 6–8 m.p.h.

We stopped at towns where the big event of the day was our arrival, just as it must have been in the 19th century when thousands of **paddlewheelers** traveled the Mississippi and Ohio. In Cincinnati, where the *Mississippi Queen* and its sister ship, the *Delta Queen,* are frequent sights, people with cameras came to see the ship at Public Landing. They stayed until the boat's whistle signaled our leaving. We left Cincinnati for a four-night cruise on the Ohio.

Unlike ocean voyages, there was constantly something to see from both sides of the boat. We passed riverside towns, **isolated** farmhouses in islands of corn, and huge factories that looked like Lego constructions. Long stretches of **wooded** riverbanks and tall hills showed no evidence that anyone had ever been there.

Our first stop was Maysville, Kentucky, 65 miles southeast of Cincinnati. School buses waited for passengers who wanted to explore the downtown area, listed on the National Register of Historic Places.

The town of 8,500 stretches between hills and the river. It's a beautiful town, **brimming** with Southern charm. There are tiny parks where **locals** meet and talk. Some of the forty-eight historic buildings and sites have graceful iron railings like those in New Orleans.

Rosemary Clooney (a well-known singer from the 50s) is one of Maysville's native daughters. She has a space in the Mason County museum and a note that her first film, *The Stars Are Singing,* was premiered in 1953 at the Russell Theater. A sign outside the building, no longer a theater, advertises hamburgers, three for $1.08.

Arriving in Maysville was **dramatic.** A few hundred people waited on the banks as the boat edged in. Ropes were tied to trees, the world's largest and loudest calliope (similar to an organ) **blared,** and the stage lowered. (The stage—a passenger ramp—traces its name to the time when entertainers performed on it.)

Our second stop was made at Huntington, West Virginia, where we spent all our time at Huntington Galleries, the state's largest art museum. We saw wonderful works of glass from artists across the country.

Our final stop was Ripley, Ohio. This tiny town was once described as an "**abolitionist** hell hole" because of its politics and its practice of helping runaway slaves.

Ripley is a small gem. Smaller than it used to be—2,400 residents now, 5,000 at its peak—Ripley is being rediscovered. Its 55-acre historic district has more buildings built before 1830 than any other place in Ohio.

The Olde Piano Factory Antique Mall was really once a piano factory. Here a dealer from New Jersey laughed about a "visit" to Ripley that began many years ago and isn't over yet.

The Ripley Museum was popular with steamboat visitors. Even more popular was the Main Street drug store that served Cokes made the old-fashioned way—with syrup and soda water—and foamy sodas.

Some of the *Mississippi Queen*'s 420 passengers never bothered to get off the boat. They were there just for the experience of traveling on this floating palace. Besides, there was a lot to do on board—bridge, bingo, trivia contests, kite flying, morning exercises, tours of the pilot house, a beauty shop, and movies, one of which was *The Adventures of Tom Sawyer.*

There were calliope tryouts, and anyone who could play a note gave it a shot. Most were awful, but everyone had a good time blasting a hole in the summer air. An open-air jacuzzi went mostly unused; the masseuse (someone who gives massages) complained she hardly had any customers.

Evenings, there were skits and music in the Grand **Saloon** with an excellent band and singers. Chad Mitchell, cruise director, once headed the Chad Mitchell Trio, singers of folk songs in the '60s.

A pianist played at dinner. Her choices ranged from Broadway musicals to long-ago favorites. Two nights in a row, she played "The Moon of Monakura." Those of us of a certain age remembered that Dorothy Lamour had sung it in one of the *Road* movies with Bing Crosby and Bob Hope.

After dinner the last night aboard, the dining room staff performed the "second line," an imitation of a traditionally lively New Orleans funeral procession, to Dixieland music. They strutted, danced, twirled umbrellas, and clowned their way through the room. If it had been a real show, they would have stopped it!

As on ocean cruises, food was a major experience on the *Mississippi Queen.* We had three generally outstanding meals in the dining room. These were **supplemented** by "health" breakfasts in the Grand Saloon, lunchtime buffets of salads, sandwiches, and barbecues, late afternoon appetizers, and midnight buffets in the Paddlewheel Bar.

Comprehension Questions

1. **The reading selection is mainly about** _____.

    a. outstanding meals   **c.** a vacation cruise
    b. museums along the Ohio River **d.** exploring the Ohio River

2. **The writer was traveling the Ohio River on** _____.

    a. an ocean liner **c.** a steamboat
    b. the *Delta Queen* **d.** a raft

3. **Some of the iron railings in Maysville, Kentucky, reminded the writer of** _____.

    a. New Orleans   **c.** a Dorothy Lamour movie
    b. Rosemary Clooney's home **d.** Ripley, Ohio

4. **This cruise varied from an ocean cruise in that** _____.

    a. there were seven luxurious decks
    b. there was always something to see on both sides of the boat
    c. there was evening entertainment on board
    d. food was a major experience

5. **The main thing this selection shows is** _____.

    a. the beauty and history of the Ohio River area
    b. how paddlewheel boats work
    c. the many important historic places near the Ohio River
    d. the varied activities and entertainment provided on the trip

Vocabulary Test

On each line, write the word that completes the sentence.

abolitionists	**isolated**	**saloon**
blared	**locals**	**supplemented**
brimming	**luxurious**	**wooded**
dramatic	**paddlewheeler**	

1. The banks of the river were ———————————; they were covered with trees.

2. The ——————————— came out of their nearby homes to see the ship.

3. Snacks ——————————— the meal.

4. The fireworks over the river were a ——————————— effect.

5. The ——————————— were responsible for putting an end to slavery.

6. If a house is all by itself, it is ———————————.

7. The trumpets ——————————— in the brass band.

8. The flooded river was ——————————— over its banks.

9. The beautiful hall where they had the reception was called a

———————————.

10. Passengers had to pay extra for the most ———————————
suites.

Allied Health

Why It's So Hard to Quit Smoking

By Christine Gorman

Vocabulary Preview

addictive: causing a compulsive physiological (or bodily) need for something

dependence: addiction or habit

fatally: in a way resulting in death

hallucinations: seeing imagined objects or visions

legitimate: in agreement with laws and requirements

nervous system: the bodily system made up of the brain, spinal cord, nerves and all their parts

opiates: drugs derived from opium; drugs that cause sleepiness, dullness, or inaction

overstimulate: to excite to too much activity

psychopharmacologist: a person who studies the effects of drugs on the mind and behavior

skyrockets: rises up suddenly and quickly

tranquilizer: a drug used to reduce mental tension and anxiety

treatable: capable of responding to treatment

Anyone who has ever tried to give up smoking cigarettes knows the meaning of being hooked. Of those who succeed in quitting for the first time, 75 percent go back to smoking. Recently, the U.S. surgeon general made official what everyone has recognized for a long time. Tobacco, like cocaine or heroin, is **addictive.**

The surgeon general not only said that "cigarettes and other forms of tobacco are addicting." He also urged that they should be treated the same as illegal street drugs.

Based on 20 years of research by 50 scientists, the surgeon general's report earned high praise from the medical community. However, the tobacco industry disagreed. "Smokers are not 'addicts,'" they replied. "People quit smoking every day," said Brennan Moran, a spokeswoman for the Tobacco Institute. "The surgeon general has mistaken the enemy," said a North Carolina senator. "In comparing tobacco—a **legitimate** and legal substance—to narcotics such as heroin and cocaine, he has politely attacked American farmers and businesspersons."

The surgeon general's reply was a strong one. "I haven't mistaken the enemy," he said. "My enemy kills 350,000 people a year." In the U.S. in 1986, smoking-related lung problems accounted for 108,000 deaths; heart disease killed 200,000 more. By comparison, the surgeon general continued, cocaine and **opiates** such as heroin kill about 6,000 a year and alcohol about 125,000. To show how addicting nicotine is, the surgeon general mentioned several national surveys that reveal that 75 to 85 percent of the nation's 51 million smokers would like to quit but have so far been unable to do so.

The panic of a heavy smoker who is out of cigarettes shows something more powerful at work than mere desire. Not long after taking up the habit, smokers' bodies accept nicotine's effects. As with heroin and cocaine, **dependence** quickly follows. Tobacco only seems safer because it is not immediately dangerous. Nicotine is not likely, for example, to **fatally overstimulate** a healthy heart. Or to cause **hallucinations.** Or to bring on a sudden "high." "People die with crack immediately," explains Alexander Glassman, a **psychopharmacologist** at the New York State Psychiatric Institute in Manhattan. "With cigarettes the problems occur 20 years down the line. Nobody lights up their first cigarette and dies."

Like many drugs that affect the **nervous system,** nicotine stimulates and relaxes the body at the same time. It takes only seven to ten seconds to reach the brain—twice as fast as intravenous (injected into a vein) drugs and three times faster than alcohol. After a few puffs, the level of nicotine in the blood **skyrockets.** The heart beats faster and blood pressure increases. Result: smokers become more alert and may actually even think faster. In addition, nicotine may produce a calming effect. It causes the body to release natural **tranquilizers** called beta-endorphins. Thus, a smoker is in two states of mind—alertness and relaxation.

Nicotine cannot be stored in the body. So smokers keep up the level in the blood by continuing to smoke. "Because you take 200 to 400 of these hits a day, they build a strong habit," says Nina Schneider, a psychopharmacologist at the University of California, Los Angeles. "The hits are easy to get. And they control mood and performance. That's what makes it so powerfully addicting."

In spite of all this, smoking can be conquered. It is true that ex-heroin users have reported that tobacco's grip was harder to break than their drug habit. But 43 million Americans have managed to quit smoking, mostly succeeding on their own. More and more, though, the one third of all Americans who still smoke are seeking help in antismoking programs. These generally stress that the tobacco habit is a **treatable** addiction.

The real key to success, however, lies in the amount of encouragement smokers get from physicians, friends, and relatives. That's what the experts tell us. Without doubt, the benefits of quitting are worth the struggle.

Comprehension Questions

1. **The main reason it is hard to quit smoking is that** _____.

   a. smoking is addictive   **c.** smokers take 200 to 400 hits a day
   b. people have no will power   **d.** it makes people more alert

2. **Surveys show that** _____ **of the country's smokers wish they could quit.**

   a. a minority   **c.** about half
   b. 75% to 85%   **d.** 90%

3. **Tobacco industry spokespersons claim that** _____ .

   a. nicotine takes a long time to reach the brain
   b. smokers are not addicts
   c. smokers have no unusual health risks
   d. smoking may cause cancer but not heart disease

4. **According to experts, tobacco seems safer than heroin or cocaine because** _____ .

   a. it is not taken by needle   **c.** so many people smoke
   b. no one dies from tobacco   **d.** the problems don't show up till later

5. **Which word expresses the basic problem discussed here?**

   a. ignorance   **c.** dependence
   b. business   **d.** support

Vocabulary Test

On each line, write the word that matches the definition.

addictive   legitimate   psychopharmacologist
dependence   nervous system   skyrockets
fatally   opiates   tranquilizer
hallucinations   overstimulate   treatable

1. _____ in agreement with laws and requirements

2. _____ to excite to too much activity

3. _____ addiction or habit

4. _____ seeing imagined objects or visions

5. _____ capable of responding to treatment

6. _____ rises suddenly and quickly

7. _____ drugs that cause sleepiness, dullness, or
   inaction

8. _____ causing a compulsive bodily need for
   something

9. _____ in a way resulting in death

10. _____ the bodily system made up of the brain,
    spinal cord, and nerves and all their
    parts

SELECTION 27

Union Station Back on Track after $120 Million Facelift

By Judi Bredemeier

Hospitality and Tourism

Vocabulary Preview

bicentennial: a 200th anniversary

commercial: having to do with business or trade

complex: a group of related units

condemned: declared unfit for use

deteriorating: becoming of worse condition

effort: work; a serious attempt

embarrassment: a feeling of being uncomfortable or nervous

history-oriented: interested in the past

possibilities: things that may happen or come true

preservation: keeping or saving from decaying or rotting

redevelopment: the process of making an old and decaying area or thing like new again

renovation: bringing back to an earlier, better condition

restoration: bringing back to an original condition

volunteer: someone who does a job for goodwill, not pay

Washington's once-proud Union Station has returned to public life. It re-opened in October 1988 after a $120 million, seven-year **restoration** and **redevelopment effort.**

Union Station will once again house Amtrak operations serving some seven million passengers every year. But the historic turn-of-the-century building also has been turned into a multi-use dining, shopping, and entertainment **complex** that developers believe will be extremely popular with both tourists and people who live in Washington.

It also brings to Capitol Hill something that has long been in short supply: special parking areas for tour buses. The garage space for tour buses should improve crowded conditions and difficult driving around the Capitol and other nearby attractions.

The historic building on Capitol Hill has been closed to the public since 1981, its design and detail covered in mold and dust. It was last used as a **Bicentennial** Visitors Center. Badly designed and located in the dim, damp center of the **deteriorating** station, it was an **embarrassment** to Washington and to the travel industry.

Union Station was once one of Washington's most famous public buildings, designed by famed Chicago architect Daniel Burnham in the grand days of rail travel. But as air travel replaced railroads after World War II, the condition of Union Station gradually became so poor that it was finally **condemned.**

A seven-year **renovation** effort since that time was the result of a partnership between the federal government and private developers. Careful historic **preservation** of the station's vivid style combined with modern **commercial** marketing transformed the structure into a model "festival marketplace" in the manner of Boston's Faneuil Hall and New York's South Street Seaport. The renovated complex will have 140 retail shops, nine theaters, and several dozen cafes and restaurants.

Tom Murphy, tourism promotion manager for the Washington Convention and Visitors Association, calls Union Station "another major selling point for the city. Washington's travel industry," he said, "is very excited about its **possibilities**—it's our newest monument."

The National Trust for Historic Preservation trains **volunteers** that offer free tours of the renovated station. The Union Station tour program is a first for the National Trust, which never before offered its architecture and **history-oriented** tours to public buildings. It does, though, give such tours of some historic houses owned by the National Trust itself.

Amtrak president W. Graham Claytor, Jr., approved the rebirth of Union Station, calling the historic building "by far the most refined transportation terminal in America."

Comprehension Questions

1. **This article is mainly about** _____.

   a. train travel to Washington, D.C.
   b. visiting the Capitol
   c. the National Trust for Historic Preservation
   d. the renovation of Washington's Union Station

2. **Union Station had been closed to the public since** _____.

   a. 1986   **c.** 1975
   b. 1981   **d.** 1969

3. **Union Station's condition became so bad that it was condemned. This happened because** _____.

   a. rail travel had been largely replaced by air travel
   b. the city could not afford to take care of the station
   c. tourists wanted a new train station
   d. no one likes old buildings

4. **The renovated station complex has many attractions, but not**
   _____.

   a. restaurants   **c.** a hotel
   b. shops   **d.** theaters

5. **The writer's main point is that** _____.

   a. trains are running again in Union Station
   b. the station complex will have parking for tour buses
   c. the fine design of Union Station has been preserved and restored into a multi-use complex
   d. Union Station should attract tourists

Vocabulary Test

On each line, write the word that completes the sentence.

bicentennial	**condemned**	**possibilities**	**renovation**
commercial	**deteriorating**	**preservation**	**restoration**
complex	**history-oriented**	**redevelopment**	**volunteers**

1. The _____ of stores and restaurants is visited by many tourists.

2. Many volunteer groups are started for the _____ of old buildings that are still in good condition.

3. A building that is no longer safe is _____ and can no longer be used.

4. In 1976, Americans celebrated the _____ of the signing of the Declaration of Independence in 1776.

5. The _____ who conduct the tours are not paid for their time.

6. The condition of many historical buildings is

   _____ because cities cannot pay for repairs.

7. Businesspeople had many _____ reasons for wanting Union Station to be a useful place again.

8. A beautiful old building like Union Station deserved a

   _____ and _____ project.

9. _____ people love to be able to see old buildings in their original condition.

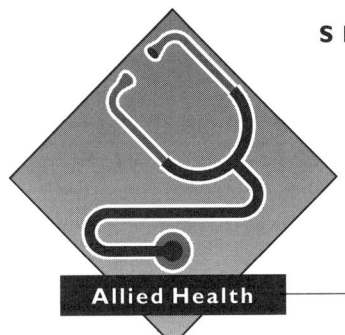

Medical Assistant

By Craig R. Ilk

Vocabulary Preview

clinical: concerned with actual observation and treatment of diseases rather than experimentation or theory

curriculum: the total of courses of study given at a school, college, or university

electrocardiogram: a graphic record of heart action used to detect heart disease

pharmaceutical: relating to the preparing of drugs and medicine

posting: entering data into an accounts ledger

transcribe: to make a written copy of something

An important member of the health care team is the medical assistant who helps the doctor care for his patients and provides an important link between the doctor and other doctors and suppliers of equipment and medications. The medical assistant performs **clinical** tasks and the tasks necessary to maintain an efficiently functioning office. Upon entering a doctor's office, the patient's first contact will probably be with the medical assistant. This assistant represents the doctor and the other office personnel and often provides the patient with the first dose of kindness and compassion that is an important part of any treatment plan. The medical assistant should not be confused with the medical secretary or the physician's assistant. The medical secretary performs administrative functions only, while the physician's assistant performs clinical tasks far beyond the scope of those provided by the medical assistant.

The following is a list of tasks that may be performed by medical assistants, adapted from that developed by the **Curriculum** Review Board of the American Association of Medical Assistants (AAMA). All duties are performed at the request and under the supervision of the doctor employing the medical assistant.

1. Schedule appointments in person and by telephone.

2. Greet and receive patients.

3. Prepare patient files for each day's appointments.

4. Take and record patients' statistical data and portions of the medical history.

5. Prepare patients for examination.

6. Take patients' blood pressure, pulse, temperature, height, and weight.

7. Collect blood samples, take **electrocardiograms,** and do other tests.

8. Give certain medications and injections.

9. Explain examinations or procedures to the patients.

10. Assist the doctor in the collection of throat cultures, Pap smears, and other similar specimens.

11. Perform simple, routine laboratory tests, such as urinalysis, and prepare other specimens to go to the laboratory.

12. Set up patient files, enter notes, and review the files for completeness and accuracy.

13. Arrange hospital admissions and/or laboratory and x-ray procedures ordered by the doctor.

14. Instruct patients on the preparation for tests ordered by the doctor.

15. Schedule surgeries.

16. Record laboratory, x-ray, and electrocardiogram results on patient charts.

17. Sterilize instruments and maintain diagnostic equipment in working order.

18. Properly dispose of contaminated items.

19. Order office, laboratory, and medical supplies and maintain inventory.

20. Be able to reach the doctor in emergencies and know how to apply first aid if necessary.

21. Answer telephone calls; check the answering service and record messages; make calls for the doctor; take reports from other doctors and laboratories.

22. Receive representatives of **pharmaceutical** companies, equipment manufacturers, and other callers.

23. Supervise maintenance personnel and see that the office is neat, attractive, and sanitary at all times.

24. Be responsible for correspondence, open and sort mail, answer mail; take medical dictation; **transcribe** shorthand or machine dictation; type all correspondence including medical reports, insurance reports, and other material as directed.

25. File all correspondence and medical records.

26. Operate business machines.

27. Perform daily **posting** of charges and collections and prepare patient bills. Assist patients in making credit arrangements and make necessary collections.

28. Arrange payments and issue receipts.

29. Keep financial records and assume banking duties.

30. Pay professional bills as directed.

31. Explain doctor's fees to patients.

32. Arrange accommodations, including travel arrangements, for the doctor's meetings and conferences.

33. Discuss insurance coverage with patient.

34. Complete all types of insurance forms including Medicare, Medicaid, Worker's Compensation, Blue Shield, and others.

35. Review and appeal, if necessary, insurance claims for which payment is denied.

A medical assistant should have a pleasant personality and skills that allow precise and caring communication with other people, as well as a sincere desire to serve people. Reliability and discreetness are also qualities that are essential for a successful career as a medical assistant.

Comprehension Questions

1. **The medical assistant's main job is to _____.**

   a. represent the doctor and to help the doctor in caring for the patients and running the office
   b. answer the phone
   c. order office and medical supplies
   d. supervise the medical secretary and the physician's assistant

2. **A medical assistant can only perform tasks _____.**

   a. that the patient wants
   b. that are on the AAMA list
   c. that the doctor requests and supervises
   d. that the physician's assistant recommends

3. **The first contact that a patient has with the medical personnel in a doctor's office will probably be with _____.**

   a. the receptionist   **b.** the medical assistant
   c. the physician's assistant **d.** the doctor

4. **A medical assistant can _____.**

   a. perform simple laboratory tests   **c.** take X rays
   b. prescribe medications   **d.** perform minor surgery

5. **The job of a medical assistant is a combination of _____.**

   a. public relations and office work
   b. secretary and doctor
   c. nurse and doctor
   d. office procedures and clinical tasks that the doctor requests

Vocabulary Test

Draw a line from each word to its correct definition.

1. **transcribe**
2. **curriculum**
3. **pharmaceutical**
4. **posting**
5. **electrocardiogram**
6. **clinical**

a. concerned with actual observation and treatment of diseases rather than experimentation or theory

b. to make a written copy

c. entering data into an accounts ledger

d. a graphic record of heart action used to detect heart disease

e. relating to the preparing of drugs and medicine

f. the total courses of study given at a school, college, or university

Temporary Employees Meet Needs of Business

By Samuel R. Sacco

Business and Computers

Vocabulary Preview

backlog: an accumulation of unfinished jobs

fiscal: relating to finances

flexibility: able to adapt to changing requirements

forefront: the first place; the very front

mandatory: by command; not voluntary

prospective: likely to happen in the future

seasonal: varying according to the time of year

temporary: not permanent; for a limited time

work force: the total number of people available for work

The nation's shift from traditional industries to industries based on service and information is written about almost daily. In the **forefront** of this shift is the **temporary** help industry. This industry helps people to enter the **work force** and even provides employee training to meet changing needs.

Temporary help is a business that provides both employees and employers with added labor **flexibility.** Currently there are more than 944,000 people employed in temporary help jobs every day. Such employment allows individuals who don't want full-time positions to adjust their work schedules to meet their needs. It also permits employers to respond quickly to temporary workloads and unexpected staff vacancies without the costs of permanent staff.

What is the difference between a temporary help company and an employment agency? The agency brings a job-seeker and **prospective** employer together for the purpose of permanent employment. A temporary help company, on the other hand, hires its own employees and assigns them to customers for limited periods of time on an as-needed basis.

As employers, temporary help companies provide all the things that employers must provide to employees: wages, benefits, payroll deductions, unemployment and workers' compensation, as well as the employer's share of social security.

The development of the temporary help industry since World War II can be divided into what might be termed three "generations." In the first generation, companies kept a record of the skills and availability of their temporary workers. They assigned them to routine work in emergency situations in which a regular worker was absent or unable to complete a sudden upsurge in work. This kept company activities flowing at a smooth pace and prevented work **backlogs.**

The second generation use of temporary help generally coincided with the 1960s. A cost-conscious business increased its use of temporary services to avoid overstaffing and to control costs. More efficient financial management became possible through the use of temporary employees on a planned basis. These employees were used to supplement the regular work force.

This use of temporaries is of great value to management in controlling costs. For example, all businesses are subject to **seasonal** demands of one kind or another: inventories, **fiscal** closing, tax season, and budget preparation. For all of these tasks, and many others, temporary employees may be the answer.

During the current—third—generation, temporary services have reached their most advanced and unusual forms of customer service. In addition to the traditional uses of temporary office personnel, firms now include almost every skill and work category.

The clerical sector (secretaries, typists, bookkeepers, clerks) still provides the largest amount of business to the industry—approximately 63%. But there is also heavy use made of temporary employees for industrial purposes such as warehouse and factory workers. Marketing (product demonstrators, interviewers, comparison shoppers) and technical (engineers, surveyors, draftsmen, computer programmers) divisions have also been developed and expanded.

Still another specialized area of the industry is health-care services. They provide licensed and registered nurses and laboratory technicians for home health, clinical and hospital care. Temporary nursing personnel in hospitals and nursing homes provides an efficient and economical management tool to control costs and provide good patient care in response to changing patient loads. At-home patients eliminate a costly hospital visit with a private-duty nurse providing professional care.

The manner in which temporary employees are put to use had also found some rather unusual applications. Typical areas might include such things as converting operations to a computer system; assembling and mailing an annual report; distributing new product samples; or mailing monthly statements.

Yet another example has to do with retirement policies. **Mandatory** retirement policies often cause a company to lose valuable and experienced employees when they are most needed. Sometimes these policies also force employees to leave before they wish to do so. But temporary help companies can save the day for everyone. By placing the retired employee on a temporary service's payroll and assigning that person to his or her former company, all parties remain happy.

There are still other new uses for temporary service. For example, smooth transitions can be achieved when such employees are used during office and plant relocations. In addition, temporaries can be used in jobs during the delays while formal written job descriptions are being drafted. Finally, temporary employees can fill essential jobs until hiring freezes are lifted.

The applications are almost limitless. As a result, temporary service firms and their customer companies are constantly working out flexible cost-saving solutions to complicated staffing and workload problems.

Comprehension Questions

1. **This article is mainly about** _____.

    a. what to expect from a temporary help company
    b. why temporary employees are better than regular employees
    c. how temporary help solves work force problems
    d. seasonal jobs for temporary help

2. **Such things as payroll deductions and workers' compensation are handled by** _____.

    a. the business using the temporary help service
    b. the individual employee
    c. a separate accounting firm
    d. the temporary help company

3. **Which work area is not mentioned among those covered by temporary help services?**

    a. health care   c. secretarial
    b. education   d. industrial

4. **One benefit a temporary help company offers workers is** _____.

    a. a chance to adjust work schedules to fit their needs
    b. not having to pay their own Social Security
    c. on-the-job training
    d. a retirement plan

5. **A summary sentence expresses one or more main points. Which of these is the best summary sentence for this article?**

    a. Temporary help companies are very much limited by the business world.
    b. The temporary help industry has expanded greatly since its beginnings.
    c. Temporary help workers sometimes take jobs from regular workers.
    d. Temporary help companies now provide industrial workers also.

Vocabulary Test

On each line, write the word that completes the sentence.

backlog	**forefront**	**seasonal**
fiscal	**mandatory**	**temporary**
flexibility	**prospective**	**work force**

1. It was _____ that she wear a uniform, and it must be black.

2. In my company, the _____ year ends June 30.

3. In an accounting office, the _____ need for extra employees is in March and April.

4. Anna enjoyed the many different experiences that come with being a _____ employee.

5. When people graduate from career school, getting a job is in the _____ of their thoughts.

6. Most students are anxious to finish school and join the

    _____.

7. A temporary employee needs to have _____.

8. An employer must be accurate in describing what he needs in a _____ temporary employee.

9. Seth was hired to clean up a _____ of orders.

Used-Car Inspection Tips

Trade and Technical

Vocabulary Preview

corrosion: the process of being worn away through chemical action

foul play: a dishonorable action

frayed: worn out, especially into shreds

odometer: an instrument for measuring and recording the distance traveled by a vehicle

Ideally, you should have a used car checked by a mechanic or diagnostic center before you buy. But you can tell a lot about a car's condition on your own by examining parts that are easily worn out. Here's what to look at:

✔*Check the odometer.* A low mileage reading can add more than $1,000 to the asking price of the car. Although federal law prohibits tampering with mileage figures, the practice is still a problem—especially in late-model cars that had been used previously as leased cars for large companies. (NHTSA estimates that **odometers** on more than 50% of all leased cars are rolled back before being resold.)

Look for signs of **foul play,** such as slightly out-of-line mileage figures or greasy fingerprints and chewed-up screw heads around the odometer unit or the dashboard. Look for lubrication stickers around door frames or under the hood; these help confirm actual mileage figures as well as how recently—and regularly—the car was maintained.

As you look over the car, be sure signs of wear are consistent with the mileage shown. When purchasing a vehicle, be certain you receive a mileage disclosure statement before the transfer of title. Also, make sure that the odometer works properly when you drive the vehicle.

✔*Check the front door on the driver's side.* Is it hard to close? Is the handle loose? Do windows rattle or operate improperly? These symptoms indicate frequent use and should not be present in a late model used car with under 30,000 miles.

✔*Examine the accelerator, brake, and clutch pedals* for worn areas and metal showing through rubber, which demonstrate heavy use.

✔*Observe the condition of seats, armrests, center consoles, carpeting, and upholstery.* Seats, for example, don't normally sag or feel mushy unless a car is aging or has suffered sustained use.

✔*Test every accessory and electrical component, one at a time.*

✔*Carefully examine the car's exterior.* Are there signs of rust in door frames, below doors, on rocker panels, or around fenders? Is there evidence of collision damage, such as bumps or waves in the metal, uneven body side molding, or uneven gaps between body panels? (Incidentally, avoid shopping in the rainy weather, which makes dents and repaints shine.)

✔*Test the suspension.* Push down on each corner of the car—front and back—to check shock absorber performance. If the car bounces several times, the shocks are worn and most likely need replacement. Stand back from the car and see if it's level. If one corner is lower than another, one of the springs may be broken or worn.

✔*Check the tires.* Do they match? Are there excessive or strange tread wear patterns? This could mean severe misalignment problems and the need to replace expensive steering/suspension parts. Check the spare tire for suspicious wear, as well.

✔*Look under the hood.* Do you see **frayed** cables, loose clamps, or **corrosion?** Are fan belts loose, cracked, or worn smooth? Do hoses feel soft or look discolored? Is the oil and antifreeze dirty or below prescribed levels? All are signs of a poorly maintained vehicle loaded with potential engine and starting problems. In automatics, check transmission fluid. A dark color or burned odor is a sign of potential transmission problems.

Comprehension Questions

1. **You have a better chance of buying a good used car if** _____.

   a. you know the previous owner
   b. it has not been driven too much
   c. it has a warranty
   d. you check on the parts that are easily worn out and have a mechanic check the car over

2. **It is against federal law to** _____.

   a. change the odometer numbers   c. hide accident damage
   b. buy a leased car   d. sell a poorly maintained vehicle

3. **Fan belts are in bad shape if they are** _____.

   a. soft and discolored   c. out of line
   b. loose, cracked, or worn smooth   d. below prescribed levels

4. **Excessive wear or strange tread-wear patterns on the tires could mean** _____.

   a. severe misalignment problems   c. cheap tires
   b. an old car   d. unbalanced tires

5. This article could also be called _____.

    a. Don't Buy Used Cars   **c.** Looking for Used-Car Problems
    b. To Buy Used or New   **d.** Good Buys in Used Cars

Vocabulary Test

Draw a line from each word to its correct definition.

1. **foul play**   **a.** worn out, especially into shreds

2. **odometer**   **b.** an instrument for measuring and recording the distance traveled by a vehicle

3. **frayed**

4. **corrosion**   **c.** a dishonorable action

                     d. the process of being worn away through chemical action

Banks Put Employees in Customers' Shoes

By Penny Lunt

Business and Computers

Vocabulary Preview

arthritis: inflammation and pain in joints of the body

consistency: the ability to stay with the same ideas or actions

curt: marked by rude shortness

defect: to leave a situation (or a company) to go over to a rival

distinguish: to make different; to set apart

empathize: to be aware of, or sensitive to, the feelings, thoughts, and experiences of others

officer: one who holds a position of trust or authority

retention: the act of keeping a customer in possession

scenario: a sequence of imagined events

universal: shared by everyone

Customers are likely to feel welcome at a branch of State Bank of Tulsa—they're often greeted with a hug. "We have a lot of older customers at that office," explains Training Director Susan Sykes. And while the bank's customer-contact people are generally encouraged to greet customers with a handshake, many customers have **arthritis** or just prefer hugs.

State Bank is one of many banks that tries to **distinguish** itself from the competition with a high level of service. Proof of its success is that during the eight months that this former savings bank was run by the Resolution Trust Corp., customer and account **retention** remained high, even though the RTC lowered deposit rates so that they were no longer competitive.

Can you teach people to be nice?

"You can't train someone to have a good attitude," says Arthur Bassin, chief service quality officer, Dime Savings Bank, New York. "You have to hire people who like people and reinforce their skills."

Bassin feels strongly that customer service training helps achieve a consistent level of service. Dime employees are in the classroom learning service skills about 5% of the time, in other words one day a month. "The right number is probably 10%," he says. This may sound expensive, but "it's more expensive not to do this," he says. "The alternative is that you don't service the customer properly the first time and have to keep trying to fix it. It may be five times more expensive to make mistakes and do it over, and have customers **defect,** than to train the person to do it right the first time."

◆ Overcoming the Workload

One **universal** obstacle to good service is that customer contact people are often overwhelmed with customers and tasks that need to be handled immediately. "Quality service is nothing more than common courtesy, but when you get busy that's the first thing you forget," says Cyndy Johnston, marketing and personnel officer at Friendly Bank of Oklahoma City.

What the bank tries to achieve through its training, which now consists mainly of a set of videotapes and workbooks from Stickler Learning, Clearwater, Fla., is **consistency.** Tellers, for example, know exactly what the bank considers good service: things like a prompt greeting, a smile, a pleasant comment, and use of the person's name. At the same time, Johnston says, "We don't want them to get too chatty, because that can make people just as angry as someone who's **curt.**"

◆ Below the Surface

There's more to being courteous than smiling or using certain words. What some training programs also try to do is help employees understand customers, and use that understanding to decide how to respond.

Employees in a classroom at First Union are mentally taken through all the steps a customer goes through in dealing with the bank, from the moment the customer pulls into the parking lot. At each point—say, waiting to see an **officer**—they discuss what the customer expects and what would be excellent service, explains Ellen Holiday.

"If you're sitting in the lobby and someone offers you a brochure you can look at while you're waiting, that might exceed your expectations," she says. First Union weaves customer service principles throughout the curriculum of its in-house training programs.

At Peoples Bank, Bridgeport, Connecticut, employees view a video **scenario** of an angry customer arguing with a teller. Then the employees discuss what might have occurred in the customer's day before the visit to the bank. "You can't control events in your customer's day or your customer's feelings, but you can control your own feelings and response," says Carole Callahan, manager of management development. Employees learn self-management techniques. "Instead of blaming themselves when faced with an angry customer, employees learn to remain calm, **empathize,** and ask themselves 'what can I do to improve the situation,'" Callahan says.

◆ Someone Is Watching

One thing that can make or break a customer service program is whether or not it is supervised and coached properly. "People do what's inspected, not what's expected," as Kent Stickler, chairman, Stickler Learning puts it. (The company sells a personal computer-based system that tracks mystery shopping programs, in which people are paid a small fee to have transactions or questions taken care of at the bank and report on the service they receive.)

Gainer Bank is in the process of writing its new service quality standards into employees' overall standards of performance. They'll be graded one to ten by their supervisor on service.

Recognition of good work is very simple at ARCS Mortgage, says Jeri Cohen: it's a bulletin board in the lunchroom. Every time the firm gets a letter from a customer that praises an employee, it posts the letter and a picture of the employee. Service is a high priority at ARCS. "Rates are rates, they might go up or down a point, but that's true for everyone," Cohen says. "What will make us stand out is outstanding service."

Comprehension Questions

1. **Many banks believe that the way to have happy customers is to** _____.

   a. raise interest rates
   b. be open more hours
   c. train employees to understand customers and treat them well
   d. teach tellers when to carry on a conversation and when to be quiet

2. **One obstacle to good service and common courtesy is** _____.

   a. being too busy   c. listening to the customer
   b. big banks   d. knowing you are being watched

3. **Every customer wants** _____.

   a. a chatty teller   c. to be known by a first name
   b. evening bank hours   d. prompt and courteous service

4. **One bank trains employees by showing them a videotape of a teller having to deal with** _____.

   a. long lines of people   c. a large deposit
   b. an angry customer   d. the drive-up window

5. Another title for this article might be _____.

    a. Videos for Bank Tellers
    b. Understand Customers to Keep Them Happy
    c. Being a Customer-Contact Person
    d. Checking on Customer Service

Vocabulary Test

On each line, write the number of the word that matches the definition.

1. **distinguish**   _____   **a.** marked by rude shortness

2. **officer**   _____   **b.** to make different; to set apart

3. **arthritis**   _____   **c.** one who holds a position of trust or authority

4. **universal**

5. **defect**   _____   **d.** a sequence of imagined events

6. **retention**   _____   **e.** a feeling of pain in joints of the body

7. **scenario**   _____   **f.** the ability to stay with the same ideas or actions

8. **curt**

9. **consistency**   _____   **g.** to leave a situation (or a company) to go over to a rival

10. **empathize**

  _____   **h.** to be aware of, or sensitive to, the feelings, thoughts, and experiences of others

  _____   **i.** the act of keeping a customer in possession

  _____   **j.** shared by everyone

Avionics Technician

Vocabulary Preview

able: marked by intelligence, knowledge, skill, or competence
advent: coming; arrival
aviation: airplane manufacture, development, or design
calibrated: adjusted; tuned
components: ingredients; parts
downturns: declines or worsening of conditions
foreseeable: knowing beforehand

◆ Definition

Avionics (a term formed by combining the words ***aviation*** and *electronics*) is the application of electronics to the operation of aircraft, spacecraft, and missiles. The field of avionics grew out of World War II applications of electronic equipment to the operation of military aircraft. As aircraft rapidly grew more complicated, the amount of electronic equipment needed for navigation and for monitoring equipment performance greatly increased. Large missiles and spacecraft require many more electronic **components** than even the largest and most sophisticated aircraft. Computerized guidance systems became especially important to the space program with the **advent** of manned flights.

◆ Nature of the Work

Avionics technicians assist avionics engineers in developing new electronic systems and components for aerospace use. They also adapt existing systems and components for application in new equipment. Most of their work, however, involves installing, testing, repairing, and maintaining navigation, communication, and control equipment in existing aircraft and spacecraft.

New equipment, once installed, must be tested and **calibrated** to prescribed specifications. Technicians also adjust the frequencies of radio sets and other communication equipment by signaling ground stations and then adjusting setscrews until the desired frequency has been achieved. Periodic maintenance checks and readjustments enable avionics technicians to keep equipment operating on proper frequencies. The technicians also complete and sign maintenance-and-overhaul documents recording the history of various equipment.

Avionics technicians involved in the design and testing of new equipment must take into account all the conditions under which the equipment will have to operate, determining its weight limitations, resistance to physical shock, atmospheric conditions it will have to withstand, and other factors. For some sophisticated design projects, technicians will have to design and make their tools first, and then use them to construct and test new avionic components.

The range of equipment in the avionics field is so broad that technicians usually specialize in one area, such as radio equipment, radar, computerized guidance, or flight-control systems. New specializations are constantly opening up as new developments occur in avionics. The development of the new specializations requires avionics technicians to keep informed about their special fields, through reading technical articles and books and through attending seminars and taking courses in new developments, often sponsored and offered by manufacturers.

Avionics technicians usually work as part of a team, especially if involved in research and testing and the development of new products. They are often required to keep detailed notes and records of their work and to write detailed reports.

◆ Advancement

Avionics technicians usually begin their careers in trainee positions, until they are thoroughly familiar with the requirements and routines of their work. Having completed their "apprenticeships," they are usually assigned to work independently, with only minimal supervision, testing and repairing avionic equipment. The most experienced and **able** technicians go on to install new equipment and to work in research and development operations. Many senior technicians may move into training, supervisory, and sales and customer relations positions.

◆ Employment Outlook

The aerospace industry as a whole is closely tied to government spending and to political change, as well as to **downturns** in the economy. The economy also affects the aircraft and airline industries strongly. The cancellation of one spacecraft program or a fall in airline travel that leads to employee cutbacks may throw a large number of avionics technicians out of work, making competition for the remaining jobs very strong.

On the positive side, avionics is a necessary and developing field for which there will be need through the **foreseeable** future, and for which more and more trained technicians will be needed.

Comprehension Questions

1. **Avionics technicians mainly _____.**

   a. supervise space flights
   b. check, repair, and install avionic equipment
   c. design new electronic systems for aerospace use
   d. specialize in computerized guidance systems

2. **The field of avionics began to develop after _____.**

   a. World War II   c. the Korean War
   b. 1975   d. the space shuttle program

3. **Most of the work avionics technicians do is with _____ aircraft and spacecraft.**

   a. experimental   c. existing
   b. military   d. outdated

4. **The number of jobs for avionics technicians depends on _____.**

   a. government spending and the economy   c. airline safety
   b. the season   d. specialization

5. **There would be no avionics technicians if there were no _____.**

   a. government   c. airlines
   b. apprenticeships   d. aircraft and spacecraft

Vocabulary Test

On each line, write the word that matches the definition.

able   **calibrated**   **downturns**
advent   **components**   **foreseeable**
aviation

1. _____   coming; arrival

2. _____   knowing beforehand

3. _____   declines or worsening of conditions

4. _____   ingredients; parts

5. _____   marked by intelligence, knowledge, skill, or competence

6. _____   adjusted; tuned

7. _____   airplane manufacture, development, or design

Allied Health

AIDS: How to Get It and How to Avoid It

By Betty Hamilton Pryce

Vocabulary Preview

bisexual: oriented toward both sexes

carrier: one who has in his or her system the cause of a disease to which he or she is immune or shows no signs of the disease

fact: a piece of true information

fiction: an invented story

fluid: a liquid

foolproof: so reliable as to leave no opportunity for mistake or failure

heterosexual: oriented toward the opposite sex

homosexual: oriented toward the same sex

immune: having or producing substances that protect against disease

syringe: an instrument that consists of a hollow tube fitted with a plunger and a hollow needle; it is used to inject fluids into or to remove fluids from the body

transfusion: the process of transferring a fluid into a vein or artery

transmitted: passed on from one person to another

vaccine: a preparation that produces or increases resistance or immunity to a disease

virus: the agent that causes an infectious disease; microscopic organisms that grow only in living cells

You don't want to get AIDS. But you know it is spreading throughout the country, and you are worried. Do you know what kinds of behavior will be most likely to expose you to AIDS? If you do, you can avoid that behavior. Do you know what kinds of behavior will *not* give you AIDS? It's important to know **facts** from **fiction.**

AIDS is spread mainly through sex and through drug needles and **syringes.** Right now, AIDS is a fatal disease. It kills everyone who gets it. Unfortunately, so far there is no **vaccine** to prevent AIDS. There is no cure when someone does get AIDS.

The word AIDS is short for Acquired Immuno-Deficiency Syndrome. It means that the body's **immune** system is not working. It has been affected by a **virus** called HIV. This virus makes the body's immune system too weak to fight diseases and infections. So the person dies from things the body would usually be able to fight.

The virus that causes AIDS is the Human Immunodeficiency Virus (HIV). It can hide in the body for years. Often people don't know they are carrying this AIDS virus for a long time after they get it. But an HIV carrier can infect others even when the **carrier** doesn't have any signs of AIDS.

◆   How Do We Get AIDS?

HIV (the AIDS virus) is spread by direct contact with blood and other body **fluids.** The two main ways are (1) by contact with infected blood and (2) by contact with various body fluids during sex.

Infected Blood

A major way of getting the AIDS virus is by sharing needles or syringes. A tiny bit of blood left on a needle or syringe infects the next person to use it.

There are other ways of getting AIDS from infected blood. One is through blood **transfusions.** Blood centers now have better tests for finding the virus in donated blood, so most donated blood is safe. However, the tests are not perfect.

Babies born to infected mothers are at risk for AIDS. Babies can get the AIDS virus from their mothers before birth, during birth, or even from breast milk. According to Joan Beck, a writer for the *Chicago Tribune,* in New York City, 1 baby out of every 61 has AIDS.

Sex

Another way to get AIDS is by having sex with a partner who is carrying the virus. This could be a friend who takes drugs, a prostitute—*anyone* who has had sex with, or shared a needle with, an infected person before having sex with you.

This sex partner may not even know that he or she is carrying the virus. Even worse, he or she may know but not tell you. The HIV is carried by men and women. They may be **heterosexual, homosexual,** or **bisexual.**

Obviously, the best ways to avoid AIDS are (1) by not sharing needles or syringes with another person and (2) not having sex with anyone who could be a carrier. Using a latex condom may help protect against AIDS, but this method is not **foolproof.**

◆   What Things Do Not Spread AIDS?

Ordinary, everyday contact will not give you AIDS. For example, you won't get AIDS just by being near someone who has it. You won't get

AIDS from hugging or kissing. The U.S. Public Health Service also tells us you won't get AIDS from flies, mosquitoes, bedbugs, or lice. You won't get it from saliva, sweat, tears, urine, or a bowel movement, either. You won't get AIDS from clothes or a telephone or a toilet seat. You won't get it by donating blood to a blood center. You won't get it from dishes or glasses, or from using the same desk or word processor, or from sharing an elevator. In other words, you don't have to worry about ordinary living or working with someone who carries HIV.

◆ What Things Should Worry You

You *do* have to worry about blood from an infected person. This means no sharing of needles or syringes. For people in health-care jobs, it means using common sense and following safety rules.

You *do* have to worry about getting AIDS from a sex partner. It is easy to get AIDS in this way because the virus is **transmitted** in body fluids during sex.

The AIDS virus (HIV) can enter the body through a very tiny break in body tissue, such as a scratch, a rash, a sore, etc. That's why risky behavior includes (1) contact with infected blood and (2) the exchange of body fluids during sex with an infected person.

If you want to avoid AIDS, you must avoid such dangerous behavior. What you do will expose you to AIDS—or it will protect you from AIDS. It's up to you.

Comprehension Questions

1. **One major warning we get from this article is that _____.**

    a. people can carry the AIDS virus without knowing it or without showing signs of it
    b. we should always ask a sex partner whether he or she has AIDS
    c. we should make sure a sex partner has an annual AIDS test
    d. all glasses and dishes used by a family member with AIDS should be sterilized

2. **The term HIV stands for _____.**

    a. the disease called AIDS for short
    b. an immunization vaccine now being tested
    c. the virus that causes AIDS
    d. a person infected with AIDS

3. Of the following, who is at high risk for getting AIDS?

   a. a parent taking care of a child with AIDS
   b. a person working with someone who is carrying the AIDS virus
   c. anyone donating blood
   d. a person having sex with someone who is carrying the AIDS virus

4. Users of needle drugs are a high-risk group because _____.

   a. they don't know what they're doing
   b. they may share infected needles and syringes
   c. drugs are sometimes contaminated with the AIDS virus
   d. they often have sex with prostitutes

5. The main point of this article is that _____.

   a. doctors and other health-care workers are often exposed to AIDS
   b. we don't get AIDS from sharing an elevator with people who have it
   c. the risk of AIDS is directly related to behavior
   d. homosexuals and drug addicts may carry the AIDS virus

Vocabulary Test

On each line, write the number of the word that matches the definition.

1. **immune**	_____	**a.**	passed on from one person to another
2. **carrier**	_____	**b.**	a liquid
3. **vaccine**	_____	**c.**	agent that causes an infectious disease
4. **bisexual**	_____	**d.**	having substances that protect against disease
5. **transmitted**			
6. **fluid**	_____	**e.**	a piece of true information
7. **virus**	_____	**f.**	oriented toward both sexes
8. **fact**	_____	**g.**	oriented toward the opposite sex
9. **foolproof**	_____	**h.**	so reliable as to leave no room for mistake or failure
10. **heterosexual**			
11. **homosexual**	_____	**i.**	preparation that produces resistance or immunity to a disease
12. **transfusion**			
	_____	**j.**	person who has the cause of a disease but shows no sign of the disease

Family Time-Fun Time in New Brunswick

By Debbie Gibson

Vocabulary Preview

Acadian: referring to Acadia, an area of eastern Canada consisting of Nova Scotia and New Brunswick

bed-and-breakfast: a place that offers home-style overnight stays and includes a large breakfast

covered bridge: a bridge that has its roadway protected by a roof and sides

endangered species: a kind of animal (or plant) threatened with extinction

Loyalist: a person who is loyal to a party, cause, government, or ruler (in this case, those loyal to England)

magnetic: possessing a power to attract metal

province: a district or division of a country

sea cucumber: an ocean animal with a long, tube-shaped body that looks like a cucumber (or pickle)

seaweed: a plant growing in the sea

trestle bridge: a bridge supported by a framework of posts connected by cross-beams

unique: unequaled; being the only one

You'll have lots of fun and learn all kinds of new things while traveling in New Brunswick, Canada. Did you know there are huge rocks shaped like flowerpots at Hopewell Cape? Instead of flowers, they have trees growing out of their tops. And there's a **covered bridge** in Hartland that's longer than *any* other covered bridge in the world. It's 391 metres (1,282 feet) long! Of course, you know that as you pass through any covered bridge, you must make a wish and hold your breath. If you manage to do that, your wish comes true. Good luck in Hartland!

Did you also know there is a hill in Moncton that makes you feel as if you're going uphill when you're really going downhill? Even the water in the brook at **Magnetic** Hill appears to run uphill. When you sit in your car at the bottom of the hill and you put the car in neutral, you will coast backwards up the hill. Be sure to try it.

Do you enjoy spending time at the shore? Just about everyone likes splashing and jumping in the waves. New Brunswick has some really great beaches, many with warm water and wonderful sand. You'll have fun playing in the salt water too, because the salt makes it so much easier to float.

Wildlife parks and zoos are terrific family activities. In New Brunswick there are several. Woolastook Recreation Park near Fredericton features animals from the Atlantic Provinces. Cherry Brook Zoo in Saint John is home to creatures from all over the world—African monkeys, lions, tigers, and camels—many of which are on the **endangered species** list. The Paradis des Animaux is located in Lameque.

If you have always wanted to ride on an old-fashioned steam train, New Brunswick has just the thing for you. The Salem Hillsborough Railroad gives you a **unique** tour of the area. On the one-hour trip, you will see all kinds of countryside and even go over a high **trestle bridge** just like in old-time movies.

Another train to try out is the Dungarvon Whooper at the Central New Brunswick Woodsmen's Museum in Boiestown. Besides the train, there are displays that tell you all about the history of those who made their living in the woods. You'll see old tools on display and also the type of buildings the men slept and ate in. This is a great place for a family to see what it was really like to be a woodsman in New Brunswick in bygone days.

Blue lobster, colored fish, and plant life from underwater can all be seen at the Shippagan Marine Centre. Watch the show the seals put on and learn all kinds of things about the Gulf of St. Lawrence, too. And if you have ever wondered what the inside of a lighthouse looks like, you can find out at the Marine Centre.

The Huntsman Marine Laboratory in St. Andrews is another place to find out about the underwater life of New Brunswick. Here you will see samples of sea life from the Bay of Fundy. There is a special "Please Touch Tank" that allows you to feel starfish, **sea cucumbers,** and **seaweed** with your own hands. There are seals and blue lobster here as well.

New Brunswick's two historical villages are great places to learn about the past. The **Acadian** Historical Village in Caraquet illustrates the early life of the Acadians in this **province,** while Kings Landing Historical Settlement shows life as it was for the **Loyalists.**

The Visiting Cousins program at Kings Landing and Les Enfants du Village at the Acadian Village allow you to live for five days, as you would have if you had lived over 100 years ago. Dressed in old-fashioned clothes, you will attend school and have chores to do like making butter or candles, going to the general store for supplies, helping with the housework, or working in the fields. You will even eat the same kind of meals as the Acadians and Loyalists used to eat. During the day you will "live" in a home with a family.

In New Brunswick, horseback riding is popular and there are trail rides in several places in the province. Cycling is another favorite activity. If you have not brought bicycles with you, there are people who rent them. Just check for details at a tourist information centre. Hiking, canoeing, sailing, and fishing are all things you can do in New Brunswick.

At Petit-Rocher, the New Brunswick Mining Interpretation Centre is an amazing place. They have displays of the many rocks and minerals in New Brunswick. Test your knowledge by trying out one of the featured games. There is even a pretend mine shaft so you can feel what it's like to be a miner.

In Les Jardins de la Republique Provincial Park, near St. Jacques, an antique automobile museum is fun for all. Old cars and other mechanical items are on display. The Match the Lights to the Car game is especially for children.

There's no doubt about it; it would be difficult not to have fun in New Brunswick. There's just so much of it around! Friendly people, clean fresh air, wide open spaces, and lots to do. Whether you are camping or staying in motels, at farm vacation homes, **bed-and-breakfast** places or country inns, you're sure to have a good time.

Comprehension Questions

1. **This article is mainly about** _____.

    a. covered bridges in Canada
    b. things to do for fun in New Brunswick
    c. how to get to New Brunswick
    d. camping in New Brunswick

2. **Magnetic Hill is in** _____.

    a. Fredericton   **c.** Hartland
    b. Caraquet   **d.** Moncton

3. **The Huntsman Marine Laboratory shows samples of sea life from the** _____.

    a. Bay of Fundy   **c.** Atlantic Provinces
    b. Gulf of St. Lawrence   **d.** Shippagon Marine Centre

4. **At Hopewell Cape, there are** _____.

    a. endangered species   **c.** Acadians and Loyalists
    b. many parks and zoos   **d.** huge rocks shaped like flowerpots

5. **Another title for this article could be** _____.

    a. New Brunswick, a Great Vacation Place
    b. Sealife in New Brunswick
    c. New Brunswick Parks
    d. 100 Years Ago in New Brunswick

Vocabulary Test

On each line, write the number of the word that matches the definition.

1. **magnetic**
2. **covered bridge**
3. **bed-and-breakfast**
4. **province**
5. **unique**
6. **seaweed**
7. **sea cucumber**
8. **Acadian**
9. **trestle bridge**
10. **endangered species**

_____   **a.**   a plant or animal threatened with extinction

_____   **b.**   possessing a power to attract metal

_____   **c.**   place that offers home-style overnight stays and includes a large breakfast

_____   **d.**   district or division of a country

_____   **e.**   a bridge that has its roadway protected by a roof and sides

_____   **f.**   referring to Acadia, an area of eastern Canada consisting of Nova Scotia and New Brunswick

_____   **g.**   a plant growing in the sea

_____   **h.**   unequaled; being the only one

_____   **i.**   a bridge supported by a framework of posts connected by crossbeams

_____   **j.**   an ocean animal with a long tube-shaped body that looks like a cucumber

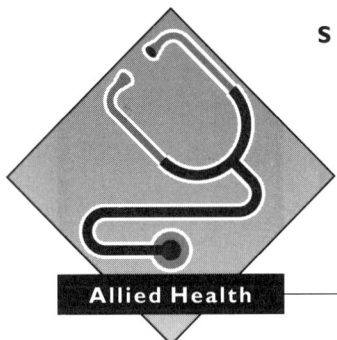

Medical-Laboratory Technician

By Craig R. Ilk

Vocabulary Preview

accredited: officially approved of

analysis: separation and identification of the ingredients or parts of a substance

bacteriology: the study of certain types of microscopic plants called bacteria and their relations to medicine and agriculture

corpuscle: a living cell that is capable of free movement in a fluid and not fixed in any one tissue

dexterity: skill in physical activity

latter: recent; closer to the end

manual: involving the hands

microorganisms: living things that can only be seen under a microscope

standardize: to bring to the same level as an accepted model

tissue: a group of similar cells taken from a particular body location or organ

The history of medical-laboratory technology shares many of its important historical milestones with the history of medicine itself. Both medicine in general and medical-laboratory technology go back to the time of the Greeks. Some significant achievements shared by both medicine and medical-laboratory technology include Jan Swammerdam's discovery of red blood **corpuscles** in 1658; Antonie van Leeuwenhoek's many observations of **microorganisms** through the microscope during the **latter** part of the seventeenth century; and the discoveries of Robert Koch and Louis Pasteur in **bacteriology** in the 1870s. Through these efforts and others like them, medical professionals became aware by the end of the nineteenth century of much valuable information and many possibilities for therapy available in the medical specialties of bacteriology (the study of microorganisms in the human body), cytology (the study of human cells), histology (the study of human tissue), and hematology (the study of human blood). The growth of these medical specialties created a steadily increasing need for laboratory personnel.

In the early part of this century, some doctors taught their assistants how to perform some of the laboratory procedures often used in their practice. Because the quality of work done by these technicians varied considerably, many doctors and medical educators became concerned with the problem of being sure that assistants did the highest-quality work possible. In 1936, one of the first attempts was made to **standardize** the training programs that were then available for the preparation of skilled assistants, in that case, the training of medical technologists. Since then, standards of training for medical laboratory technicians have been set. There are more than one hundred **accredited** educational programs offered in community, junior, and technical colleges for the training of medical laboratory technicians.

Medical-laboratory technicians perform routine tests in medical laboratories to help doctors, surgeons, and other professional medical personnel in the diagnosis and treatment of disease. They prepare samples of patients' **tissues;** execute laboratory tests, such as urinalysis and blood counts; and make **analyses** of samples of cells, tissues, blood, or other body specimens. They usually work under the supervision of a medical technologist or a laboratory director. Medical-laboratory technicians may work in many fields, or they may specialize in one area of medical-laboratory work, such as cytology, hematology, or histology. These technicians must have good **manual dexterity,** normal color vision, the ability to follow orders, and a tolerance for working under pressure.

Comprehension Questions

1. **The overall job of a medical-laboratory technician is to** _____.

   a. keep track of a patient's blood tests
   b. perform tests that aid in the diagnosis and treatment of disease
   c. work with doctors
   d. check specimens carefully

2. **Cytology is the study of** _____.

   a. human cells   **c.** microorganisms
   b. human blood   **d.** bacteria

3. **Red blood corpuscles were discovered by** _____.

   a. Louis Pasteur   **c.** van Leeuwenhoek
   b. Robert Koch   **d.** Swammerdam

4. **Medical-laboratory technicians do *not*** _____.

   a. prepare samples of patients' tissues   **c.** take X rays
   b. analyze blood   **d.** check urine samples

5. **The earliest medical-laboratory technicians were** _____.

   a. doctors' assistants   **c.** Greek
   b. nurses   **d.** required to take tests

Vocabulary Test

On each line, write the word that matches the definition.

accredited	dexterity	microorganisms
analysis	latter	standardize
bacteriology	manual	tissue
corpuscle		

1. _____ recent; closer to the end

2. _____ a group of similar cells taken from a particular body location or organ

3. _____ skill in physical activity

4. _____ to bring to the same level as an accepted model

5. _____ the study of certain types of microscopic plants called bacteria and their relations to medicine and agriculture

6. _____ separation and identification of the ingredients or parts of a substance

7. _____ involving the hands

8. _____ living things that can only be seen under a microscope

9. _____ a living cell that is capable of free movement in a fluid and not fixed in any one tissue

10. _____ officially approved of

The Language of Industry

Trade and Technical

Vocabulary Preview

cultural: having to do with customs, beliefs, and arts of a group of people

draftsman: a person who draws plans or designs for buildings, machines, and so on

hieroglyphics: written Egyptian language that was made up of pictures rather than letters

impressed: made by pressure

instruments: measuring and writing tools and devices

practices: usual ways of doing things

standards: things established by authorities as models or examples

Since earliest times, people have used drawings to communicate ideas to others and to record these ideas so that they would not be forgotten. The earliest forms of writing, such as Egyptian **hieroglyphics,** were picture forms.

The word *graphic* means "the expression of ideas by lines or marks **impressed** on a surface." A drawing is a graphic representation of a real thing. Drafting, therefore, is a graphic language because it uses pictures to communicate thoughts and ideas. Because these pictures can be understood by residents of different nations, drafting is referred to as a "universal language."

People have developed drawing along two distinct lines, using each form for a different purpose. Artistic drawing is mainly concerned with the expression of real or imagined ideas of a **cultural** nature. On the other hand, technical drawing is concerned with the expression of technical ideas or ideas of a practical nature, and is used in all branches of technical industry.

Even highly developed word languages are inadequate for describing the size, shape, and relationships of physical objects. For every manufactured object there are drawings that describe its physical shape completely and accurately, communicating the **draftsman**'s ideas to the worker. For this reason, drafting is referred to as the "language of industry."

Throughout the long history of drafting, many symbols, terms, abbreviations, and **practices** have come into common use. Different draftsmen must use the same practices if drafting is to serve as a reliable means of communicating technical theories and ideas. Mechanical engineering representatives from government and industry have published and revised recommended drafting practices.

Since many thousands of drawings presently being used in industry follow the older drawing practices, a draftsman must become acquainted with these drawing **standards** as well as the newest ones. It is expected that any new drawings will closely follow the latest drawing standards. However, when a draftsman is called upon to make changes or revisions to a drawing already in existence, he or she must stick to the drawing standards that appear on the drawing being used.

Because a drawing is a set of instructions that a worker must follow, it must be clear, correct, accurate, and complete. The ability to draw does not in itself make a person a draftsman. A draftsman must have creative ability, a wide range of technical knowledge, and specialized knowledge in his or her own field. The various specialized fields are as different as the branches of industry. Some of the main areas of drafting are mechanical, architectural, structural, and electrical drafting. Technical drawing is the term applied to any drawings used to express technical ideas. When drawings are made with the use of **instruments,** they are referred to as instrumental drawings. If instruments are not used, drawings are referred to as sketches. The ability to sketch ideas and designs and to make accurate instrumental drawings is a fundamental part of this graphic language.

Only a small percentage of students taking a drafting course will make drafting a lifetime occupation. However, a thorough understanding of this precise language is necessary for anyone who intends to work in the highly technical manufacturing and construction industries, or plans to become a professional engineer. Many more people are required who can read drawings than who can make them.

In daily living, a knowledge of drafting is very helpful in understanding house plans; assembly, maintenance, and operating instructions for many manufactured products; and plans and specifications for many hobbies and other leisure activities.

Comprehension Questions

1. **One of the main ideas presented here is that the basic difference between artistic and technical drawing is that _____.**

   a. drafting uses pictures to communicate thoughts
   b. each form is developed for a different purpose
   c. technical drawing is a universal language
   d. artistic drawing uses symbolism, and technical drawing uses symbols

2. **Drafting practices** _____.

    a. have remained the same since the earliest days of technical drawing
    b. have usually been tied to the language spoken in a particular country
    c. are explained in German because of the influence of German engineers
    d. have been revised by experts in mechanical engineering

3. _____ **taking a drafting course will be draftsmen for the rest of their working lives.**

    a. Most of the people
    b. It is estimated that about half of the people
    c. A small percentage of the people
    d. We have no idea how many people

4. **When instruments are not used, the drawings are called** _____.

    a. sketches   **c.** technical drawings
    b. preliminary plans   **d.** graphics

5. **This selection gives us the firm idea that** _____.

    a. there will be a problem when draftsmen familiar with earlier standards retire
    b. mistakes can easily be made when using technical drawings made by other draftsmen
    c. most people in the construction industry should know how to make technical drawings
    d. many people in manufacturing, engineering, and construction need to know how to read drawings even if they can't make them

Vocabulary Test

On each line, write the number of the word that matches the definition.

1. **practices**
2. **hieroglyphics**
3. **cultural**
4. **standards**
5. **instruments**
6. **impressed**
7. **draftsman**

_____ **a.** a person who draws plans for buildings, machines, and so on

_____ **b.** made by pressure

_____ **c.** usual ways of doing things

_____ **d.** having to do with a people's customs, beliefs, and arts

_____ **e.** written Egyptian picture language

_____ **f.** things established by authorities as models

_____ **g.** measuring and writing tools and devices

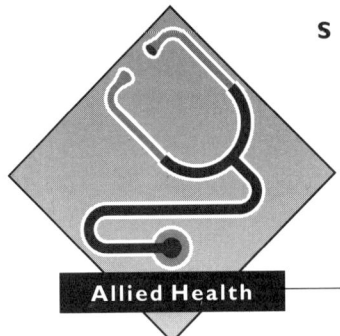

SELECTION 37

Cardiology Technologist

By Craig R. Ilk

Vocabulary Preview

cardiac: relating to the heart

catheterization: insertion of a tube into canals, vessels, passageways, or body cavities, usually to permit fluids to be put into or withdrawn from the body

noninvasive: not involving placing a needle or any other instruments into the patient's body

rounds: a series of daily visits to hospitals made by a doctor or a nurse

routine: part of an established procedure

stress test: a test to see how the heart reacts under the strain of exercise

A cardiology technologist is an individual trained to perform or assist with various tests of the human heart. These tests are primarily **noninvasive** in nature and require the technologist to make measurements of heart functions without placing a needle or other instrument into the patient's body. The most common example of this is the electrocardiogram (ECG), which measures the electrical activity of the heart. Some cardiology technologists assist physicians in laboratories where **cardiac catheterizations,** which require insertion of certain diagnostic instruments into the patient's body, are performed.

A variety of tasks are performed during a cardiology technologist's day. Some of these duties take place in the hospital cardiology laboratory, and others are done in patients' rooms. A technologist may begin the day by making hospital **rounds** and taking electrocardiograms (ECGs) on patients who were admitted the day before or who require repeat studies. By inspecting a properly recorded ECG, a physician may be able to determine whether the patient has a heart problem. Wires, or electrodes, are placed on specific parts of the body and connected to the electrocardiograph machine by the technologist. The machine is then operated and a permanent record, or tracing, of the electrical activity of the patient's heart is made.

With the **routine** ECGs completed, the technologist may return to the laboratory to help the physician take a stress test. The **stress test** again requires that electrodes be placed on the patient's body. The patient then exercises in some manner while the doctor carefully watches for any changes in the function of the heart. The technologist must stand by to assure that, from a technical point of view, a test of the highest possible quality is obtained. An echocardiogram might also be required. In this test, the technologist operates a machine that uses sound waves to help the physician check some other functions of the heart. Again, the technologist's main objective is to perform this test correctly and to obtain a high-quality result for the maximum benefit to the patient.

Before the end of the day, the technologist may be required to respond to an emergency call for an ECG to be done on a patient who is complaining of chest pain or on a patient who may be having a severe heart attack. These situations, as well as the other nonemergency situations described, require the technologist to perform certain tests in a very responsible and proper manner.

The common factor is that all tests performed require that the technologist work directly with the patient. The ability to work with and care for people is an absolute necessity.

Comprehension Questions

1. **A cardiology technologist performs or assists with tests of the** _____.

   a. lungs   **c.** human heart
   b. blood vessels **d.** brain

2. **A test that a cardiology technologist performs often is the** _____.

   a. electroencephalogram   **c.** cholesterol screening
   b. electrocardiogram   **d.** mammogram

3. **A noninvasive test is a test that does not require** _____.

   a. any instruments to be placed in the patient's body
   b. any blood work
   c. X rays
   d. that the patient go without food

4. **An electrocardiogram may tell a doctor if a patient** _____.

   a. is overweight   **c.** has a heart problem
   b. has cancer   **d.** can handle stress

5. **A cardiology technologist must be able to work with and care for people because the technologist** _____.

   a. is doing what the doctor wants
   b. needs to make the patient comfortable
   c. wants to keep the job
   d. works directly with the patients

Vocabulary Test

Draw a line from each word to its correct definition.

1. **routine**
2. **cardiac**
3. **catheterization**
4. **rounds**
5. **stress test**
6. **noninvasive**

a. a series of daily visits to hospital patients made by a doctor or a nurse

b. a test to see how the heart reacts under the strain of exercise

c. part of an established procedure

d. relating to the heart

e. not involving placing a needle or any other instrument into the patient's body

f. insertion of a tube into canals, vessels, passageways, or body cavities, usually to permit fluids to be put into or withdrawn from the body

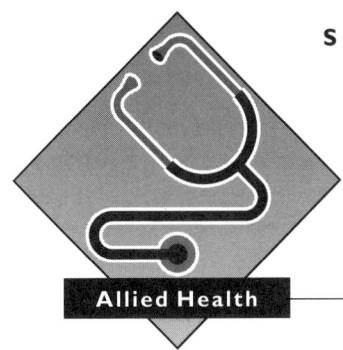

SELECTION 38

Rx for Good Health: Get a Pet

By Gordon E. Rowley

Vocabulary Preview

antisocial: disliking the company of other people

companionship: the state of having someone to accompany another; doing things together

confide: tell confidentially; share secrets

contentedly: satisfied with a situation

criminally inclined: likely to do something illegal

depression: a disorder characterized by extreme sadness, inactivity, and difficulty in thinking, concentrating, and sleeping

population: the total number of people in an area or in a sample under consideration

relieve: to lessen or bring about the removal of

spouse: husband or wife

therapy: a treatment aimed at making something better

well-being: the state of being healthy

Want to feel better, reduce the stress of modern living, avoid a heart attack, and live longer? Get a pet, say a growing number of physicians, psychologists, psychiatrists, and veterinarians.

Twenty years ago, the suggestion that a person could be healthier and lengthen his or her life by getting a dog or cat would have been laughed at by most members of the medical community. But research begun in the early 1970s has proven that pets promote both physical and mental **well-being.**

One of the earliest studies in so-called pet **therapy** was conducted by a British researcher who wished to measure the effects on lonely elderly women of having an animal companion. Each member of one group was given a parakeet, while each in a second group was given a flowering plant. Those with a bird developed a better outlook on life than those with a plant.

On this side of the Atlantic, autistic children (children who are unable to communicate) were invited by the World Dolphin Foundation in Miami to play with dolphins. Soon they began to speak more often and even come out of their private world long enough to feed the animals.

Other programs have also had successful results. These programs have included patients with Alzheimer's disease, the mentally disturbed, the extremely **antisocial,** even the **criminally inclined.**

More important for the general **population,** however, are studies that have tried to find a link between pets and heart disease. In 1977, Dr. Erika Friedman began studying the influence of several social factors on heart disease survival rates.

As Friedman had expected, human contact was one of the most important factors, but having a pet also was important. The death rate among people with pets was one third that of patients without pets.

This result was so surprising that the data were rechecked. Perhaps, thought the researcher, having a dog forced the patient to walk and, thereby, increased the recovery rate for dog owners only. But no, the results were the same for owners of cats, birds, rabbits, even tropical fish.

Doctors had determined the health benefits of having a pet. Now psychiatrists and psychologists began to identify the reasons why. Having a pet helps to **relieve** stress. It can also prevent cases of extreme depression in which people feel that their lives cannot be improved and are not worth living. In short, pets give many people a reason to live.

The fact that a pet needs us "pulls us into life," write Drs. Alan Beck and Aaron Katcher in their book *Between Pets and People.* When we don't want to get up in the morning, we do so because the dog wants to go out or the cat is crying to be fed. Those little acts of caring—feeding, watering, taking the dog for a walk, playing games—make us feel needed. They protect us against **depression.**

Pets also provide **companionship,** another living creature to go for a walk with or to greet you at the door after a hard day at school, at the office, or in the factory. Even worrying about our pets can be a positive experience, say psychologists, because worry is the result of caring.

The companionship of a pet is different from that of a **spouse,** close friend, or a child. A pet is blind to our faults. Pets don't care about our income or status, our looks, whether we have changed our clothes or taken a shower lately. They are not impressed by youthful appearances, money, mink coats, expensive automobiles, or university degrees.

When they greet us at the door, they don't tell us what a bad day they had. They welcome us happily, wagging their tails or purring **contentedly.** And in doing so, they make us forget our bad day.

We talk to our pets (nearly 99 percent of the pet owners surveyed at the University of Pennsylvania veterinary clinic said they talk to their pets). We **confide** in them, telling them secrets we wouldn't tell to another living human.

It is not surprising that we treat them as well as, sometimes better than, our fellow human beings. In return we get companionship. We get loyalty.

We get pleasure when we stroke their fur or feathers. We get a reason for exercise and an excuse for play. We get a reason to laugh and the feeling of being needed. And we get better health.

Comprehension Questions

1. **The basic idea of this article is that _____.**

    a. doctors recommend pets for certain problems
    b. pets do not find fault or judge us by our possessions
    c. pets give many people a reason to live
    d. pets can help improve mental and physical health

2. **One study shows that the death rate among heart disease patients _____.**

    a. decreased when people were given plants to take care of
    b. was lower when people had pets to be exercised
    c. was related to human contact, not pets
    d. was much lower for people who had pets

3. **Psychologists say taking care of a pet can _____.**

    a. cure people of Alzheimer's disease
    b. help to relieve stress
    c. allow criminals an early parole
    d. be better than having a husband or wife

4. **In cases of severe depression, people feel _____.**

    a. no one likes them   c. their lives are not worth living
    b. they are mentally disturbed   d. they have a fatal disease

5. **Which title best fits this article?**

    a. Pets: Another Kind of Medicine
    b. Talking to Your Pet
    c. Pets and Disease
    d. The Advantages of Having a Pet in the Home

Vocabulary Test

On each line, write the number of the word that matches the definition.

1. **therapy**
2. **depression**
3. **spouse**
4. **antisocial**
5. **well-being**
6. **companionship**
7. **contentedly**
8. **relieve**
9. **confide**
10. **population**

_____ **a.** disliking the company of other people

_____ **b.** doing things together

_____ **c.** tell confidentially; share secrets

_____ **d.** satisfied with a situation

_____ **e.** a disorder characterized by extreme sadness and inactivity

_____ **f.** the total number of people in an area

_____ **g.** to lessen or bring about the removal of

_____ **h.** husband or wife

_____ **i.** treatment aimed at making something better

_____ **j.** the state of being healthy

Troubleshooting Automatic Transmissions

By Paul Weissler

Vocabulary Preview

chassis: the frame on which the body of a car is mounted

flushing: washing out with a sudden flow of water

franchised: licensed to sell a certain product under a certain corporation's name

gasket: any seal used between machine parts to prevent the escape of a gas or fluid

powertrain: the mechanism by which power is transmitted from the engine to the axle that it drives

torque: a twisting force (like the force used to twist a lid off a jar)

trade: an organization limited to businesses in a certain industry

Keeping cool may be the last thing on your mind during the winter months. But when it comes to your car's automatic transmission, excess heat is as likely on a snowy winter day as it is during a long summer-vacation drive. It's why winter and summer are the busiest times of the year for transmission-repair shops.

"Engines run hotter during the summer and in warmer parts of the country," says Bob Chernnay, technical director of the Automatic Transmission Service Group, a Florida-based information and training center. "Add a trailer, a carload of passengers and vacation gear, and an automatic's lubricating oil can get hot enough to damage critical seals, clutches and bands."

The story is often the same in winter, when many drivers overheat transmission fluid while trying to "rock" a car out of snow or ice. Repair bills, says Chernnay, typically range from $350 to overhaul a rear-drive three-speed unit to upwards of $2,000 for some four-speed front-drive transaxles.

To help you avoid major repairs—and get your money's worth when they're needed—we'll cover the basics of how your car's automatic transmission works and how to keep it healthy. We'll also detail the usual trouble signs and how to choose the right transmission repair shop.

◆ Preventing Problems

The most common trouble signs are oil leak, low oil pressure, no drive or reverse gear, hard shifting, slippage, missed shifts, early or late shifting, excess noise, poor fuel economy, poor low-speed acceleration, engine stalls, and surging. Many of those symptoms stem from minor problems such as improper oil level, improper cable adjustment and—on computer-controlled automatics—a bad electrical connection. What's more, most internal transmission damage is caused by overheated transmission oil or improper oil level.

These simple maintenance steps can help keep your transmission's vital parts intact:

- Have the transmission oil and filter changed at least every two years—annually if you pull a trailer or routinely carry heavy loads.

- If you change the oil and filter yourself, prevent leaks by installing a new pan **gasket** and tightening pan bolts to factory settings with a **torque** wrench.

- Periodically lube external shift-linkage joints with silicone lubricant or **chassis** grease.

- Check for transmission-fluid leaks at the vacuum modulator, speedometer-drive gear, oil dipstick tube, and other external components. Take the car to a shop if you find any leaks.

- Stay within the maximum towing and carrying capacities listed in your car's owner's manual.

- If you can't "rock" out of mud or snow after a few tries, call a tow truck. Otherwise, you'll overheat the transmission oil and damage seals, causing leaks as well as premature band and clutch wear.

◆ Dealing with the Pros

You have four basic choices when your car's automatic transmission needs professional help: (1) the independent garage that performs your other car service, (2) an independent garage that specializes in transmission work, (3) a **franchised** transmission shop, and (4) a car dealer.

Each of these facilities typically has strengths and weaknesses that often depend on the problem at hand. We'll cover the pros and cons of each to help you choose the right one for your needs.

The Independent Garage

This is the obvious choice for routine maintenance, such as oil and filter changes. Independent garages are also a good bet for small repairs such as fixing a leak. They also tend to have the general experience needed for diagnosing transmission problems related to the engine and **powertrain** computer.

If you don't have a favorite garage, ask a friend or neighbor for a recommendation. Be sure the shop has experience with a specific repair, rather than a complete overhaul or reseal, since a repair is usually all that's needed.

The Independent Transmission Shop

This is the next step if your usual shop doesn't repair transmissions or if the repair is extensive.

Before agreeing to a repair, find out if the shop is a member of a **trade** organization such as the Automatic Transmission Rebuilders Association (ATRA) or the transmission section of the Automotive Service Association (ASA). Such organizations provide the shop with technical training as well as a hotline service for difficult problems. ATRA also has a national warranty program.

The Franchised Transmission Shop

These have received a lot of bad press over the years. Such shops must help pay for their national organizations' costly ad budgets, which means there's a good chance they're eager to sell you the expensive "security" of guaranteed overhauls.

On the positive side, many of these franchises have qualified, experienced technicians. They also offer a choice of convenient locations and a national warranty. Generally, franchised transmission shops charge only slightly more than independent shops.

The Car Dealer

This is often regarded as the most expensive option and, for minor repairs, it is. But if your local garage is recommending an overhaul, the dealer may be worth considering. More and more dealers now install transmissions from factory-authorized rebuilders with ready access to improved parts. The result is a transmission that's often more durable than one rebuilt by the competition. Costs are about the same.

Whichever option you choose, keep the following warnings and suggestions in mind:

- Get a firm diagnosis and a written estimate before work begins. If a shop insists on disassembling the transmission before giving you a price, go somewhere else.

- Avoid a complete external seal replacement unless it's part of a necessary overhaul. One leaking seal doesn't necessarily mean the others need replacement.

- If a transmission overhaul is needed, be sure there's a warranty, and find out if there's a deductible or a service charge involved.
- Find out if an overhaul includes a rebuilt torque converter. If it doesn't, check whether the existing converter and its clutch are covered under the warranty.
- Be sure the overhaul includes **flushing** the transmission cooler and cooler lines.
- Finally, see if the technician who will work on your car is certified by the National Institute for Automotive Excellence (ASE). While ASE certification doesn't guarantee a good repair, it does imply professional competence.

Comprehension Questions

1. **One of the main points of this article is that _____.**

   a. transmission repairs are expensive
   b. proper care can help avoid transmission problems
   c. only one kind of transmission shop is any good
   d. transmission problems only happen in the summer

2. **Most internal transmission damage is caused by _____.**

   a. overheating   c. age
   b. a bad filter   d. worn seals

3. **If your transmission needs only a small repair, you should probably go to _____.**

   a. an independent garage
   b. an independent transmission shop
   c. a franchised transmission shop
   d. a car dealer

4. **You should have the transmission oil and filter changed at least _____.**

   a. every six months   c. every two years
   b. every year   d. every 50,000 miles

5. **Keeping a transmission working well is a matter of _____.**

   a. having it overhauled   c. checking the warranty
   b. choosing the right garage   d. simple maintenance steps

Vocabulary Test

On each line, write the word that matches the definition.

chassis   **gasket**   **trade organization**
flushing   **powertrain**   **vital**
franchised   **torque**   **warranty**

1. _____ very important, essential

2. _____ the mechanism by which power is transmitted from the engine to the axle that it drives

3. _____ a written guarantee

4. _____ licensed to sell a certain product under a certain corporation's name

5. _____ an organization limited to businesses in a certain industry

6. _____ the frame on which the body of a car is mounted

7. _____ washing out with a sudden flow of water

8. _____ any seal used between machine parts to prevent the escape of a gas or fluid

9. _____ a twisting force

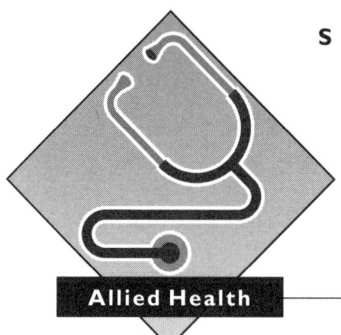

SELECTION 40

Medical Record Technician

Vocabulary Preview

ambulatory-care facilities: places that serve patients who are able to walk

census: information about characteristics of someone (height, weight, age, sex, etc.)

extended-care: providing nursing care for people recovering from illness

practitioner: a person engaged in the practice of a profession or occupation

precise: exactly or sharply defined or stated

sophisticated: complex or intricate

third-party reimbursement: the paying back of expenses by an agent such as Blue Cross-Blue Shield or medicare to a patient or doctor (the first and second parties)

tolerance: capacity to put up with something

Medical **practitioners** have been writing down information about their patients' illnesses and treatments for hundreds of years. Before the twentieth century, such records were kept mostly to help the practitioners learn as much as possible from their own experience. By the early 1900s, medical record keeping was changing, along with many other aspects of medicine. Medicine was more **sophisticated,** more scientific, and more successful in helping patients. Hospitals were increasingly accepted as the conventional place for middle-class patients to go for care. As a consequence, hospitals became more numerous and better organized, and medical record keeping became more important and time-consuming.

The personnel responsible for this work, who used to be called medical record librarians, eventually became differentiated into two basic professional categories—medical record administrator and medical record technician.

Medical record technicians help perform the technical tasks associated with compiling, maintaining, and using these records. Each patient's individual medical record describes in detail his or her condition over time, including any illness and injuries, operations, treatments, outpatient visits, and the progress of hospital stays. Medical record technicians review records for completeness and accuracy; assign codes to the diseases, operations, diagnoses, and treatments according to detailed coding systems; and post the codes on the medical record, so the information on the record is easier to retrieve and analyze. They copy medical reports; maintain indices of patients, diseases, operations, and other categories of information; compile patient **census** data; and file records or supervise other personnel who do so. In addition, they may direct the day-to-day operations of the medical records department. They maintain the flow of records and reports to and from other departments, and sometimes assist medical staff in special studies or research that draws on information in the records.

In recent years a trend toward computerization of records, the growing importance of privacy and freedom of information issues, and the changing requirements of **third-party reimbursement** organizations have all had major impacts on the field of medical records technology. These areas can be expected to continue to reshape the field in future years.

Most opportunities for employment will be found in hospitals; however, opportunities will also be found in **extended-care** facilities, **ambulatory-care facilities,** health maintenance organizations (HMOs), medical group practices, nursing homes, and home-health agencies. Technicians are also finding opportunities with computer firms, consulting firms, and government agencies. The importance of complete and well-organized medical records for financial management of health-care institutions is especially likely to lead to increased demand for medical record technicians in almost all types of facilities.

People who work in the medical records field must have an inclination to be very **precise** and a high **tolerance** for detail work. They must also feel comfortable about dealing with a variety of people, including medical staff members, hospital administrators, other health-care professionals, attorneys, and insurance agents.

In many settings, the medical record technician is under pressure caused by a heavy work load. As health-care institutions come under increasing demands for cost containment and productivity, medical record technicians will be required to produce, in short periods of time, a significant volume of high quality.

Nonetheless, the knowledge that their work is significant for patients and for medical research can be personally very satisfying for medical record technicians.

Comprehension Questions

1. **Another name for a medical record technician might be**
    _____.

    a. medical computer operator
    b. medical secretary
    c. patient file-keeper, finder, and organizer
    d. medical file clerk

2. **As used in this article, the meaning of the word** *record* **is most close-ly like that of** _____.

    a. historical document
    b. diary
    c. list
    d. public information

3. **Two hundred years ago, medical records were kept by**

    _____.

    a. hospitals
    b. doctors
    c. patients
    d. no one

4. **The job of medical record technician grew out of the job of**

    _____.

    a. medical secretary
    b. physician's assistant
    c. nurse
    d. medical librarian

5. **The machine that has affected medical record technology the most is the** _____.

    a. typewriter
    b. word processor
    c. computer
    d. tape recorder

Vocabulary Test

On each line, write the word that matches the definition.

ambulatory-care facilities   **practitioner**   **third-party reimbursement**
census   **precise**   **tolerance**
extended-care   **sophisticated**

1. _____   information about characteristics of someone

2. _____   a person engaged in the practice of a profession or occupation

3. _____   exactly or sharply defined or stated

4. _____   health or nursing care for people recovering from illness

5. _____   the paying back of expenses by an agent such as Blue Cross-Blue Shield or medicare to a patient or doctor (the first and second parties)

6. _____   places that serve patients who are able to walk

7. _____   complex or intricate

8. _____   capacity to put up with something

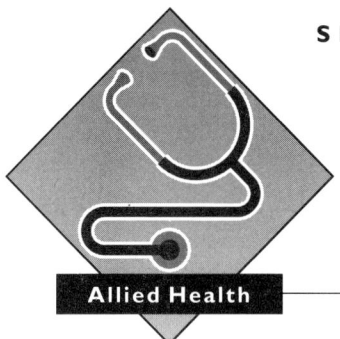

Allied Health

How to Age Gracefully

By Ruth A. Mack

Vocabulary Preview

absorption: the act or process of taking in or soaking up
cardiovascular: relating to the heart or blood vessels
chronic: continuing a long time or coming back frequently
enhance: to make greater; improve
geriatric: relating to aged people
marathon: a long-distance race measuring 26 miles, 385 yards
nutrient: something that nourishes
sedentary: inactive; accustomed to sitting or resting
stature: level of achievement

Which age group benefits the most from exercise?

(a) toddlers

(b) teens

(c) middle-age adults

(d) older adults

The answer is *d,* according to William Evans, author of *Biomarkers,* a book about exercise and aging.

Senior citizens don't have to run **marathons** to reap the benefits of physical fitness. Brisk walking, swimming, and simple weight-lifting benefit people at any age. Recent studies show that even leisure activities—gardening and bowling, for instance—burn off calories and help maintain overall fitness. What's most important, say experts, is to find an enjoyable activity, exercise on a regular basis, and consult with a physician before you leap into a program—regardless of your previous athletic **stature.**

◆ Prime the Pump

If you are an older adult, it is important to start slow and pace yourself. Dr. Evan W. Kligman, director of the **geriatric** program at the University of Arizona College of Medicine, says exercise can help your heart pump more efficiently, strengthen muscles and bones, improve flexibility, help maintain balance, **enhance** oxygen intake, lower blood pressure, and normalize blood sugar. Aerobic exercise—any activity done repetitively for about 20 minutes and at least three times a week—improves heart rate and, according to studies, benefits overall life span.

Aerobics in waist-deep water or swimming laps provides **cardiovascular** benefits and builds stamina without stress on joints. Other activities that do not overly tax the body include bicycling, rowing, dancing, and skating. According to studies by Dr. Thomas Hickey of the University of Michigan, exercise lowers blood pressure and reduces arthritic pain, even in people with **chronic** conditions who previously were overweight and **sedentary.**

On the behavioral side, exercise reduces stress and depression. It can enhance mental sharpness and improve the quality of sleep. "It's not just physical; it's a psychological mechanism as well. You'll feel better about yourself with exercise," notes Dr. David A. Baron, a clinical director of the National Institute of Mental Health in Bethesda, Md. Even more important to older adults, exercise provides opportunities to socialize.

◆ Eat Wisely

A healthy diet is crucial to combat heart disease—the No. 1 killer of Americans—and chronic illnesses like hypertension, arthritis, and diabetes. Nutrition experts say to keep it simple: Eat a well-balanced diet from a variety of foods. However, keep in mind that as we age, our need for calories declines while our nutritional needs stay the same.

"Select foods that are rich in **nutrients,** such as meat, vegetables, and fruit, because it takes fewer calories to maintain weight," advises Ronni M. Chernoff, Ph.D., nutrition professor at the University of Arkansas.

Eat plenty of protein: dairy products, meat, fish, poultry, eggs, nuts, beans, and peas. Choose lean cuts of meat that are low in saturated fat; try to eat cholesterol-rich egg yolks no more than three times a week.

Complex carbohydrates are essential to a healthy diet. They can be found in breads and cereals; dried beans and peas; starchy foods, such as potatoes, rice, and pasta; and fruits and vegetables. Complex carbohydrates supply energy, vitamins, and minerals. When you substitute complex carbohydrates for high-fat foods, they can even help reduce cholesterol.

Because many older adults eat too little, nutritionists recommend a multimineral, multivitamin supplement to ensure necessary nutrients. Nutritional supplements, however, should never substitute for a good diet.

Many older adults take medications to combat a range of illnesses. But food can interfere with the **absorption** of medications, and medications can interfere with the absorption of nutrients from food. Even over-the-counter medicines, such as antacids and laxatives, can cause problems. Read labels carefully, follow instructions, and consult with your doctor about which medicines can interfere with nutrients.

◆ Keep a Positive Outlook

As you age, you undoubtedly experience losses from death, retirement, mobility, and children leaving home. But it is the symbolic losses, such as the realization that you will never be CEO of the company, that most often cause sadness. Depression is not inevitable with aging, however.

Strong social and family ties are critical. "Be in situations where you can socialize with people of all ages," says Baron. With age, your opportunities to travel, resume education, and pursue hobbies are often increased. And while retirement can be a wonderful opportunity to develop new interests, it is by no means mandatory at any age. The message from experts is: Be flexible.

To combat feelings of sadness and isolation, look within your community for networks of support and to find meaningful activities. Experts stress individually tailored solutions. For example, studies show that pets help older adults socialize, exercise, feel safer and more needed, and even lower blood pressure. But a dog or cat isn't right for everyone. If you adopt an animal, be sure it is one you are able to physically handle.

Libraries across the country offer special programs for seniors, carry large-print books and increasingly furnish videocassettes that provide instruction and education, as well as entertainment—all available with a library card.

◆ Update Yourself

Doctors stress the importance of routine checkups to maintain health and detect illnesses early. Be sure to have a yearly physical that includes tests for chronic illnesses—diabetes, high blood pressure, and vision and hearing impairments. Also be sure to have regular immunizations. And check with your physician to learn about safe use of drugs if you take multiple medications.

Falls are the leading cause of accidental death among adults over age 65. Be aware that exercise, wise use of medications, reduced alcohol consumption, and safe home environments can decrease your chances of falling. Make sure rugs and furniture are secure, lighting is adequate, and bathtubs are equipped with nonslip surfaces.

Experts stress the importance of staying productive, creative, and optimistic through leisure activities. By volunteering, older adults can do meaningful work, socialize, and stay active. In fact, recent research shows that people who volunteer live longer and are healthier.

There is no perfect prescription for achieving a healthy, active lifestyle in our later years. But however you pursue it, vitality will surely be rewarded.

Comprehension Questions

1. **The main idea in this article is that** _____.

    a. an informed and active older person can have a good life
    b. older adults should take multivitamins
    c. volunteer work is good for health
    d. socialization with people and pets keeps you young

2. **The leading cause of accidental death in people over 65 is** _____.

    a. cancer   **c.** stress
    b. heart attacks   **d.** falls

3. **The most important thing about exercise is that it should** _____.

    a. speed up your heart   **c.** not overtax your body
    b. be enjoyable and done regularly   **d.** help you sleep better

4. **Older adults need** _____ **but have the same nutritional needs.**

    a. more carbohydrates   **c.** fewer calories
    b. several medications   **d.** less protein

5. **Another title for this article could be** _____.

    a. Diets for Senior Citizens
    b. Reducing Risks for Older Adults
    c. You Don't Have to Run a Marathon!
    d. Growing Older and Enjoying It

Vocabulary Test

On each line, write the number of the word that matches the definition.

1. **enhance**
2. **nutrient**
3. **absorption**
4. **stature**
5. **cardiovascular**
6. **marathon**
7. **chronic**
8. **sedentary**
9. **geriatric**

_____ **a.** a long-distance race measuring 26 miles, 385 yards

_____ **b.** to make greater; improve

_____ **c.** inactive; accustomed to sitting or resting

_____ **d.** something that nourishes

_____ **e.** relating to the heart or blood vessels

_____ **f.** the act or process of taking in or soaking up

_____ **g.** level of achievement

_____ **h.** continuing a long time or coming back frequently

_____ **i.** relating to aged people

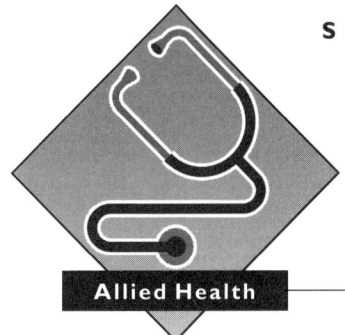

Allied Health

SELECTION 42

Exporting Health—and Hope

By Jacquelyn Hanson, RN, BSN

Vocabulary Preview

airborne: off the ground and flying

bilateral: affecting both sides

cleft lip: a lip that is partially split or divided

clinic: a place that gives medical help to patients not staying in a hospital

heartrending: heartbreaking; causing intense sorrow or distress

hemangioma: a usually noncancerous tumor that appears as a slightly raised, purplish or reddish area of skin.

hypertensive: having abnormally high blood pressure

impetigo: a contagious skin disease characterized by blisters and crusted areas

limbs: a leg or arm of a human being

meningitis: a disease in which there is inflammation of the brain's or spinal cord's membrane

polio: short for poliomyelitis—a viral disease that causes fever and paralysis and often permanent damage to the muscles

recurrences: acts of coming back time after time

"Five zero whiskey, clear for takeoff."

"Five zero whiskey." My brother Ed acknowledges the control tower's transmission and pours on the power. Moments later we are **airborne,** en route to Guaymas, Mexico, on the first leg of our monthly trip with Liga.

Liga International, also known as the Flying Doctors of Mercy, is a volunteer group based in Santa Ana, California. Since 1935, doctors, nurses, and other medical personnel have been bringing much-needed medical care to rural Mexico. We maintain six **clinics** in southern Sonora and northern Sinaloa. On the first weekend of every month, 25 to 30 planes take off for these clinics, each carrying people, medicine, and supplies.

We nurses do everything from assisting in surgery to counting pills. We tell patients how to take the medicine prescribed for them, and we explain how important it is. We make it clear why handwashing is essential to prevent **recurrences** of internal parasites. We help the **hypertensive** patient with his diet and teach the new mother how to feed her baby.

I've been flying with Liga since 1982. I'd wanted to do something like this ever since the late '60s when, as a public health nurse in central California, I'd come to love the Mexican people. I'd never known a group so hardworking, so honest, and so giving of themselves.

What I encountered on my first trip overwhelmed me. Hundreds of patients had been waiting for us since early morning. Many had traveled long distances by train or bus, on horseback, even on foot. Some of them carried children with severe deformities.

In the years since then, I've often—too often—had to tell these people we have no cure to offer. I grieve with them as I watch all hope fade from their eyes: the mother of brain-damaged Juan, the grandmother of Ana, who has leukemia, the parents of little Tonia, her legs withered. Some of the things we see are especially **heartrending** because they're so easily preventable now, like **limbs** paralyzed by **polio** or **meningitis.**

But many times we *can* help. Take 10-year-old Lupita. She had suffered with **impetigo** for two years. It covered most of her face and one shoulder, and had started down her back. We gave her antibiotics, and by our next visit she was almost completely well.

Carla, age 3, had a **hemangioma** the size of an orange above her left eye. Surgery turned her almost instantly from a fretful, unhappy child into a bouncing, sparkly eyed little girl.

Roberto, one of my favorites, was 8 months old when he was brought to us with severe **bilateral** clubfeet. We brought him back to California for surgery. On our return, his father and grandmother burst into tears of joy. We all had a good cry, with Roberto in the center of our huddle wondering what all the fuss was about.

Tears of joy are not reserved for the young. José had spent all of his 26 years looking—and feeling—like a monster. One of our surgeons repaired the **cleft lip** he was born with under local anesthesia. When we gave him a mirror afterwards, he stared at his "new" face for several moments, then tears started rolling down his cheeks.

Like José's surgery, many of the operations we do, and take for granted in the States, are unavailable locally even to people who could pay for them. We also provide general clinic care to people who haven't seen a doctor in years, if ever.

I'm often asked why I do this every month. My teenage son has a simple explanation: "My mom's crazy." He may have a point because, unlike my brother—who lives to fly—I'm kind of nervous when I'm not on the ground. But the smiles and hugs that greet us make everything worthwhile.

Nothing can equal watching Roberto run on his two sound feet. Or seeing pretty Raquel, whose right leg was badly crippled, wearing a new dress that shows off two straight limbs.

To be able to bring hope as well as health to people who respond to our care with love and gratitude is a high unlike any other—one that you can't really understand until you experience it for yourself.

Comprehension Questions

1. **The author's main message is that** _____.

    a. volunteers are needed everywhere
    b. taking medical treatment to poor areas helps the people and rewards the medical people
    c. not everyone can always be helped
    d. you have to be a little crazy to go to poor areas

2. **The volunteer nurses** _____.

    a. perform operations
    b. instruct people about cleanliness and taking medicines
    c. give up their vacations
    d. drive to Mexico

3. **The author has loved Mexican people since** _____.

    a. 1982
    b. 1935
    c. she became a nurse
    d. she was a public health nurse in central California

4. **It is especially sad to see the sick people because** _____.

    a. many of the diseases can be prevented today
    b. the children are so cute
    c. they have to walk to the clinic
    d. they are only treated once a month

5. **The medical personnel of Liga International help the people of rural Mexico because** _____.

    a. the group likes Mexico
    b. they like to fly
    c. the people need the medical care
    d. the doctors and nurses need the work

Vocabulary Test

On each line, write the word that matches the definition.

airborne	clinic	hypertensive	meningitis
bilateral	heartrending	impetigo	polio
cleft lip	hemangioma	limbs	recurrences

1. _____ a contagious skin disease characterized by blisters and crusted areas

2. _____ legs or arms of human beings

3. _____ heartbreaking; causing intense sorrow or distress

4. _____ acts of coming back time after time

5. _____ affecting both sides

6. _____ a disease that can cause paralysis, damage to the muscles, and sometimes death

7. _____ a place that gives medical help to patients not staying in a hospital

8. _____ a disease in which inflammation of the brain's or spinal cord's membranes occurs

9. _____ off the ground and flying

10. _____ having abnormally high blood pressure

The Office at Home

By Lynie Arden

Business and Computers

Vocabulary Preview

bureau: a branch or subdivision of a business

database: a collection of information organized for rapid search and retrieval by a computer

electronic bulletin board: a list of messages, maintained by a computer, that can be both posted and read by someone at a computer connected to other computers by means of telephone lines

electronically: by means of terminals linked by telephone lines

inbound: headed inward

mailings: the batch of letters, fliers, or catalogs sent at one time by someone

outbound: headed outward

personalized: addressed to a particular person (not just "Dear Student" or "Resident")

registered: formally enrolled or signed up

software: computer programs (as opposed to hardware—that is, machines and equipment)

telemarketing: selling goods or services by telephone

How can I use a computer to help market my product? That's a question a lot of home and small-business owners ask. Indeed, a lot of good products and good ideas fail for lack of good marketing.

You can, of course, use your computer, a **database,** and a word processor to prepare large **mailings.** Selling by mail is a key part of many marketing plans. But there are less obvious ways a computer can tell possible customers about your product and even help fill orders. Most require a modem, that tool that links your computer—by way of telephone lines and satellites—to the outside world. Here's a look at some ideas that may be suited for your business.

◆ Automated Call Taker

You've probably heard of, or experienced, automated **outbound telemarketing.** That's when the computer is programmed to call you and deliver a sales pitch. It's not the nicest side of high-tech marketing. The flip side is an automated **inbound** marketing service **bureau.** It is very useful for the business owner and "soft" enough not to annoy people. It's often called Audio Storage and Dial Access Retrieval (ASDAR).

Let's say you place an ad in a magazine to sell a certain product. Included in the ad is a toll-free number. Rather than hiring an operator to answer questions and take orders, you could use an ASDAR system. The system would use your voice to create a script. It will cost you at least 50 to 60 percent less than a live operator would. Callers can be guided to give a name, address, phone number, credit card number, and product order. The service bureau that receives the information then sends the data to you **electronically.**

◆ Telemarketing Software

Still, for the most part, telemarketing works best when there's a human involved. There are all kinds of telemarketing **software** packages around now. Some of them are loaded with features.

One highly rated package, Tele Magic, can track one billion contact names and phone numbers. It can tell you when they were called last and what was discussed. It can also let you know when you should call again. Tele Magic can print out **personalized** form letters, envelopes, bills, packing slips, labels, and thank-you notes. It can keep track of goods in stock.

◆ Paperback Marketer

Word-of-mouth advertising is vital to the home-based business person. Using **electronic bulletin boards** is one of the best ways to encourage it.

Anyone can list a "for sale" message on a computer bulletin board. But Jaron Summers showed more creativity than that. When his paperback *Safety Catch* was published, he worried that his book would be removed from the racks in less than eight weeks. He was determined not to let that happen.

The plot of the book itself inspired his marketing brainstorm. The hero in Summers' detective story saves the day when he taps into a computer system. Since the story involved a computer, it seemed likely that computer owners would be interested.

Summers offered the first chapter of *Safety Catch* free to anyone who wanted it through CompuServe and The Source. The idea was to create enough interest to move the reader to go out and buy the book and maybe tell friends about it.

But that was only the beginning. Summers also offered $5 to anyone who would post the first chapter on one of the thousands of free electronic bulletin boards. Chapter one was posted on more than 400 bulletin boards. Each had more than 1,000 users.

The result? *Safety Catch* went into its second printing and sold more than 100,000 copies. Summers later sold movie rights. Not bad for a novel that would typically have sold less than 8,000 copies!

◆ Shareware

Giving away a sample is one thing, but how about giving away the whole thing? Would you believe you could make a profit?

That's exactly what happens with shareware. Shareware is software that is available free to anyone who wants to try it. If you like it, you're expected to **"register"** as a user and pay for it (at rates reduced). There are almost no marketing and manufacturing costs.

Once a program is developed, all the author has to do is put it onto as many electronic bulletin boards as he can find. One success story is that of Tom Smith and Bruce Barkelew. Their company, Datastorm Technologies, Inc., has produced *ProComm,* an IBM communications software product.

ProComm has been available on hundreds of electronic bulletin boards. More than 35,000 users—an estimated 3 to 7 percent of the total users—have registered.

Comprehension Questions

1. **Each of these ideas can be found in the reading selection. But only one expresses the main point that is being made. Which one?**

    a. There's more to computer marketing than just mass mailings.
    b. Lots of good products are not being marketed properly.
    c. The modem is a remarkable omni-useful tool for computer users.
    d. Mass mailings are a key part of many marketing campaigns.

2. **Jason Summers used an electronic bulletin board _____.**

    a. to meet new people   **c.** to sell books
    b. to market shareware   **d.** to promote ProComm

3. **Most of the marketing methods in this selection require _____.**

    a. dial access retrieval   **c.** a large amount of hard-disk storage space
    b. a modem   **d.** customized questions

4. **The ASDAR system _____.**

    a. helps sales by giving information to the human operator
    b. works through a service bureau
    c. asks users to register and pay at lower rates
    d. mostly does mass mailings

5. **The general idea of this reading selection is that** _____.

   a. most small-business owners aren't using good marketing practices
   b. there are many marketing possibilities available through your computer
   c. a small business probably needs some kind of telemarketing arrangement
   d. computer marketing systems require substantial financial investment

Vocabulary Test

On each line, write the number of the word that matches the definition.

1. **bureau**	_____ **a.**	headed inward
2. **database**	_____ **b.**	selling goods or services by telephone
3. **electronically**		
4. **inbound**	_____ **c.**	a branch or subdivision of a business
5. **mailings**	_____ **d.**	addressed to a particular person
6. **outbound**	_____ **e.**	computer programs
7. **personalized**	_____ **f.**	headed outward
8. **registered**	_____ **g.**	by means of terminals linked by telephone lines
9. **software**		
10. **telemarketing**	_____ **h.**	the batch of mail sent by someone at one time
	_____ **i.**	formally enrolled or signed up
	_____ **j.**	a collection of information organized for rapid search and retrieval by a computer

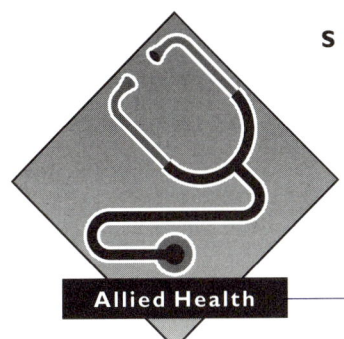

SELECTION 44

Emergency Medical Technician-Paramedic

By Craig R. Ilk

Vocabulary Preview

accreditation: recognition for maintaining standards that qualify graduates for professional practice

assess: to determine the importance or seriousness of something

electrocardiographic: having to do with the recording of changes in electrical energy in the heart

life-support skills: skills in keeping someone alive

paramedic: one who is trained to give first aid or other health care in the absence of a physician

pertinent: relating to the matter at hand

splint: to hold in place by using a thin piece of wood

stabilization: the act of putting firmly in position

◆ Definition

The emergency medical technician-**paramedic** (EMT-P) is a person who is qualified to recognize, **assess,** and manage medical emergencies under the supervision and direction of a licensed physician. The EMT-P should not be confused with the emergency medical technician-ambulance (EMT-A), an individual trained only to provide basic **life-support skills.**

◆ History

The emergency medical technician profession is relatively new. It originated in 1970 when the Federal Department of Transportation and the National Highway Traffic Safety Administration developed a curriculum for the emergency medical technician-ambulance. It consisted of 81 hours of classroom work, practical experience, and hospital work. Topics studied in the EMT-A curriculum included the management of heart-attack patients; cardiopulmonary resuscitation (CPR); airway obstruction; bleeding and shock management; wound care; chest, abdominal, and soft tissue injuries; **stabilization** of broken bones; medical emergencies such as diabetic coma, emergency childbirth, removal of injured persons from vehicles, communications, and other necessary skills. After completing this curriculum, the EMT-A was ready for certification examination and on-the-job experience leading to state certification.

It soon became apparent to physicians, administrators, government officials, and the general public that the EMTs were saving many lives. Supporters of the profession urged development of more advanced training programs so additional lives could be saved. In response to this urging, EMTs in Los Angeles, California, Seattle, Washington, and Jacksonville, Florida, were given increased responsibility, and ultimately a standardized EMT-P curriculum was developed and released in 1977.

◆ Duties

The emergency medical technician-paramedic is usually the first individual to arrive at the scene of an accident or illness who is capable of providing emergency care. Upon arrival, the EMT-P will try to obtain a **pertinent** medical history from the patient, relatives, or bystanders. The EMT-P will then examine the injured person, keeping in mind the medical history. If necessary, efforts are begun immediately to get a patient breathing. For some patients, the physician, with whom the EMT is in constant communication, may order the start of an intravenous solution, with or without specific medications. Oxygen through a mask or other device might be ordered and, in certain critical cases, the EMT-P will insert a tube into the patient's lungs in order to provide oxygen. Patients who have heart problems are often encountered by the EMT-P, who is able to take an accurate **electrocardiographic** tracing of the heart's activity and interpret some of the abnormal findings. When a patient's heart stops pumping effectively, the EMT-P, still under the direction of a physician, will apply a strong electrical shock to the patient in an attempt to prompt the heart to work again. Many of the calls answered will be for less serious injuries or diseases, but the EMT-P must use learned skills to **splint** broken bones, bandage wounds, and provide additional help as needed.

When the call is completed, after the patient is safely delivered to the hospital, the EMT-P must know enough about the lifesaving equipment on the ambulance to be able to clean it, check for proper operation, and have the unit ready for the next call. Written reports are then filed, including details about the patient and the situation. After these tasks are completed, the EMT-P waits to be called upon again to offer lifesaving, or other necessary assistance to sick or injured patients.

◆ Employment

EMT-Ps are employed by emergency medical services systems within cities or counties, fire departments, police departments, or private ambulance companies. Shift work is the rule since staffing is necessary 24 hours per day.

The EMT-P provides a vital link in the emergency medical care chain. The recognition of the need for **accreditation** of programs, national and state certifying examinations, and the requirement for continuing education after certification all attest to the importance of this relatively new allied health profession.

Comprehension Questions

1. **The main idea of this article is that the profession of emergency medical technician-paramedic was developed to _____.**

   a. help doctors
   b. get to accidents fast
   c. save lives
   d. replace nurses

2. **The title "emergency medical technician-paramedic" did not exist until _____.**

   a. 1950
   b. 1970
   c. 1977
   d. 1990

3. **The first person with medical skills to arrive at an accident is usually _____.**

   a. an emergency medical technician-paramedic
   b. an ambulance driver
   c. a nurse
   d. a doctor

4. **The EMT-P's job is finished when _____.**

   a. the police arrive
   b. the patient is in the ambulance
   c. the patient's heart is stabilized
   d. the patient is safely delivered to the hospital

5. **Another title for this article might be _____.**

   a. New Healthcare Technicians
   b. Modern Life Savers
   c. Professional First Aid
   d. Help for Accident Victims

Vocabulary Test

On each line, write the number of the word that matches the definition.

1. **splint**
2. **accreditation**
3. **electrocardiographic**
4. **pertinent**
5. **life-support skills**
6. **assess**
7. **stabilization**
8. **paramedic**

_____ **a.** the act of putting firmly in position

_____ **b.** one who is trained to give first aid or other health care in the absence of a physician

_____ **c.** skills in keeping someone alive

_____ **d.** recognition for maintaining standards that qualify graduates for professional practice

_____ **e.** having to do with the recording of changes in electrical energy in the heart

_____ **f.** relating to the matter at hand

_____ **g.** to hold in place by using a thin piece of wood

_____ **h.** to determine the importance or seriousness of something

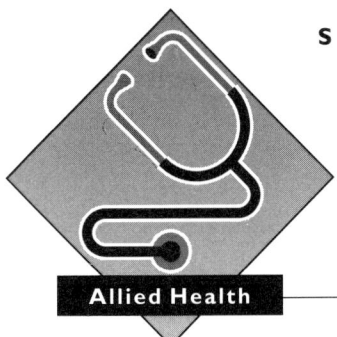

Dental Assistant

By Craig R. Ilk

Vocabulary Preview

clinic: a place, usually connected with a hospital, that gives medical help to patients not staying in the hospital, usually for little or no fee

diagnostic: used in the act or process of examining persons carefully to find out what is wrong with them

impressions: imprints of the teeth and nearby portions of the jaw for use in dentistry

operative field: the area of the body where an operation or procedure takes place

practice: the continuous exercise of a profession

suture: a strand or fiber used to sew part of the human body

The dental assistant is a trained professional who assists the dentist with dental treatment procedures. The new concept of the dental assistant far surpasses the receptionist-chore girl image of the past. The dental assistant of today develops skills that are not only used to assist the dentist at chairside, but also used to produce **diagnostic** aids for the dentist's interpretation, provide oral health instructions for patients, and perform treatment procedures (expanded functions) where state law allows the dentist to assign these services. Dental assistants also develop skills in business office procedures.

Basic functions include the sterilization of equipment; transfer of instruments during surgical procedures; maintaining a clear **operative field** by the use of suction devices, cotton, and retainer devices; preparation of filling materials; and basic laboratory procedures.

Expanded functions vary from state to state. More than 30 states allow dental assistants to expose and develop X rays, place rubber dams for specialized procedures, and remove **sutures.** Over 20 states allow assistants to make **impressions** for study models of teeth and to polish teeth. Eight states allow assistants, with supervision, to place and carve restorations.

It is estimated by the U.S. Department of Labor that there will be increased demand for dental assistants, especially those who are graduates of accredited educational programs. Dental assistants may work in one of several dental specialties, including oral (mouth) surgery, orthodontics (straightening teeth), pedodontics (children's dentistry), periodontics (dealing with gum disease), oral pathology (mouth disease), prosthodontics (artificial teeth), and dental public health.

At this time, there are approximately 150,000 dental assistants who are actively employed in the United States. Most dental assistants work in private and group dental **practices** as employees for one or more dentists. Other opportunities for employment are in hospital dental departments; federal, state, and community **clinics;** dental school clinics; and the armed services.

Comprehension Questions

1. **This article is mainly about _____.**

    a. taking care of teeth
    b. what a dentist does
    c. becoming a dental assistant
    d. how a dental assistant helps a dentist

2. **Most dental assistants work _____.**

    a. for the government
    b. in private and group dental practices
    c. in a community clinic
    d. in a hospital

3. **A pedodontist _____.**

    a. straightens teeth
    b. does surgery in the mouth
    c. is a children's dentist
    d. fits artificial teeth

4. **Many of the procedures a dental assistant is allowed to perform are regulated by _____.**

    a. the state
    b. the dentist
    c. common sense
    d. dental schools

5. **Another title for this article could be _____.**

    a. In a Dentist's Office
    b. The Dental Assistant of Today
    c. Regulations for a Dental Assistant
    d. Oral Health

Vocabulary Test

On each line, write the word that matches the definition.

| **clinic** | **impressions** | **practice** |
| **diagnostic** | **operative field** | **suture** |

1. _____   the continuous exercise of a profession

2. _____   a place, usually connected with a hospital, that gives medical help to patients not staying in the hospital, usually for little or no fee

3. _____   the area of the body where an operation or procedure takes place

4. _____   used in the act or process of examining persons carefully to find out what is wrong with them

5. _____   imprints of the teeth and nearby portions of the jaw for use in dentistry

6. _____   a strand or fiber used to sew parts of the human body

Developing a Sales Personality

Business and Computers

Vocabulary Preview

assiduously: with attentive and persistent care

aura: feeling; sensation

cultivate: encourage the growth of

emanate: give off; emit

empathy: the action of understanding, being aware of, being sensitive to the feelings, thoughts, and expressions of another

endearing: making one loved or admired

latent: existing but not now visible or active

scrutiny: a searching look; examination

timidity: lack of courage or self-confidence

unearth: discover

virtuoso: one who excels in the technique of an art

The basic steps involved in developing a sales personality are the breaking of bad habits and the replacing of them with good ones. This takes self-control, self-determination, and willpower. We all have enough of these traits. It is well worth our while to **cultivate** them. The goals are high. A person cannot automatically change, but slow improvement in outer evidences of one's character can result in establishing good habits.

To begin, an honest self-inventory is necessary. Combine this with an inventory of successful salespeople that are worth emulating.

Are your personal habits in cleanliness and grooming desirable ones? If not, this is simple to remedy. Always be well dressed and well groomed. There is room for individual tastes and style, but the finished product must be businesslike.

The next personal observation may be more painful to the ego. Do you have any distracting or unpleasant habits or mannerisms? These can be most subtle and not necessarily only the more obvious ones such as nail biting and teeth gnashing. Many people are normally unaware of having these habits, and it requires a close personal **scrutiny** to **unearth** mannerisms that drive others to distraction.

If an honest self-inventory indicates the existence of these undesirable practices, break yourself of them at all costs.

Learn to develop an interest in others. If you can establish true **empathy** with those with whom you come in contact, you have taken a big stride towards sales personality.

Practice your smile. A smile must not be a smile of the lips only—it must show in the eyes. Spend a period of time every day in front of the mirror smiling at yourself. Do not discontinue this until you can honestly say to yourself that your smile is sincere, friendly, and warming.

Your handshake should be firm but not a bone crusher. This too can be achieved with practice.

Your voice and speech habits can be cultivated and improved if you try. Speak in an empty room and use a tape recorder. Satisfy yourself that your voice and diction reach the desired levels. If your vocabulary is limited, practice can improve this, too. Everytime you hear or read a new word, make a note of it and remember the context of its use. At the end of each day, look the words up in the dictionary plus additional new words selected at random from the dictionary to total a minimum of 20 new words a day. Write the words and their meaning down five times and repeat them aloud five times that evening. The amount of new words that will enter your vocabulary will amaze you. Improving your reading habits will also be a helpful factor in conjunction with this practice.

Build your memory. If necessary, take a memory course. Try never to forget a name or a face. This remembering is an **endearing** quality in the sales personality, and failure to remember a name can, at times, cost a sale.

The rest of the traits that must be developed to achieve an outstanding sales personality are traits of character. These must be worked at much more **assiduously.** You must be determined and concentrate on being who you want to be.

Have faith in yourself and in what you have to sell. This will eliminate **timidity** and enable you to **emanate** an **aura** of confidence, enthusiasm, and assuredness. This will enable you also to be truly convincing, sincere, and persuasive. With these traits, you can develop the strength of character to keep from yielding when you should not and the good judgment to yield when you should.

When your personality has the strength and confidence required, avoid the swinging of the pendulum too far in the opposite direction. Many people, who in this manner succeed in conditioning their thinking, do develop all of these desirable traits. However some go to an extreme and find themselves with a new group of undesirable characteristics. They may become brash, opinionated, or conceited, or come across as superior. Keep checking on yourself, and see to it that you are who and what you want to be.

In very few words, strive to have that indefinable asset called "class," and combine this with all of the other favorable characteristics that will enable you to motivate people.

All of this takes work and practice. A violin **virtuoso** achieves his high degree of success by long hours of playing and correcting. He starts with a hidden talent and brings it to its artistic heights through hard work. Everyone has the talent of an obvious or **latent** sales personality. For those who want to achieve success in the sales field, this talent can be brought out or improved by the same type of effort.

Comprehension Questions

1. **The main point of this article is that** _____.

   a. good salespeople are just born that way
   b. selling is an easy job
   c. appearance is everything to a good salesperson
   d. anyone can develop a good sales personality

2. **The writer believes that bad habits** _____.

   a. are permanent
   b. can be replaced with good ones
   c. are a problem
   d. are learned when you are young

3. **The article states that sometimes a sale can be lost by** _____.

   a. failure to remember a name
   b. too strong a handshake
   c. poor vocabulary
   d. the wrong clothes

4. **All salespeople should dress** _____.

   a. alike
   b. in gray
   c. in a businesslike style
   d. any way, as long as they are clean

5. **This article could be called** _____.

   a. Born to Sell
   b. Developing a Sales Vocabulary
   c. You Can Have a Good Sales Personality
   d. Making Good Habits

Vocabulary Test

On each line, write the number of the word that matches the definition.

1. **emanate**   _____   **a.** one who excels in the technique of an art
2. **scrutiny**
3. **assiduously**   _____   **b.** to give off; emit
4. **latent**   _____   **c.** making one loved or admired
5. **virtuoso**   _____   **d.** encourage the growth of
6. **timidity**   _____   **e.** with attentive and persistent care
7. **unearth**   _____   **f.** feeling; sensation
8. **endearing**   _____   **g.** discover
9. **aura**   _____   **h.** existing but not now visible or active
10. **cultivate**   _____   **i.** a searching look; examination
                      _____   **j.** lack of courage or self-confidence

Data-Processing Technician

Vocabulary Preview

census: an official count of the people of a country

computer language: system of coding and organization in which programs are written

debugging: eliminating errors (bugs) from a computer program

flow chart: a diagram that shows the step-by-step progression and organization of a computer program

mainframe: a large central computer with the greatest capacity for storing data and performing many tasks at once (minicomputers and microcomputers can operate on their own or can hook into a mainframe for data and operation use; computer terminals usually operate only by being attached to a mainframe)

personnel: the people who work for a company, business, or organization

programming: giving a computer (in a particular computer language) a set of steps to accomplish a task

segment: a piece of something; part

Data-processing technicians occupy a relatively new **segment** of the working population. In the 1930s, the forerunners of the first computer were being developed in university research centers. Twenty years later, in 1951, the first computer was used to process the U.S. **census.** In 1954, the first computer was used in private business. Since then, public and private industries, universities, and other research centers have been developing different kinds of computers. Many new discoveries have been made in information processing, storage, analysis, and application to solve problems faster and more accurately than ever before.

To understand the work of data-processing technicians and the professionals whom they assist, it is necessary to understand computers and know how they are used to perform the complex processes of modern data processing. These remarkable machines can do thousands of tasks and more. But they cannot do any of them without one essential thing: instructions. A computer needs to be told how to do what it does. A human being has to tell the computer how to become a word processor, a gas gauge, a speedometer, an automatic dialer, a timer, or a welder. In fact, the only thing any computer can do by itself is accept instructions and carry them out. For this reason, most of the specialized activities involved in using computers are associated with giving them instructions. Giving instructions to a computer is called **programming.** Most computer courses and training programs focus on the various levels and kinds of programming methods.

Computers that are the central data processor in large data-processing systems are called **mainframe** computers. They were the first types of computers to be developed. Later, smaller computers called minicomputers were developed. They were used to manage the program or list of instructions for the operation of complex programs for large mainframe computers. They also were used for relatively limited data-processing tasks.

Still more recently, the most modern and smallest computers, called microcomputers or microprocessors, were developed. They perform the same work as minicomputers did in large systems, and in addition are used for many small, independent computer applications in small businesses, offices, schools, or even as personal computers in the home.

The **personnel** in large data-processing centers generally include machine operators, technicians who may be called junior programmers or programmers, senior programmers, and analysts.

A computer program originates from the definition of a problem. Data-processing technicians receive the problem definition, the computer system and units to be used, and the **computer language** to be used as an assignment from the analyst and the senior programmer. The technicians then design the necessary **flow charts** and input-output forms. They collect necessary data and translate the problem definition into a set of instructions called a program.

Programs are written in systems of coding and organization called computer languages. There are many computer languages, and specific computers accept specific languages. One of the simplest languages is called BASIC. It is elementary, and new computer users learn programming with it. For business data processing, the most common language is COBOL, which means "Common Business Oriented Language." In the mid-1980s, more than half of all business programs used COBOL. Although other languages are gaining popularity, business data-processing technicians need to have a working knowledge of this language.

It is the responsibility of the programmer to write the program in the language most suited to the problem definition and the computer involved. These are usually specified to the technician by the system analyst or senior programmer. In addition to writing new programs, technicians constantly modify existing programs to meet new requirements or increase operating efficiency. Technicians also spend a lot of time in the computer room, checking on programs to be certain they have no errors and that the answers coming from the program are correct.

Under the technician's supervision, machine operators perform the actual tasks of computer operating required to produce the desired output. Both operator and technician must know the operating characteristics of the computer and be able to identify problems. The greatest part of the operator's time is spent in the computer room with the technician or other responsible programmers.

When the program has been run for the first time, the programmer analyzes the results. Often, some step in the program leads to a mistake and changes or corrections need to be made. This is called **debugging.** After all of the debugging is done, the program provides the answer or process it was planned to perform, and the technician moves on to another problem.

Comprehension Questions

1. **A data-processing technician could also be called a** _____.

   a. systems analyst
   b. computer repairperson
   c. information processing engineer
   d. data-processing programmer

2. **A computer cannot do anything without** _____.

   a. paper
   b. instructions
   c. a problem
   d. files

3. **Giving instructions to a computer is called** _____.

   a. programming
   b. debugging
   c. analyzing
   d. flow-charting

4. **The smallest and most modern computers are called**

   _____.

   a. minicomputers
   b. mainframe computers
   c. central computers
   d. microcomputers

5. **This article could also be titled** _____.

   a. Organizing Information to Solve Problems
   b. Operating Computers
   c. How to Become a Systems Analyst
   d. Writing Computer Programs

Vocabulary Test

On each line, write the number of the word that matches the definition.

1. **mainframe**
2. **debugging**
3. **personnel**
4. **segment**
5. **census**
6. **programming**
7. **flow chart**
8. **computer language**

_____ **a.** large central computer with the greatest capacity for storing data and performing many tasks at once

_____ **b.** diagram that shows the step-by-step progression and organization of a computer program

_____ **c.** piece of something; part

_____ **d.** an official count of the people of a country

_____ **e.** eliminating errors (bugs) from a computer program

_____ **f.** systems of coding and organization in which programs are written

_____ **g.** giving a computer a set of steps to accomplish a task

_____ **h.** the people who work for a company, business, or organization

Improving Hospitality

By Gen La Greca

Hospitality and Tourism

Vocabulary Preview

commitment: an agreement to do something in the future
eye contact: looking directly into a person's eyes
posture: the way a body is held
preside: to exercise guidance, direction, or control
refrain: to keep oneself from doing something
survey: a questionnaire for collecting data

According to the dictionary, a host or hostess is a person who is in charge of a social event and makes sure that guests are comfortable and entertained. This is a very important job. Do your hosts realize the importance of their job and perform it properly? The training of hosts and hostesses should be given careful attention.

◆ Appearance

Stress its importance. Give your hosts and hostesses a brief **survey** to fill out and ask them if they make your best-dressed list. They should answer "always, sometimes, or never" to such statements as: "My hands are clean and my nails are scrubbed and manicured"; "I **refrain** from chewing gum while on duty"; and "My hair is clean and attractively styled."

Ask your hosts and hostesses to rate themselves honestly. Ask each one to make a **commitment** to improving appearance, and call on each person to tell you what that commitment is.

◆ Hospitality

You may have another questionnaire for the hosts to fill out by which to judge their hospitality. It might contain statements such as "I smile and make **eye contact** with guests"; "I greet guests before asking how many in the party"; and "I say goodbye to guests who are leaving." The hosts should answer "always, sometimes, or never."

Again, ask them to be honest. (Even if they aren't, they will still get a message about what you expect of them.) Ask for a commitment from them that explains how they will improve their hospitality in the future.

◆ Greeting the Guest

Points that usually need to be made include: Greeting the guest immediately; smiling; making eye contact; greeting the guest before asking how many in the party; properly handling a wait and being accurate in estimates of wait time; staying "glued" to the entrance; and standing with good **posture.** Have these staff members practice greeting each other in a class role-playing exercise.

◆ Seating the Guest

Important points here generally include: Seating guests only at clean tables; walking to the table with or only slightly ahead of guests; pulling out chairs to assist with seating; handing menus to the guests (opening them, too); and making a selling suggestion.

Posing difficult situations that come up at your restaurant will give you a chance to discuss with your hosts and hostesses how you would like each one handled.

How do you make the training "stick"? By being a good role model yourself in your dealings with guests. If you do not seat guests, for example, as you explained in class, do not expect your staff to take it seriously. Watch and correct them when they do not follow your procedures. Mystery guests can also be asked to describe to you how they were greeted and seated by your staff.

Training programs such as the one described can be enjoyable for everyone and quite helpful in teaching your standards to those who **preside** over your dining room.

Comprehension Questions

1. **This article is written to _____.**

   a. tell a host or hostess how to make a restaurant better
   b. make sure hosts and hostesses do not annoy customers
   c. help restaurants get more business
   d. help a restaurant owner properly train the hosts and hostesses

2. **A host or hostess should** _____.

   a. be ready to take guests' orders
   b. be clean and well dressed
   c. tell the waiters and waitresses what to do
   d. never suggest special foods

3. **Greeting the guests does not include** _____.

   a. smiling
   b. cleaning the table
   c. always staying at the entrance
   d. being a good judge of waiting times

4. **One way to have hostesses and hosts learn good skills is to have them** _____.

   a. practice with each other in a role-playing exercise
   b. make up questionnaires
   c. work overtime
   d. be a waiter or waitress first

5. **Another title for this article could be** _____.

   a. Training Good Hosts and Hostesses
   b. How Restaurants Can Be Better
   c. Why Hosts and Hostesses Are Important
   d. Making Training "Stick"

Vocabulary Test

On each line, write the number of the word that matches the definition.

1. **eye contact**   _____
2. **posture**
3. **refrain**   _____
4. **preside**
5. **commitment**   _____
6. **survey**

   _____

   _____

   a. the way of carrying one's body in a vertical position

   b. to keep oneself from doing something

   c. a questionnaire for collecting data

   d. an agreement to do something in the future

   e. to exercise guidance, direction, and control

   f. looking directly into a person's eyes

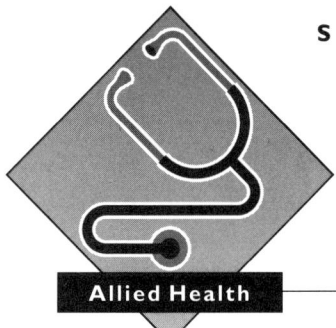

Home Health Technician

Allied Health

Vocabulary Preview

convalescent: recovering health and strength gradually after an illness

dressings: material (such as gauze) used to cover a wound

fluid: substance, such as water, that flows easily

respiration: breathing

surgical: of or relating to surgery or operations

walker: a framework designed to support a crippled or handicapped person while walking

---

Home health technicians work with elderly, handicapped, and **convalescent** patients and their families in their homes. With appropriate help from these technicians, elderly or disabled people may be able to continue living at home instead of going to a nursing home, and the sick may return home from the hospital sooner. The technicians are part of a health-care team and work under the direction of a medical professional such as a physician or registered nurse.

The duties of home health technicians fall into three main areas: personal services, medical services, and instruction. They aid patients, some of whom must stay in bed, with routine personal activities (dressing, eating, bathing, exercising, for example). The technicians may transfer patients to and from wheelchairs, and they may help them walk to and from the bathroom.

In providing routine medical services, the technicians must utilize their knowledge of proper medical techniques and of the structure and function of body systems. This care may include changing **surgical dressings,** caring for wounds, and administering massages, hot and cold applications, enemas, and oral and injected medications. The technicians periodically gather basic information on the patients' progress and make observations such as blood pressure, pulse, temperature, **respiration** rate, and **fluid** intake and output, for reporting to the supervising medical professionals.

The home health technician might teach patients and families skills and techniques that are useful in coping with illness and disability at home. At the same time, they also provide encouragement and the stability needed to help patients make the best possible adjustment to their situation. They instruct patients in how to use such devices as **walkers** and wheelchairs. They suggest and demonstrate methods of housekeeping and of meal planning and preparation that are adapted to the patients' physical and economic needs and limitations.

People interested in becoming home health technicians can expect to undergo one to two years of post-high school training. They should be good at following written and oral instructions, interested in attending to the specific needs of individuals, and in good physical and emotional health.

Comprehension Questions

1. **A home health technician mainly works with** _____.

   a. doctors
   b. patients in nursing homes
   c. children
   d. patients and their families in their homes

2. **If a hospital patient has a home health technician, that patient might** _____.

   a. get well faster
   b. return home from the hospital sooner
   c. not need a doctor
   d. learn to cook

3. **Education to be a home health technician is** _____.

   a. one or two years after high school
   b. the same as that for a nurse
   c. like premedical training
   d. not much

4. **A home health technician works** _____.

   a. alone
   b. as part of a health-care team
   c. in a hospital
   d. long hours

5. **The main job of a home health technician is to** _____.

   a. give medications
   b. help families cope with illness
   c. assist and train patients so they can continue to live at home
   d. show patients how to cook and clean

Vocabulary Test

On each line, write the number of the word that matches the definition.

1. **surgical**   _____   **a.** a framework designed to support a crippled or handicapped person while walking

2. **dressings**

3. **fluid**   _____   **b.** of or relating to surgery or operations

4. **walker**   _____   **c.** material (such as gauze) used to cover a wound

5. **convalescent**

6. **respiration**   _____   **d.** recovering health and strength gradually after an illness

                         _____   **e.** substance, such as water, that flows easily

                         _____   **f.** breathing

Be Your Own Tax Guru

By Tom Morton

Vocabulary Preview

accountant: someone skilled in the systems of recording and keeping track of business credits and debts, or incoming money and outgoing money

checklist: a complete list of items used for inventory by checking items off

deduction: an amount that may be subtracted from income or taxes in income tax forms

eligible: qualified for or entitled to

fellow: equal in rank or power

intimidated: made shy or frightened; put off by

itemized: listed; written down in detail

liable: obligated according to law; responsible

replica: copy; duplicate

schedules: supplementary tax forms for special situations

sole: only

spreadsheets: the ledger layout modeled by a computer

violate: disobey

worksheet: a form for doing calculations

At the risk of upsetting **fellow accountants,** I'm going to tell you a little secret: Even though accountants can give you important tax advice, their calculators and computers aren't any smarter than yours are. I'll tell you another secret: You probably know more about taxes than you give yourself credit for. During the tax season, offices, homes, and restaurants across the country will be discussing 1040s, Schedule Cs, and **itemized deductions.** If you ask me, many of you enjoy talking about taxes.

Yet, too many taxpayers take their boxes of receipts, paycheck stubs, bank statements, W-4s, and other items to their accountants' offices, say "Get me back as much money as you can," and walk out. No questions asked.

Maybe your tax problems are very complicated or maybe you really don't care to know—about tax laws. If so, you'll always need your accountant. But if you're just a bit **intimidated** by tax forms or just a bit lazy, you should take a closer look at tax-preparation software.

Tax-prep software is for people who want to prepare their own individual income tax returns. They want to do them more accurately. (These programs are also good for individuals who want to prepare their own draft tax returns and then ask accountants for advice.) In fact, some of the best programs available for tax preparation, such as HowardSoft's *Tax Preparer* and SoftView's *MacInTax* and *TaxView,* were created by nontax professionals who wanted to make tax preparation less painful.

Over the last couple of years, I've looked at a number of tax-preparation packages that were written for individual taxpayers. (With the new tax code, some of the tax-software publishers have taken the rewriting required as an opportunity to make their programs better.) Below, I've created a **checklist** of questions to ask when you're shopping for a suitable tax-preparation package. The more "yes" answers you give, the better the program will be for you. If you can't answer these questions by looking at the package, flip through the manual or ask a salesperson for assistance. If you still can't find out everything you'd like to know, try calling the software publisher's customer service phone number.

◆ What to Look For

- Is the package written specifically for individuals? Packages intended for accountants and professional tax preparers are generally too expensive, too complex, and too confusing for the average user.

- Is the manual complete, yet easy to understand? The manual should clearly describe the program's features, and it should include clear explanations of the tax laws and of all the forms.

- Has the program sold well in the past? Does the package indicate that it's made best-seller lists?

- Will you be able to get updates of the program each year? For a reasonable price? Because tax laws change, tax-preparation programs need yearly updating.

- Does the program give tax advice?

- Is there any on-line help? With Best Programs' PC/TaxCut, for instance, if you have a question about your child's interest income, you simply touch the question mark key, and the program gives you the rules regarding interest earned by a child and tells you the special forms you need to fill out.

- Does the program show **replicas** of the tax forms on-screen?

- Does the package perform the calculations for all of the forms, **schedules,** and **worksheets** that you may need? For instance, if you are paying off a mortgage, you'll need Schedule A so that you can deduct your home-mortgage interest. Employees who claim business expenses on their personal tax returns need Form 2106; those who are self-employed would use Schedule C.

- If you operate a home-based business, does your package include the forms and schedules you need to deduct the expenses of a home office?

- If you are **sole** owner or involved in a partnership, can you use the program?

- Are forms, schedules, and worksheets all linked together and computations made automatically? If they are, you may find that a form you didn't know about will spew out of the printer. "People are always surprised when it comes time to print their returns because the program automatically completes numerous built-in worksheets and generates forms and schedules that they never knew they were **eligible** or **liable** for," says HowardSoft president and founder Dr. J. E. Howard.

- Does the program automatically check for inconsistencies and errors and let users know when Internal Revenue Service (IRS) rules have been **violated?**

- Can the package accept data from other software, such as **spreadsheets?**

- Does the program change your tax liability each time you plug in a new figure? This feature lets you make estimates. For instance, you can instantly see how much money you'll save if you put $2,000 into an IRA, instead of $1,000 or nothing at all.

- Can the program create and print out an IRS-approved 1040, 1040EZ, or 1040A? (Any tax forms that have to be signed need special approval from the IRS.)

- Does the program let you create and print out other forms, worksheets, and schedules that can be mailed to the IRS?

- If the package doesn't create its own forms and schedules, will it let you print information onto tax forms that you can feed through your printer?

◆ Make April Less Taxing

I won't promise you that completing your tax returns on your computer is any faster than doing it by hand. If you're trading in a human tax preparer for software, computerized tax preparation may not even be cheaper. But tax-preparation software *will* help you be better organized, more complete, and more accurate.

Comprehension Questions

1. **The general idea of this selection is that** _____.

    a. some people will always need an accountant
    b. accountants may not like what the writer says
    c. there's no sense in using a tax-preparation program if you are going to consult an accountant
    d. tax-preparation software should be chosen carefully

2. **The writer says programs intended for accountants are**

    _____.

    a. the best kind to buy
    b. confusing for the average user
    c. generally well written
    d. not correct for individuals

3. **Doing your tax returns with a computer program will**

    _____.

    a. save you time
    b. improve your accuracy
    c. cost less than using a professional tax preparer
    d. prevent mistakes

4. **According to the writer, some of the best tax programs were made by** _____.

    a. accountants
    b. H&R Block
    c. nontax professionals
    d. tax lawyers

5. **This selection mainly offers** _____.

    a. comments and suggestions for choosing the right program
    b. arguments for doing tax returns by computer
    c. preparation for filing IRS returns electronically
    d. a discussion of recent changes in the income tax laws

Vocabulary Test

On each line, write the number of the word that matches the definition.

1. **accountant** _____
2. **eligible** _____
3. **itemized** _____
4. **intimidated** _____
5. **liable**
6. **schedules** _____
7. **sole** _____
8. **spreadsheet** _____
9. **violate** _____
10. **worksheet** _____
11. **fellow** _____
_____

a. obligated according to law

b. listed; written down in detail

c. disobey

d. supplementary tax forms for special situations

e. made shy or frightened

f. qualified for or entitled to

g. ledger layout modeled by a computer

h. a form for doing calculations

i. only

j. equal in rank or power

k. someone skilled in the systems of recording and keeping track of incoming and outgoing money

Answer Key

PART 1

Chapter 1

LESSON 1.1

1. computer	**2.** color	**3.** week
4. dictate	**5.** standard	**6.** chip
7. arrange	**8.** fold	**9.** labor
10. assist	**11.** valid	**12.** place
13. accept	**14.** indicate	**15.** delete
16. horizon	**17.** script	**18.** impose
19. inform	**20.** origin	

LESSON 1.2

1. **mal-** means "bad, badly," so malfunction means "function or perform badly."
2. **un-** means "not," so untitled means "not titled."
3. **de-** means "from," so depart means "part from (leave)."
4. **re-** means "again," so reformat means "format again."
5. **pre-** means "before," so preset means "set before."
6. **bi-** means "two," so bimonthly means "(every) two months."
7. **trans-** means "across," so transatlantic means "across the Atlantic (ocean)."
8. **im-** means "not," so immovable means "not movable."
9. **extra-** means "beyond," so extralegal means "beyond legal" (beyond the law).
10. **co-** means "with," so co-worker means "with a worker."
11. **dis-** means "separation," so disassociate means "separation (from) an associate."
12. **sub-** means "under," so subtitle means "a title under (another title)."
13. **multi-** means "many," so multistage means "many stages."
14. **mis-** means "badly," so mismanage means "manage badly."
15. **mono-** means "one," so monosyllable means "one syllable."
16. **anti-** means "against," so antifraud means "against fraud."
17. **mini-** means "very small," so minivan means "very small van."
18. **inter-** means "between," so interbranch means "between branches (of an office or company)."
19. **ultra-** means "extremely," so ultramodern means "extremely modern."
20. **semi-** means "half," so semiannual means "half annual (every half year)."

LESSON 1.3

1. **-ate** means "to cause to become," so activate means "to cause to become active."
2. **-ion** means "act (of)," so instruction means "act (of) instructing."
3. **-ment** means "result of," so replacement means "result of replacing."
4. **-ize** means "cause to be," so sterilize means "cause to be sterile."
5. **-ese** means "pertaining to," so computerese means "pertaining to a computer."
6. **-ery** means "place of," so bindery means "place of binding."
7. **-ance** means "action of," so assistance means "action of assisting."
8. **-ee** means "receiver of," so employee means "receiver of employ(ment)."
9. **-or** means "one who," so auditor means "one who audits."
10. **-al** means "of," so seasonal means "of the season."
11. **-able** means "capable of," so translatable means "capable of (being) translated."
12. **-er** means "one who," so printer means "one who prints."
13. **-ness** means "state of (being)," so usefulness means "state of (being) useful."

    OR **-ful** means "full of" and -ness means "state of (being)," so usefulness means "state of (being) full of use."
14. **-ant** means "one who," so accountant means "one who accounts (or does accounts)."
15. **-ful** means "full of," so successful means "full of success."
16. **-ous** means "full of," so poisonous means "full of poison."
17. **-ship** means "position of (being a)," so judgeship means "position of (being a) judge."
18. **-ic** means "having the nature of," so energetic means "having the nature of energy."
19. **-ly** means "in the manner of," so capably means "in the manner of (being) capable."
20. **-like** means "having the quality of," so viruslike means "having the quality of a virus."

LESSON 1.4

1. d   2. b   3. c   4. b   5. c

LESSON 1.5

1. cursor—a figure on a computer screen that indicates where data is to be entered; it is usually controlled by hand.
2. brief—a summary of a client's case made out for the instruction of the lawyer in a trial.
3. pipe—a long, hollow tube for the transporting of liquids or gases.
4. pen—an instrument for writing with ink.
5. crown—an artificial substitute for the part of a tooth that is seen above the gums.

6. reservation—an arrangement by which places (or tickets or seats) are secured in advance.
7. program—a computer-coded procedure for solving a problem or handling information.
8. patient—a person under medical treatment.
9. outlet—a holder, mounted to a wall, that is attached to a power source and into which plugs of electrical appliances are put.
10. counter—a level surface on which goods are displayed.
11. order—instructions to buy.
12. pressure—the continuous force by one thing on another.
13. run—flow and spread.
14. diet—a person's usual food and drink.
15. hardware—the actual machinery and components.
16. breaker—an automatic device that stops the flow of electricity.
17. frame—to enclose with glass and a rigid border.
18. officer—one who has a position of trust and authority.
19. manual—using human, rather than electrical, energy.
20. tissue—a group of similar cells.

Chapter 2

LESSON 2.1

1. tool
2. career
3. book
4. lodging places
5. vacation
6. typed things
7. auto parts
8. computer command
9. vital signs
10. stores

LESSON 2.2

1. Employees must learn self-management techniques.
2. Tobacco, like cocaine or heroin, is addictive.
3. There is so much equipment in the avionics field that technicians usually specialize in one area.
4. In the past 25 years, it has changed more than it did in its first 200 years.
5. In other words, you don't have to worry about ordinary living or working with someone who carries HIV.

LESSON 2.3

1. B   2. A   3. B   4. A

LESSON 2.4

1. No   2. Yes   3. No   4. No

LESSON 2.5

5, 3, 2, 7, 1, 4, 8, 9, 10, 6

(It is also possible to put 10 before the sentence "Replace gas cap on car's tank." Then the order would be 5, 3, 2, 7, 1, 4, 10, 8, 9, 6.)

1. **b.** Behind all computer games is a designer who performs a series of steps that are both technical and tedious.
2. **e.** For some, it's a lonely, frustrating job.
3. **a.** Others believe it's the best type of work imaginable.
4. **h.** How the work is done depends on which company the designer works for.
5. **c.** At big companies, designers use state-of-the-art equipment.
6. **g.** At small companies, they may work with little more than home computers.
7. **f.** Freelance designers work for themselves.
8. **d.** Using whatever equipment they can afford, they try to invent games that will catch the fancy of game companies.

Chapter 3

LESSON 3.1

1. A   2. A   3. A   4. B

LESSON 3.2

1. page 40	2. No	3. Goal Setting
4. 1¾	5. No change	6. No
7. Yes	8. Yes	

Chapter 4

LESSON 4.1

1. Highway Robbery: The Scandal of Auto Repair in America
   How people are robbed when they have their cars repaired in the United States.
   The author feels that the auto-repair industry has an embarrassingly bad reputation.
2. Introduction
   The "Prevent" Defense
   A Regular Customer
   Symptoms
   Written Estimate
   Useful Complaining
3. owner's manual   second opinion
   regular maintenance plan   written estimate
   check before you drive   scare tactics
   regularly   complain
   specific   complain in writing
   test drive
4. Trade and Technical

5. Know your car and read the owner's manual.
6. If you get ripped off, complain in writing to a consumer organization.
7. a. Get to know and understand your car, and do basic maintenance regularly.
   b. Find an honest garage that does good work, and use it regularly.
   c. Give the mechanic a good description of what seems to be wrong with the car.
   d. Get a written estimate of all work.
   e. Complain in writing to a consumer organization about any bad work.

LESSON 4.2

Answers will vary. Students should state in complete sentences the material that answers the questions.

LESSON 4.3

The students will go to the actual first reading selection on page 61 for the Vocabulary Preview.

Then they will go through the guided reading using the selection as it was printed on pages 43–44.

LESSON 4.4

The students will use the selection as it is printed on page 61 to follow the guided review.

LESSON 4.5

Details will vary. The students will use the selection as it is printed on page 61.

The students should refer to the Comprehension Questions on page 63.

PART 2   SELECTION I

Comprehension Questions
1. c
2. d
3. a
4. a
5. b

Vocabulary Test
In order: consumer, fraud, odometer, opinion, vital, tactics, wary, random, precautions

SELECTION 2

Comprehension Questions
1. b
2. a
3. d
4. d
5. c

Vocabulary Test
1. prerequisite
2. fraught
3. upkeep
4. proliferating
5. bellhop
6. accommodations
7. metropolitan
8. maître d'
9. stamina
10. refurbishment

SELECTION 3

Comprehension Questions
1. a
2. c
3. b
4. d
5. b

Vocabulary Test
a. 7
b. 6
c. 1
d. 2
e. 5
f. 3
g. 4
h. 8

SELECTION 4

Comprehension Questions
1. b
2. a
3. c
4. d
5. b

Vocabulary Test
a. 2
b. 9
c. 5
d. 8
e. 3
f. 10
g. 6
h. 7
i. 1
j. 4

SELECTION 5

Comprehension Questions
1. d
2. b
3. d
4. d
5. a

Vocabulary Test
a. 4
b. 7
c. 1
d. 3
e. 8
f. 6
g. 2
h. 9
i. 5
j. 10

SELECTION 6

Comprehension Questions
1. d
2. d
3. a
4. d
5. a

Vocabulary Test
1. columns
2. radon
3. furnace
4. virgin
5. consulting
6. camped
7. assessor
8. niceties
9. thermostat
10. dedicated

SELECTION 7

Comprehension Questions
1. c
2. d
3. a
4. b
5. b

Vocabulary Test
1. screening
2. malnourished
3. respondents
4. neurological
5. dentures
6. dyspnea
7. coalition
8. routine
9. geriatric

SELECTION 8

Comprehension Questions
1. d
2. c
3. b
4. a
5. b

Vocabulary Test
1. swamp
2. standard
3. relics
4. climate
5. cottage
6. marsh
7. Creole
8. thoroughbred

SELECTION 9

Comprehension Questions
1. b
2. a
3. b
4. a
5. d

Vocabulary Test
1. ongoing
2. epileptic
3. correlated
4. electrode
5. convulsive seizure
6. impulses
7. neurosurgeon
8. combative

SELECTION 10

Comprehension Questions
1. d
2. a
3. b
4. c
5. c

Vocabulary Test
1. coil
2. cupped
3. refrigerant
4. vent
5. condenser
6. residential
7. duct tape
8. deliberation
9. obstruction
10. duct

SELECTION 11

Comprehension Questions
1. d
2. d
3. b
4. c
5. c

Vocabulary Test
1. reluctantly
2. oral
3. insistent
4. accessible
5. likelihood
6. stethoscope
7. bulimia
8. malignancy
9. periodontist
10. barometer

SELECTION 12

Comprehension Questions

1. d
2. a
3. c
4. d
5. b

Vocabulary Test

a.	4	f.	2
b.	5	g.	10
c.	7	h.	3
d.	9	i.	1
e.	8	j.	6

SELECTION 13

Comprehension Questions

1. b
2. d
3. a
4. d
5. c

Vocabulary Test

1.	crude	5.	components
2.	transistor	6.	calibrate
3.	circuitry	7.	consumer
4.	electron	8.	vacuum

SELECTION 14

Comprehension Questions

1. d
2. a
3. c
4. b
5. b

Vocabulary Test

a.	8	e.	2
b.	7	f.	3
c.	4	g.	1
d.	6	h.	5

SELECTION 15

Comprehension Questions

1. c
2. b
3. d
4. a
5. a

Vocabulary Test

In order: accurate, gauge, rotation, tread, punctures, impact, adequate

SELECTION 16

Comprehension Questions

1. d
2. b
3. c
4. a
5. c

Vocabulary Test

a.	5	e.	6
b.	4	f.	7
c.	2	g.	3
d.	1		

SELECTION 17

Comprehension Questions
1. d
2. c
3. b
4. b
5. a

Vocabulary Test
a. 2   f. 10
b. 6   g. 4
c. 5   h. 1
d. 7   i. 9
e. 8   j. 3

SELECTION 18

Comprehension Questions
1. c
2. d
3. b
4. a
5. b

Vocabulary Test
1. e   5. c
2. d   6. b
3. g   7. a
4. f

SELECTION 19

Comprehension Questions
1. d
2. b
3. c
4. b
5. d

Vocabulary Test
1. d   5. a
2. g   6. c
3. h   7. b
4. e   8. f

SELECTION 20

Comprehension Questions
1. d
2. a
3. b
4. d
5. b

Vocabulary Test
a. 4   e. 2
b. 7   f. 8
c. 1   g. 5
d. 6   h. 3

SELECTION 21

Comprehension Questions
1. b
2. c
3. a
4. d
5. a

Vocabulary Test
1. compressor   6. energy-efficient
2. initial   7. humidity
3. duct   8. accumulate
4. accessible   9. frost
5. capacity   10. grounded

SELECTION 22

Comprehension Questions
1. b
2. a
3. d
4. b
5. c

Vocabulary Test
1. drafting
2. craftsworker
3. fused
4. dexterity
5. brazing
6. metallurgical
7. welding

SELECTION 23

Comprehension Questions
1. b
2. c
3. b
4. d
5. c

Vocabulary Test
a. 6   e. 3
b. 8   f. 2
c. 7   g. 5
d. 1   h. 4

SELECTION 24

Comprehension Questions
1. c
2. b
3. d
4. a
5. b

Vocabulary Test
1. revolutionary
2. upgrade
3. hype
4. in-depth
5. mouse
6. explanatory
7. database
8. vendor
9. modem
10. on-line

SELECTION 25

Comprehension Questions
1. c
2. c
3. a
4. b
5. d

Vocabulary Test
1. wooded
2. locals
3. supplemented
4. dramatic
5. abolitionists
6. isolated
7. blared
8. brimming
9. saloon
10. luxurious

SELECTION 26

Comprehension Questions
1. a
2. b
3. b
4. d
5. c

Vocabulary Test
1. legitimate
2. overstimulate
3. dependence
4. hallucinations
5. treatable
6. skyrockets
7. opiates
8. addictive
9. fatally
10. nervous system

SELECTION 27

Comprehension Questions
1. d
2. b
3. a
4. c
5. c

Vocabulary Test
1. complex
2. preservation
3. condemned
4. bicentennial
5. volunteers
6. deteriorating
7. commercial
8. redevelopment, restoration
9. history-oriented

SELECTION 28

Comprehension Questions
1. a
2. c
3. b
4. a
5. d

Vocabulary Test
1. b
2. f
3. e
4. c
5. d
6. a

SELECTION 29

Comprehension Questions
1. c
2. d
3. b
4. a
5. b

Vocabulary Test
1. mandatory
2. fiscal
3. seasonal
4. temporary
5. forefront
6. work force
7. flexibility
8. prospective
9. backlog

SELECTION 30

Comprehension Questions
1. d
2. a
3. b
4. a
5. c

Vocabulary Test
1. c
2. b
3. a
4. d

SELECTION 31

Comprehension Questions
1. c
2. a
3. d
4. b
5. b

Vocabulary Test
a. 8
b. 1
c. 2
d. 7
e. 3
f. 9
g. 5
h. 10
i. 6
j. 4

SELECTION 32

Comprehension Questions

1. b
2. a
3. c
4. a
5. d

Vocabulary Test

1. advent
2. foreseeable
3. downturns
4. components
5. able
6. calibrated
7. aviation

SELECTION 33

Comprehension Questions

1. a
2. c
3. d
4. b
5. c

Vocabulary Test

a. 5
b. 6
c. 7
d. 1
e. 8
f. 4
g. 10
h. 9
i. 3
j. 2

SELECTION 34

Comprehension Questions

1. b
2. d
3. a
4. d
5. a

Vocabulary Test

a. 10
b. 1
c. 3
d. 4
e. 2
f. 8
g. 6
h. 5
i. 9
j. 7

SELECTION 35

Comprehension Questions

1. b
2. a
3. d
4. c
5. c

Vocabulary Test

1. latter
2. tissue
3. dexterity
4. standardize
5. bacteriology
6. analysis
7. manual
8. microorganisms
9. corpuscle
10. accredited

SELECTION 36

Comprehension Questions

1. b
2. d
3. c
4. a
5. d

Vocabulary Test

a. 7
b. 6
c. 1
d. 3
e. 2
f. 4
g. 5

SELECTION 37

Comprehension Questions
1. c
2. b
3. a
4. c
5. d

Vocabulary Test
1. c
2. d
3. f
4. a
5. b
6. e

SELECTION 38

Comprehension Questions
1. d
2. d
3. b
4. c
5. a

Vocabulary Test
a. 4
b. 6
c. 9
d. 7
e. 2
f. 10
g. 8
h. 3
i. 1
j. 5

SELECTION 39

Comprehension Questions
1. b
2. a
3. a
4. c
5. d

Vocabulary Test
1. vital
2. powertrain
3. warranty
4. franchised
5. trade organization
6. chassis
7. flushing
8. gasket
9. torque

SELECTION 40

Comprehension Questions
1. c
2. a
3. b
4. d
5. c

Vocabulary Test
1. census
2. practitioner
3. precise
4. extended-care
5. third-party reimbursement
6. ambulatory-care facilities
7. sophisticated
8. tolerance

SELECTION 41

Comprehension Questions
1. a
2. d
3. b
4. c
5. d

Vocabulary Test
a. 6
b. 1
c. 8
d. 2
e. 5
f. 3
g. 4
h. 7
i. 9

SELECTION 42

Comprehension Questions
1. b
2. b
3. d
4. a
5. c

Vocabulary Test
1. impetigo
2. limbs
3. heartrending
4. recurrences
5. bilateral
6. polio
7. clinic
8. meningitis
9. airborne
10. hypertensive

SELECTION 43

Comprehension Questions
1. a
2. c
3. b
4. b
5. b

Vocabulary Test
a. 4
b. 10
c. 1
d. 7
e. 9
f. 6
g. 3
h. 5
i. 8
j. 2

SELECTION 44

Comprehension Questions
1. c
2. c
3. a
4. d
5. b

Vocabulary Test
a. 7
b. 8
c. 5
d. 2
e. 3
f. 4
g. 1
h. 6

SELECTION 45

Comprehension Questions
1. d
2. b
3. c
4. a
5. b

Vocabulary Test
1. practice
2. clinic
3. operative field
4. diagnostic
5. impressions
6. suture

SELECTION 46

Comprehension Questions
1. d
2. b
3. a
4. c
5. c

Vocabulary Test
a. 5
b. 1
c. 8
d. 10
e. 3
f. 9
g. 7
h. 4
i. 2
j. 6

SELECTION 47

Comprehension Questions	Vocabulary Test

Comprehension Questions
1. d
2. b
3. a
4. d
5. a

Vocabulary Test

a.	1	e.	2
b.	7	f.	8
c.	4	g.	6
d.	5	h.	3

SELECTION 48

Comprehension Questions
1. d
2. b
3. b
4. a
5. a

Vocabulary Test

a.	2	d.	5
b.	3	e.	4
c.	6	f.	1

SELECTION 49

Comprehension Questions
1. d
2. b
3. a
4. b
5. c

Vocabulary Test

a.	4	d.	5
b.	1	e.	3
c.	2	f.	6

SELECTION 50

Comprehension Questions
1. d
2. b
3. b
4. c
5. a

Vocabulary Test

a.	5	f.	2
b.	3	g.	8
c.	9	h.	10
d.	6	i.	7
e.	4	j.	11
		k.	1

◆ **Progress Chart**

Selection

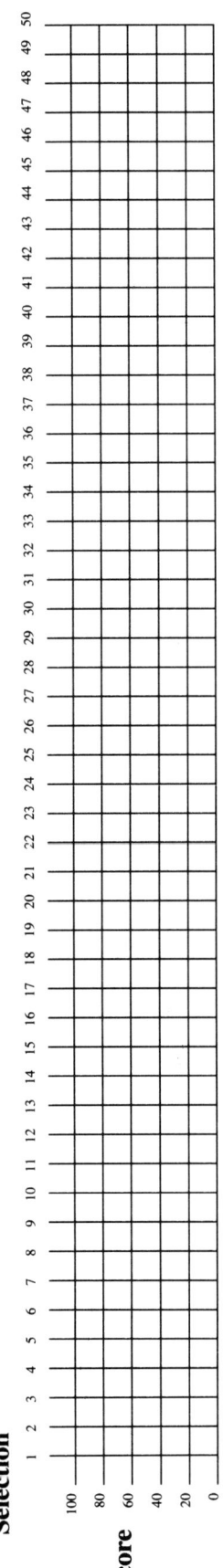

On the line provided for each selection, mark your score with a dot (•). As you progress, connect your Comprehension Questions score dots with lines (——).

CREDITS

Selection 1

Reprinted with permission from the author, Robert Sikorsky.

Selection 2

Copyright 1980 by Arnold R. Deutsch.

Selection 3

Reprinted with permission of J. G. Ferguson Publishing Co.

Selection 4

Reprinted by permission of *Boys' Life* magazine, published by the Boy Scouts of America.

Selection 5

Reprinted with permission of the Louisiana Office of Tourism.

Selection 6

Copyright 1991 by Word Association, Inc.

Selection 7

Published in *RN*. Copyright 1990 by Medical Economics Publishing, Montvale, N.J. Reprinted by permission.

Selection 8

Reprinted with permission of the Louisiana Office of Tourism.

Selection 9

From the book *Student's Career Guide to a Future in the Allied Health Professions* by Craig R. Ilk, B.S., P.A.-C., copyright 1992.

Selection 10

Reprinted with permission from the *Family Handyman* magazine, Home Service Publications, Inc., an affiliate of the Reader's Digest Association, Inc., 7900 International Drive, Suite 950, Minneapolis, Minn. 55425, copyright 1988.

Selection 11

Reprinted from *The Saturday Evening Post,* copyright 1986.

Selection 12

Copyright 1980 by Arnold R. Deutsch.

Selection 13

Reprinted with permission of J. G. Ferguson Publishing Co.

Selection 14

Reprinted with permission of *Remodeling Magazine*.

Selection 15

Reprinted with permission of the Firestone Tire and Rubber Co.

Selection 16

Reprinted with permission of J. G. Ferguson Publishing Co.

Selection 17

Reprinted with permission from *Working Woman* magazine, copyright 1988 by W. W. T. Partnership

Selection 36

Reprinted with permission of the McGraw-Hill Company of Canada Ltd.

Selection 37

From the book: *Student's Career Guide to a Future in the Allied Health Professions* by Craig R. Ilk, B.S., P.A.-C., copyright 1992.

Selection 38

Reprinted with permission from the author, Gordon E. Rowley.

Selection 39

Reprinted from *Home Mechanix* magazine. Copyright 1991 by Times Mirror Magazines.

Selection 40

Reprinted with permission of J. G. Ferguson Publishing Co.

Selection 41

Reprinted with permission from *Family Safety and Health,* published by the National Safety Council, 1121 Spring Lake Drive, Itasca, Ill. 60143, and from the author, Ruth A. Mack.

Selection 42

Published in *RN.* Copyright 1990 by Medical Economics Publishing, Montvale, N.J. Reprinted by permission.

Selection 43

From *Home Office Computing,* May 1988 issue, copyright 1988 by Scholastic Magazines, Inc. Reprinted by permission of the publisher.

Selection 44

From the book: *Student's Career Guide to a Future in the Allied Health Professions* by Craig R. Ilk, B.S., P.A.-C., copyright 1992.

Selection 45

From the book: *Student's Career Guide to a Future in the Allied Health Professions* by Craig R. Ilk, B.S., P.A.-C., copyright 1992.

Selection 46

Reprinted with permission of Oceana Publications, Inc.

Selection 47

Reprinted with permission of J. G. Ferguson Publishing Co.

Selection 48

Reprinted with permission of *Restaurant Business.*

Selection 49

Reprinted with permission of J. G. Ferguson Publishing Co.

Selection 50

From *Home Office Computing,* March 1988 issue, copyright 1988 by Scholastic Magazines, Inc. Reprinted by permission of the publisher.

Career Reading Index